Alexander
August 201

CW00431739

Material Markets

The Clarendon Lectures in Management Studies are jointly organized by Oxford University Press and the Saïd Business School. Every year a leading international academic is invited to give a series of lectures on a topic related to management education and research, broadly defined. The lectures form the basis of a book subsequently published by Oxford University Press.

Clarendon Lectures in Management Studies:

The Modern Firm
Organizational Design for Performance and Growth
John Roberts

Managing Intellectual Capital
Organizational, Strategic, and Policy Dimensions
David Teece

The Political Determinants of Corporate Governance
Political Context, Corporate Impact
Mark Roe

The Internet Galaxy
Reflections on the Internet, Business, and Society
Manuel Castells

Brokerage and Closure
An Introduction to Social Capital
Ron Burt

Reassembling the Social
An Introduction to Actor-Network-Theory
Bruno Latour

Gatekeepers
The Role of the Professions in Corporate Governance
John C. Coffee

Science, Innovation, and Economic Growth (forthcoming)
Walter W. Powell

The Logic of Position, The Measure of Leadership
Position and Information in the Market (forthcoming)
Joel Podolny

Global Companies in the 20th Century (forthcoming)
Leslie Hannah

Material Markets

How Economic Agents Are Constructed

Donald MacKenzie

OXFORD

UNIVERSITY PRESS

OXFORD
UNIVERSITY PRESS

Great Clarendon Street, Oxford OX2 6DP

Oxford University Press is a department of the University of Oxford.
It furthers the University's objective of excellence in research, scholarship,
and education by publishing worldwide in

Oxford New York

Auckland Cape Town Dar es Salaam Hong Kong Karachi
Kuala Lumpur Madrid Melbourne Mexico City Nairobi
New Delhi Shanghai Taipei Toronto

With offices in

Argentina Austria Brazil Chile Czech Republic France Greece
Guatemala Hungary Italy Japan Poland Portugal Singapore
South Korea Switzerland Thailand Turkey Ukraine Vietnam

Oxford is a registered trade mark of Oxford University Press
in the UK and in certain other countries

Published in the United States
by Oxford University Press Inc., New York

© Oxford University Press 2009

The moral rights of the author have been asserted
Database right Oxford University Press (maker)

First published 2009

All rights reserved. No part of this publication may be reproduced,
stored in a retrieval system, or transmitted, in any form or by any means,
without the prior permission in writing of Oxford University Press,
or as expressly permitted by law, or under terms agreed with the appropriate
reprographics rights organization. Enquiries concerning reproduction
outside the scope of the above should be sent to the Rights Department,
Oxford University Press, at the address above

You must not circulate this book in any other binding or cover
and you must impose the same condition on any acquirer

British Library Cataloguing in Publication Data

Data available

Library of Congress Cataloging in Publication Data

Data available

Typeset by SPI Publisher Services, Pondicherry, India
Printed in Great Britain
on acid-free paper by
CPI Antony Rowe, Chippenham, Wiltshire

ISBN 978–0–19–927815–2

10 9 8 7 6 5 4 3 2 1

To Barbara, Moyra, and Robin

CONTENTS

ACKNOWLEDGEMENTS

I am extremely grateful to the Saïd Business School, University of Oxford, and to Oxford University Press for their invitation to deliver the Clarendon Lectures in Management Studies, on which this book is based. I would also like to thank the UK Economic and Social Research Council for their award of a Professorial Fellowship on 'Social Studies of Finance' (RES-051-27-0062), which made possible both the writing of this book and the bulk of the research that underpins it. My gratitude too to the Institute of Advanced Study, Durham University, for a term's fellowship that helped me bring the book to completion, and to Innogen, the ESRC Centre for Social and Economic Research on Innovation in Genomics, for supporting the underlying work on the construction of economic agents.

I have also incurred many more personal debts of gratitude: to Iain Hardie and Daniel Beunza (co-authors of Chapters 3 and 5), for allowing me to reuse our joint work here; to Moyra Forrest, who provided me with copies of the vast majority of the publications that form this book's references; to Barbara Silander, who word-processed its text and bibliography; and to Robin Williams, who has been a steadfast supporter of my work for many years. Robin has also been a wonderful friend, and Barbara and Moyra deserve special, long-term thanks: they have now worked with me on five books.

The input of the many interviewees whose testimony forms the book's main empirical underpinning was essential. The nature of the book's subject matter—and, in many cases, interviewees' preferences—mean that their contributions are generally anonymous. They were vitally important nevertheless. I am particularly grateful to those who allowed me to watch LIBOR being calculated and to the hedge fund that permitted the observations by Iain Hardie and myself that form the basis of Chapter 3.

Three chapters build directly upon articles published elsewhere: Chapter 3 is a revised version of Hardie and MacKenzie (2007); Chapter 4 of MacKenzie (2007a); and Chapter 5 of Beunza, Hardie, and MacKenzie (2006). Other work I have drawn on includes Hatherly, Leung, and MacKenzie (forthcoming) and

MacKenzie (2007b; 2008). The Glossary draws upon MacKenzie (2006). I am grateful to the copyright holders for permission to make use of this material here. Sections of Chapter 5 written by Beunza similarly draw on material in Beunza and Stark (2004).

As always, though, I save my most heartfelt thanks of all for my family: Caroline, Alice, and Iain.

LIST OF FIGURES

1

Introduction

Just after 11.00 a.m., every weekday that is not a bank holiday, an apparently mundane calculation is performed at a couple of desks in an unremarkable open-plan office in London's Docklands. Small sets of numbers arrive electronically or by telephone. The two people orchestrating the calculation correct obvious typing mistakes and check less clear-cut discrepancies by telephone calls: 'Hello, it's [X]. Just want to check the one-week on the Danish [Krone]. You guys are quoting 2.51. You want to keep it around that?' or 'Everyone else is coming in a good bit under that.' Sometimes they telephone and remind those who should have provided figures. Once half the necessary numbers have been input into the computer system that performs the calculation, it begins to process them. On the day I was watching, all the inputs had been received and checked, and the processing completed, by 11.43, and one of the two staff members involved then said to his colleague: 'You can publish away.'

This undramatic sequence of events produces what is, from the viewpoint of the amount of money hingeing directly on its outcome, one of the world's most consequential set of numbers: British Bankers' Association LIBOR (London Interbank Offered Rate), the dominant global benchmark for interest rates. On the day on which I watched LIBOR being set, over $170 trillion of the world's financial 'derivatives' (the equivalent of around $26,000 for every human being on earth) were indexed to LIBOR, fluctuating in value as it changed from day to day.[1] The importance of the calculation is reflected in the arrangements if a terrorist incident or other event disrupts the office in which I witnessed it. A nearby, similarly equipped office building is kept in constant readiness; dedicated lines have been laid into the homes of those responsible for the calculation; a permanently staffed back-up site, over 250 km away, can also calculate LIBOR. Ordinarily, LIBOR is of interest to market participants alone, but as the 'credit crisis' began in 2007 its values started to be discussed in TV news bulletins, because the market turmoil suddenly highlighted the crucial importance of whether banks were prepared to lend to each other and at what rates of interest.

I begin with LIBOR because attention to it is an instance of what is distinctive about the approach to markets explored in this book. That approach is currently best exemplified in 'social studies of finance'. The term came into use first amongst young scholars in Paris in the late 1990s. In its broad meaning, it signals the application to financial markets of social science disciplines beyond economics (and also wider than those approaches to 'behavioural finance' that are rooted in individual psychology), such as anthropology, gender studies, human geography, political science, and sociology. Small numbers of scholars in these fields have been interested in financial markets for many years,[2] but recently such interest has grown and coalesced as those involved have become aware of what their peers in other disciplines are doing.[3]

A more specific meaning of 'social studies of finance' is, however, more pertinent here. In this meaning, the term refers to approaches to markets that are inspired by social science research on science and technology.[4] Perhaps the most prominent name for the latter research is 'social studies of science', hence the analogous expression 'social studies of finance'. Those who have worked in the social studies of science and technology tend to acquire sensitivities, interests, and intellectual resources that differ at least to a degree from those of the wider disciplines to which we belong. (Of course, we also always borrow from the social sciences more generally, and I have done so here. Sectarianism is never a virtue.)

What is perhaps most characteristic of a perspective rooted in the social studies of science and technology is its concern with the *materiality* of markets: their physicality, corporeality, technicality.[5] Even a financial market, trading as it does tokens of rights and obligations rather than goods or services that can be consumed directly, is made up of physical artefacts and technologies. For example, as emphasized in Chapter 5, a price must take physical form— spoken or written numbers, electronic signals, and so on—if it is to be conveyed from one human being or computer system to another, and the physical form it takes is consequential.

An emphasis on materiality points, however, to more than the importance of objects and technologies. The human actors who make up markets are not disembodied agents or abstract information processors, however convenient it may be for economics to model them as such. They are embodied human beings, and bodies are material entities. The capacities and limitations of these material entities (including those of human brains) are hugely important to how markets are constructed. The fact, for example, that a brain is not an information processor with infinite capacity means that conceptual tools that simplify the cognitive task of grasping what is going on in a market can be enormously important. The interbank market, for example, is diverse and hugely complicated, as one quickly learns by sitting beside the traders and brokers who spend all day, every day, seeking to understand it and act within it. Yet LIBOR condenses all that complication into a single set of numbers, making it possible, for instance, to index $170 trillion of derivatives to conditions in the interbank market. Such a tool is more than a representation of a market: it is a constitutive part of economic action, shaping such action and its consequences for market processes.

Above all, perhaps, what one might call the 'material sociology' inspired by the social studies of science and technology emphasizes the technicality of markets. The properties of artefacts, technological systems, conceptual tools, and so on are not 'details' that sociological analyses should set aside: fully rounded analyses need to incorporate them. Take, for example, Wayne Baker's superb study of the Chicago Board Options Exchange (Baker 1981; 1984a; 1984b), still exemplary nearly three decades after its completion.[6] (An 'option' is a security that gives its holder a right but not an obligation, for example to buy a set number of shares or other assets at a set price.) Baker demonstrates beautifully, using interviews, network analysis, and price data, the consequentiality of social relations amongst option traders. Yet it is also important that trading on the exchange was influenced by economic models of option pricing, notably the Black–Scholes model developed by economists Fischer Black, Myron Scholes, and Robert C. Merton. Black and others sold paper sheets of theoretical option prices, which many traders used to inform their trading decisions, and I have argued (in MacKenzie 2006) that amongst the effects was to shift patterns of option prices towards the model.

The case of options trading exemplifies a central aspect of what is distinctive about looking at markets from the viewpoint of the social studies of science and technology. Economic agents such as Chicago option traders are not just 'naked' human beings, nor simply human beings embedded in social networks. Their 'equipment' matters. A trader equipped with Black's sheets was a different economic agent from one trading on the basis of intuition and experience alone. The Black–Scholes model was indeed technical, but it was not a 'mere technicality': it was a consequential part of how economic agents were constructed. (The 'agent' of this book's title is any economic actor, not merely one who acts on behalf of another.)

The chapters that follow aim to elaborate and illustrate the 'social studies of finance', in this sense of perspectives inspired by social science research on science and technology. Chapter 2 does this by formulating a set of precepts of work of this kind. It is a set of precepts.[7] Many of them are, I think, widely shared by those who come to the study of markets from a background in the social studies of science and technology, but any such set is bound to be idiosyncratic, and I have no wish to foist these precepts on my colleagues (or even on the co-authors of Chapters 3 and 5). Furthermore, my chosen set of precepts is clearly incomplete (especially when one shifts focus to markets in spheres other than finance), nor are they all illustrated equally in the chapters that follow. Nonetheless, I hope the precepts help to flesh out the approach to the understanding of markets I am advocating.

Chapters 3 to 7 are primarily case studies, each broadly within the framework outlined in Chapter 2. Chapter 3, written jointly with Iain Hardie, is organized around one of the central ideas discussed in Chapter 2: Michel Callon's idea of treating economic actors as made up of *agencements*, of combinations of human beings, material objects, technical systems, texts, algorithms, and so on. Hardie and I apply the notion of *agencement* to a category of agent that is of growing importance in financial markets: a hedge fund. (The Glossary explains financial market terms such as 'hedge fund', and the more important such terms are also discussed in the chapters.) Our account is based upon a brief period of observation of one particular fund's trading, on interviews conducted with the partners in the fund, and on a wider set of interviews with traders in other hedge funds and in investment banks, and also with those who supply vital services to hedge funds, such as the 'funds of funds' that channel capital to them.

Like almost all sophisticated traders, the fund Hardie and I studied traded not just basic assets such as bonds but also 'derivatives' of those assets: contracts or securities the value of which depends on the price of the underlying asset, or on other parameters such as the probability of an issuer of bonds defaulting. Chapter 4 examines the development of exchanges devoted to the trading of financial derivatives. As recently as 1970, there was no financial-derivatives exchange anywhere in the world. By the end of June 2006, contracts outstanding on such exchanges totalled $84.4 trillion, around $13,000 for every person on the planet. The limited literature beyond economics on derivatives often emphasizes their 'virtual' nature as 'money's "new imaginary"' (Pryke and Allen 2000). Drawing upon oral history interviews with key figures in the development of organized derivatives trading in the USA and UK, Chapter 4 examines how those 'virtual' products have been brought into material existence. It explores the similarities and differences between technological innovation and innovation in derivatives, and discusses the role of the 'internal' cultures of financial markets and of the wider culture (in particular, the legal traces of hostility to gambling). The chapter also examines how the fact-generation mechanisms of financial markets are crucial to derivatives trading.

Chapter 5, co-authored with Daniel Beunza and Iain Hardie, examines a specific form of trading that is central to how derivatives exchanges produce facts, as well as having many other roles in financial markets: arbitrage, in other words trading that exploits discrepancies in relative prices, for example between an asset and a derivative of that asset. Drawing on work conducted by Hardie and myself, and on an ethnography of a Wall Street arbitrage trading room by Beunza and David Stark (2003; 2004; 2005), the chapter emphasizes both the materiality of prices (as noted above, prices are physical entities, and the extent and speed of their mobility are crucial to arbitrage) and the delicate social relations that exist amongst arbitrageurs and between them and others.

Chapter 6 shifts focus from financial markets themselves to the processes that provide crucial data for those markets: the book-keeping and accounting that produce corporate financial statements, especially corporate earnings ('profits'). The chapter draws upon a body of literature in accounting, little known outside the field, on 'earnings management', and on a brief case study of a particular accounting classification by a firm heavily involved in earnings management to emphasize the applicability to accounting of another of the ideas discussed in Chapter 2: finitism. In the finitist perspective explored in that chapter, '[w]e *could* take our concepts or rules anywhere' (Bloor 1997: 19) when we perform classifications, measure items, and follow rules, all of which are activities central to accounting. Given that, what keeps accounting (relatively) orderly? Chapter 6 suggests that the answer to this question is intrinsically sociotechnical: it involves both people—not just as individuals, but as members of the cultures of book-keeping and of accounting—and technical systems.

Chapter 7 moves outside the sphere of finance in a narrow sense to examine markets in pollution permits, particularly greenhouse-gas markets. It emphasizes several of the issues discussed in Chapter 2, such as the active role of economics and of economists in bringing markets into being (rather than studying them as already-existing, external 'things') and especially the political nature of the detailed design of markets. Indeed, the chapter suggests that emissions markets *are* politics. In particular, they are ways of undermining inertia and achieving apparent consensus; but they also seem to displace conflict, which shifts focus to the rules governing trading (especially governing the crucial matter of the allocation of permits). The 'economic experiment' (Muniesa and Callon 2007) of European carbon trading has so far had a mixed outcome: for example, limited environmental impact, but a surprising degree of success in 'technicizing' the politics of allocation.

Chapter 8 is the book's conclusion. It emphasizes the modest, exploratory nature of the previous chapters, and returns to the overall question informing the book: what can an approach rooted in the social studies of science and technology contribute to an understanding of markets? The chapter examines the relations of social studies of finance to economic sociology more generally, and makes explicit the possibility hinted at in Chapter 7: that an approach to markets that draws upon the social studies of science and technology can become 'public social science', analogous to what Burawoy (2005) calls 'public sociology'.

A Note re. Interview Sources

The main data source drawn on in the chapters that follow is a set of 189 interviews with people involved in financial and emissions markets as traders, managers, brokers, market designers, providers of administrative and other services, accountants, and auditors. (Twenty-three of these interviews were conducted by my colleague Iain Hardie, and sixty-six have already been drawn upon in MacKenzie 2006.) Apart from in cases in which the identity of the interviewee is important to an historical episode being discussed, I have followed the preference of most of my interviewees and cited interview data anonymously.

2

Ten Precepts for the Social
Studies of Finance

What might be involved in an approach to the study of markets, especially of financial markets, that is inspired by the social studies of science and technology? This chapter builds on Chapter 1's brief discussion of that question by sketching ten precepts that might underpin research of this kind, research that focuses on the physicality, the corporeality, and the technicality of markets.

Precept 1: Facts Matter

Let me begin with a crucial facet of the technicality of markets: the role in them of the production and circulation of facts. A 'fact' is 'A thing known ... to have occurred or to be true',[1] and facts are obviously a crucial topic of the social studies of science. That field does not ask whether claimed scientific facts are 'really true', which is a question only science, not sociology, can answer. Instead, the sociology of scientific knowledge is interested in questions such as how facts are produced and what secures their facticity, in other words their status as facts. 'Produced' is the right word: scientific facts are not in general simply 'out there', awaiting the fortunate discoverer who stumbles over them. As the Latin root of 'fact'—*facere*, to make, to do—reminds us, scientific facts are made: by experiment, by intellectual work, and by observation that is normally technologically mediated and typically is disciplined and goal-oriented rather than haphazard.

The 'career' of a fact tends to make the history of its production vanish. Full-fledged scientific facts are public, collective, 'social' facts, not simply private facts: their status as facts is assessed by scientific communities, not just by individuals.[2] As one of the classic ethnographies of the production of scientific facts emphasizes, to become a fact a statement must lose the 'trace of authorship' in the sense of being 'freed from the circumstances of its production' (Latour and Woolgar 1986: 82 and 105). If it cannot be freed from those circumstances—if, for example, a phenomenon can be exhibited only by a specific person or a particular laboratory, and not by others—it is normally fated to be classed instead as an 'artefact': not a truth about the world, but the spurious result of the particular procedures used in its production.

The facts that circulate in financial markets might seem weak and vulnerable compared to those produced by a mature science. But consider British Bankers' Association LIBOR, London Interbank Offered Rate. The low-key declaration, 'You can publish away', which I heard when standing in the London office in which LIBOR is calculated, initiated its electronic dissemination via multiple data providers. Almost instantaneously, it was possible at more than half a million terminals across the globe to click a mouse a few times and/or strike a handful of computer keys, and prompt a flow of electrical signals that would cause the numbers calculated in the London office to appear on screen.[3]

As far as I can tell, those who do this have until very recently treated the numbers that appear as unproblematic. They have been, for example, content to have huge sums of money change hands on the basis of what appears on screen. Like scientific facts, LIBOR is produced rather than stumbled upon—its production is described in Chapter 4—but like them it had been freed almost entirely from the particular circumstances of its production. (Controversy over LIBOR did, however, erupt in 2007–8 as a result of the credit crisis, as described in Chapter 4.) Surprisingly—given the amount of money that depends on them—no real controversy normally surrounded the numbers that flow out of that London office.

Of course, not all efforts to give 'market numbers' factual status are successful. Consider, for example, another daily 'price fixing': the 10.00 a.m. Cheddar cheese auction conducted on the floor of the Chicago Mercantile Exchange. A cheese auction may seem an esoteric matter of no wider interest, but the results of the auction are inputs into the formula that has been used since the 1930s to set the government-mandated minimum milk price received by farmers in the United States, and they thus help determine the consumer prices of dairy products in the USA. In the summer of 2006, fierce controversy erupted in the USA over the auction. One farmers' spokesperson claimed: 'There are very few buyers who are setting the price in a very thin market.' Another said there was 'deep scepticism' about the mechanism's 'legitimacy ... as a true reflector of supply and demand', and in July 2006 six senators, including Hillary Rodham Clinton, demanded a government investigation (Grant 2006). The accusation, contested vigorously by traders on the Chicago Mercantile Exchange and by others, was in effect that the results of the auction were artefacts, not facts.[4]

Whether market numbers achieve the status of facts is consequential. As discussed in Chapter 4, it is, for example, a major influence on whether derivatives markets can successfully be constructed. More generally, facticity is often a precondition for liquid markets. As Carruthers and Stinchcombe put it, 'liquidity is ... an issue in the sociology of knowledge' (1999: 393). A market is 'liquid' if the items traded in it can readily be bought and sold in substantial quantity at or close to prevailing market prices, without undue delay or heavy transaction costs, and achieving liquidity typically requires standardization of the items traded and, crucially, a degree of consensus on their characteristics. The market for interest-rate derivatives, for example, would not be liquid if each contract required the resolution of a disagreement over how interest rates are to be measured, if each subsequent payment was vulnerable to litigation over the adequacy of the measurement that determined its size, or if one feared that one's counterparties might be able to manipulate the measurement in their favour. The contribution of the facticity of British Bankers' Association LIBOR to the liquidity of the interest-rate derivatives markets has been that all these messy obstacles are avoided.

Precept 2: Actors Are Embodied

All markets, whether liquid or not, are combinations of human beings and physical objects. It may seem too obvious to need saying (until one realizes that few analyses of markets develop the point), but human beings have bodies, *are* bodies. Corporeality—in the sense of the material capacities and limitations of those bodies and brains—is critical to how markets function.

In some markets, embodiment can hardly pass unnoticed. Take an 'open-outcry' trading pit, a stepped amphitheatre in which deals are done by voice or by eye contact and hand signals (see, e.g., Zaloom 2006). Crucial skills for pit traders are to be able to detect the bodily signs of fear, which often indicate a trader who is desperate to exit a position, and to suppress the signs of one's own fear. Where one stands in such a pit matters economically: the top rung is best, because lines of sight are better there, and because it is advantageous to be close to the big brokers, with their large volumes of customer orders, who stand there. For that very reason, bodily position is contested. One frequently gets jostled, or has to jostle, and fist fights aren't uncommon. Physical height matters, both to seeing and especially to being seen. The pit is a place of *male* bodies, with women forming no more than a small minority.

It is of course the exotic nature of pit trading that makes its embodiment stand out. As pits have declined, they have been replaced by screen-based trading, and trading by telephone already has a long history. It's particularly easy implicitly to posit a disembodied actor when studying such trading, because the bodily actions involved are mostly familiar to any office worker. Much of the time, for instance, one would be hard pushed to distinguish the physical actions of a trader in a bank's dealing room from those of an academic at his or her desk. There's a lot of sitting and staring at a screen, typing and moving a computer mouse about, talking on the telephone, reading, chatting, and drinking coffee. Disappointingly from the viewpoint of exoticism, shouting, swearing, and raucous behaviour in dealing rooms are now far rarer in actuality than in film portrayals.

Bodily capacities still matter, however. Let me again use the example of LIBOR, which is pertinent here because it is an apparently disembodied set of numbers. As described in Chapter 4, the inputs to the LIBOR calculation come from bank dealing rooms, but they are heavily influenced by interdealer brokers. Although brokers increasingly give their clients the capacity to trade electronically, the core of their business was (and to a significant extent still is) 'voice broking'. A firm's brokers in a given market (for example, the sterling interbank market) sit close together at a cluster of desks, with nearby clusters handling related markets such as in interest-rate swaps. Each broker has on his desk (it is another predominantly male niche) a 'voicebox'—a combination of microphone, speaker, and switches—connected by dedicated telephone lines to each of his clients.

Interdealer brokers do not themselves trade: if a client bank wants to borrow money, the broker's job is to find a bank that will lend (or vice versa). So the key skill is knowing who wants to do what and who is prepared to do what. It is partly a matter of fostering relationships with clients. I was repeatedly told by interdealer brokers that theirs is 'a relationship business'. As one of them said to me, a broker in the 'money market' (the market about which LIBOR is a 'fact') might 'speak to his big clients ... have conversations with them maybe twenty-five times a day, which is twenty-five times as often as they speak to their wives'.

There's also, however, a crucial bodily skill in interdealer broking, a skill those involved call 'broker's ear': the capacity aurally to monitor what is being said by all the other brokers at a cluster of desks, while oneself holding a voicebox conversation with a client. As an interviewee put it:

When you're on the desk you're expected to hear everyone else's conversations as well, because they're all relevant to you, and if you're on the phone speaking to someone about what's going on in the market there could be a hot piece of information coming in with one of your colleagues that you would want to tell your clients, so you've got to be able to hear it coming in as you're speaking to the person.

When interviewing brokers at their desks, I sometimes found 'broker's ear' disconcerting. Someone could apparently be paying full attention to his conversation with me, when he would suddenly respond to a comment or question from five or six desks away that I simply hadn't heard. (The multiple conversations make brokers' offices noisy, and they're more closely packed and more raucous places than banks' dealing rooms.) Broker's ear is an acquired skill: as one told me, 'you don't just do it from day one.... Some people never make it.'

Broker's ear helps brokers quickly to match borrowers and lenders (or in other markets, buyers and sellers), thus contributing to the liquidity of the interbank market, and the information that broker's ear aggregates also helps brokers' clients—many of whom make the inputs to LIBOR—to understand what are sometimes rapidly changing conditions in the interbank market. As noted in Chapter 4, there's no fully algorithmic way of generating an appropriate LIBOR input. Judgement, based on an understanding of market conditions, is involved, and broker's ear is one bodily foundation of that judgement.

Precept 3: Equipment Matters

As emphasized in Chapter 1, human bodies and brains have their limitations as well as their remarkable capacities such as broker's ear, and this makes their supplementation by 'equipment' (physical and 'cognitive') crucial. A central conjecture of the social studies of finance is that equipment matters: it changes the nature of the economic agent, of economic action, and of markets.

Consider, for example, physical equipment such as the stock ticker (Preda 2006) or trading screens connected in electronic networks (see Knorr Cetina and Bruegger 2000; 2002a; 2002b; Knorr Cetina 2005). Tickers and trading screens partially circumvent the most basic of all bodily limitations—the inability to be in two places at once—and their introduction did not simply make existing forms of behaviour in markets more efficient: it reshaped markets.

Tickers were telegraphic price-dissemination systems, at the receiving end of which the abbreviated names of securities, their prices, and the volumes of trades were printed out onto paper tape. They made fine-grained knowledge of price movements available in close to real time to geographically dispersed market participants (at least if those participants were able to congregate in the offices of brokers with tickers), when previously such knowledge required one to be present physically in the exchanges where securities were traded. Preda (2004b; 2006) conjectures, for instance, that the ticker helped prompt the rise of 'chartism' or 'technical analysis': the belief—still widespread—that patterns can be found in price graphs that have predictive value. The introduction of trading screens was at least equally consequential: ' "the market" no longer resided in a network of many places, but only in one, the screen, which could be represented identically in all places' (Knorr Cetina 2005: 51). For example, as briefly discussed in Chapter 5, this altered how the pervasive market activity of 'arbitrage' (the exploitation of price discrepancies) had to be conducted.

Actors' equipment goes beyond physical technologies: their 'conceptual equipment' also matters, or so the social studies of finance posits. Financial markets are, as noted in Chapter 1, complicated places, especially in the contemporary world of bewildering arrays of products and of price data that change second by second. Given the limited memory and computational capacity of the human brain, economic agents must develop and acquire systematic ways of making sense of markets that reduce this complication to a level that is mentally tractable. Organizations must develop procedures for interacting with markets, and to an increasing extent those procedures are implemented in algorithms in automated pricing, trading, and risk-management systems. Sometimes, the ways of thinking, procedures, and algorithms that are employed derive from financial economics, such as the theory of options touched on in Chapter 1. Probably more often, however, practitioners' ways of thinking and associated ways of acting have no direct connection to academic economics or indeed are regarded by economists as mistaken. Chartism—using graphs of price movements to attempt to predict future movements—is an example of the latter: financial economists regard it as on a par with astrology, but many traders take it seriously, and act on the basis of it.

That conceptual equipment matters is a conjecture, not a presumption. Although individual economists (for example, Merton and Bodie 2005) have noted its potential importance, financial economics does not treat this equipment in any systematic way. It models a world in which, for example, market processes force option prices to their 'correct' values, without explicit consideration of the effects on those processes of whether actors have option theory available to them. The evidence concerning the effects of its availability is not unequivocal, but in my view supports the conclusion that actors' deployment of option theory did affect prices.[5] It also seems likely that chartist beliefs and procedures, if followed sufficiently widely, will affect price movements (this is one reason that even traders sceptical of chartism cite for taking it seriously), though there is again limited direct evidence on the point.[6]

Actors' conceptual equipment can also have effects that are subtler than influencing prices directly. One of the ways in which financial markets are complicated is that the members of a class of products often vary in consequential ways in their detailed characteristics. Thus options even on the same underlying asset will differ: some will be 'calls' (options to buy the asset), and some 'puts' (options to sell it), and their expiration dates will vary, as will their exercise price (the price at which they give the right to buy or to sell the asset in question). An important role of option theory is in permitting the reduction of that complication to a common underlying metric: 'implied volatility', the volatility (extent of fluctuations) of the price of the underlying asset consistent with the prices of the option, according to an option-pricing model. Translating option prices into levels of implied volatility allows the easy comparison of options with different characteristics (the implied volatility of this option is 17 per cent, of that option 19 per cent . . .), and indeed price quotations for options are sometimes expressed as implied volatility levels rather than amounts in dollars or other currencies. Although it would be hard to demonstrate it quantitatively, it seems plausible that the availability of this metric contributes to the liquidity of the options market.

'Implied volatility' is not unique in its role as a simplifying metric and facili-tator of communication about the properties of financial products. Chapter 3, for example, conjectures that the 'yield' of a bond plays the same role, although the notion of 'yield' and the original techniques for calculating it are old and come from 'mixed' (applied) mathematics rather than economics (Hawawini and Vora 2007). Another example comes from the market for 'credit derivatives' such as collateralized debt obligations (CDOs), contracts the value of which depends on the risk of default by each of a large set of corporations or other issuers of debt (perhaps a hundred or more issuers); on the likely extent of the pay-out, if any, to debt holders after default; and on the extent to which the risk of default by one issuer is correlated with the risk of default by the others. In the credit-derivatives market—which in the years preceding 2007's credit crisis was the 'hot' area of derivatives—the metric of 'base correlation'[7] seems to have a function similar to that of 'implied volatil-ity' as a communicative tool. For example, it facilitates negotiation amongst sophisticated participants. The base correlation implied by a CDO quotation can be used as the basis for a reasoned argument why the quotation needs to be altered.

The availability of conceptual equipment can matter even if the theory underpinning the equipment is not understood—software systems allow traders with only a rough grasp of the theory of options or of CDOs to cal-culate implied volatilities or base correlations—or not believed. Those who do understand the models that are used in such calculations frequently view them as oversimplifications. I have, for example, yet to interview a credit-derivatives trader who regards as adequate the 'single-factor Gaussian cop-ula' model normally used in credit correlation calculations. Nevertheless, the simple models remain in wide use. More complex models face formidable barriers as communicative tools, because for full communication both parties must be using the same model, and that is seldom the case once one moves beyond simple models. Furthermore, the simple models typically have just one free parameter—'implied volatility', for example—with the other para-meters being either fixed by market convention (CDO pricing, for example, was often done by assuming a recovery rate after default of 40 per cent, whatever the corporation that has issued the debt in question) or regarded as empirically observable facts. When numbers of free parameters are larger, or parameters do not have intuitive interpretations—as is often the case with more complex models—communication and negotiation become much harder.

Precept 4: Cognition and Calculation Are Distributed and Material

'Public facts' such as LIBOR, technical equipment such as stock tickers, graphical representations such as those used by chartists, and 'conceptual equipment' such as 'implied volatility' or 'base correlation' are all aspects of the diverse cognitive and calculative processes that take place in financial markets. These processes are 'distributed' in the sense that a given task is often performed not by a single unaided human being but by multiple human beings, objects, and technical systems—an aspect that has been examined in other spheres in the literature on distributed cognition (see, above all, Hutchins 1995a; 1995b).[8]

The social studies of finance inherits the basic conjecture of the literature on distributed cognition. Not only can combinations of multiple human beings and objects do things an unaided individual cannot, but the performance of the same task by an unaided individual can be expected to have different properties from its performance by a combination of this sort. Hutchins puts the underlying point eloquently, deploying as his prime example navigation as conducted in US warships. Human beings, he argues, 'create their cognitive powers by creating the environments in which they exercise those powers'. To understand cognition that involves multiple collaborating human beings and/or interaction with objects and technical systems, one must go beyond the psychological or cognitive-science analysis 'of the individual bounded by the skin'. '[L]ocal functional systems composed of a person in interaction with a tool have cognitive properties that are radically different from the cognitive properties of the person alone', and a 'group performing [a] cognitive task may have cognitive properties that differ from the cognitive properties of any individual' (Hutchins 1995a: xvi, 176, and 289).

For example, a single human being can produce a LIBOR, but not a LIBOR that would have the status of a fact. To have a sufficient 'feel' for intra-day and day-to-day changes in conditions in the interbank market, he or she would need to be an active participant in that market—one, for example, to whom brokers would regard it worth their while relaying up-to-date information: not just prices, but the nature of the underlying transactions (and some-times even which particular banks had done what). But that participation would make him or her an interested party. That multiple human beings are involved in the production of LIBOR—that its production is in that sense 'distributed'—in such a way that there is a good chance of their interests 'cancelling out' is an essential aspect of it being a fact, as discussed in Chapter 4. Something similar is true of the production of corporate accounts, as outlined in Chapter 6. Not only is that production (for any other than the smallest of companies) beyond the powers of an individual, but such limited 'hardness' as the resultant numbers possess is intrinsically bound up with the involvement of multiple human beings in roles that are structured in part technologically.

All cognition and all calculation are physical processes (the brain is a bio-logical organ), but the materiality of calculation is perhaps most clearly seen when it involves extensive numerical computation. For example, theoretical models of the value of CDOs seldom yield equations that can be solved, other than very slowly, with the traditional material tools of pencil and paper.[9] The models used for pricing CDOs run fairly quickly on modern computers, but calculations of hedging ratios and risk-management parameters are more demanding. Even using grids of several hundred interconnected computers, the risk calculations can take several hours. A physical constraint becomes relevant: heat. Many banks want crucial computations to be performed in or close to main offices, trading floors, and risk managers, because even fibre-optic connections are still too slow for some purposes to allow all compu-tation to take place in distant sites. In London, though, those main offices are often in the City, where expansion is frequently impossible or hugely expensive. One can't keep packing more and more computers into any given computer room, because the heat they generate will eventually exceed the capacity to remove it by air-conditioning. So those who sell computer hard-ware to investment banks are aware that 'performance per watt' is now one of the parameters on which that hardware is judged.

A risk-analysis computer run is a calculation 'internal' to a financial market. But all such markets are connected to processes outside themselves, and this too involves distributed cognition and material calculation. Take the emissions markets discussed in Chapter 7, for example. As the US Environmental Protection Agency (EPA), which coordinates the market in sulphur-dioxide emissions, points out: 'An essential feature of smoothly operating markets is a method for measuring the commodity being traded.'[10] Unaided human senses cannot tell how much sulphur dioxide is being emitted by a smokestack, yet for a market to work the quantity of the smokestack's emissions must be a fact.

Hence the importance to markets (not just in emissions, but in a huge range of other commodities too) of 'metrology': of the science and technology of measurement, in particular of standardized units and measurement procedures that ensure an ohm, a centimetre, or a gram measured in one place and at one time is sufficiently like the same quantity measured at a different place and time.[11] Each smokestack of every coal-fired or oil-fired electric power plant in the USA (other than the very smallest such plants) now has to contain equipment to measure the flow of gases through it (Levin and Espeland 2002). This equipment must also sample those gases every 15 minutes, determine the concentration of sulphur dioxide in the sample,[12] and produce an electronic record of the measurement results, which is captured by a data acquisition and handling system and averaged to produce hourly records. The data files containing these records are transmitted electronically to the EPA every three months, and published via its website.[13]

Beneath the first layer of metrology in the sulphur-dioxide market is another: the metrology that provides assurance that the meters are correctly calibrated, for example by checking the output of a monitor when fed a sample of gas not from its smokestack but from a 'calibration cylinder' containing a known concentration of sulphur dioxide. Beneath that layer is yet another: the tests and statistical procedures that measure the composition of the contents of calibration cylinders by comparing them to standardized gas samples from the federal agency with overall responsibility for metrological matters such as standard reference materials, weight, and measures, the National Institute of Standards and Technology.[14] This pyramid of metrology makes sulphur-dioxide pollution measurable: it produces facts about it, thus making the market in emissions permits possible.

Metrology isn't just a 'physical' matter; it is also political. Sulphur-dioxide emissions could, for example, have been measured more cheaply by the method of 'mass balance': by recording the amounts of coal or oil consumed and their sulphur content (a standard commercial datum), and then applying correction factors—factors that were 'well known based on engineering studies' (Ellerman et al. 2000: 248)—to take into account the retention of sulphur in ash and its removal by 'scrubbers' in smokestacks. But the resultant facts would not have been hard enough.

Many environmentalists in the USA had deep concerns about the wisdom and ethics of markets in pollution permits, and would have feared that utilities could manipulate emissions data calculated in this way. Those fears might well have tipped the political balance against the proposed market. An expensive, largely automatic measurement system, in which corruptible human beings played only a limited direct role, 'was the price of assuaging environmentalist concerns about emissions trading' (Ellerman et al. 2000: 249). Another motivation for the system was to increase market liquidity. Economist Richard Sandor, who had long experience of the Chicago derivatives markets described in Chapter 4, advised the EPA that it was essential that emissions measurements be made public as quickly and as frequently as possible. Otherwise the speculators who would provide liquidity would be deterred from entering the market by the fear that the utility companies knew too much more than they did. In Sandor's view, only automated measurement, not mass-balance calculations, could avoid a situation of 'asymmetric information' that would damage liquidity (Sandor, interviewed by author, 19 February 2007).

Precept 5: Actors Are *Agencements*

One way of expressing the hypothesis that actors' equipment is consequential and the observation that calculation is distributed and material is to say that actors are *agencements*. Although the notion of *agencement* is drawn from Deleuze (for example, Deleuze and Guattari 2004; see Wise 2005), the sense in which I use the term is more directly that in which it has been used by Michel Callon, whose work on markets has been a major resource for the social studies of finance.

Callon's approach is rooted in the 'actor-network theory' that he developed with Bruno Latour (Callon and Latour 1981; Callon 1986; Latour 1987; 2005) and with others such as Madeleine Akrich, John Law, and Vololona Rabeharisoa. The theory is currently perhaps the single most prominent form of what in Chapter 1 I called 'material sociology'. Its most distinctive feature is its agnosticism as to the nature of agents or actors, which are taken as potentially including non-human entities as well as human beings. (With the general reader in mind, I have used the word 'agent', not 'actor', in the title of this book, but do not intend any systematic distinction between the two.)

The actor-network notion of 'actor' is thus quite different from the standard sociological use of the term, which refers only to human beings. In one sense, the actor-network notion of 'actor'—also the related notion of 'actant'—simply follows how those terms are used in semiotics, especially the semiotics of A. J. Greimas.[15] (As Latour 2005: 53 puts it, some entities that 'modify a state of affairs by making a difference' are 'actants', not 'actors'. The difference is that the latter have and the former have not 'been provided in the account with some ... features that make them have some form or shape'.) The actors and actants in narratives are plainly not all human beings: 'The concept of actant ... applies not only to human beings but also to animals, objects, or concepts' (Greimas and Courtés 1982: 5). Where actor-network theory differs from traditional semiotics is in applying such notions more broadly than to narratives and other texts. As John Law puts it, '*semiotics* ... tells that entities take their form and acquire their attributes as a result of their relations with other entities ... actor-network theory may be understood as a *semiotics of materiality*. It takes the semiotic insight ... and applies this ruthlessly to all materials—and not simply to those that are linguistic' (Law 1999: 3–4, emphases in original).

Thus Callon argues that action, 'including its reflexive dimension that produces meaning, takes place in hybrid collectives': combinations of 'material and technical devices, texts, etc.' and human beings. In Callon's analysis, therefore, an economic actor is not an individual human being, nor even a human being 'embedded in institutions, conventions, personal relationships or groups' (as economic sociology posits). For Callon, an actor is 'made up of human bodies but also of prostheses, tools, equipment, technical devices, algorithms, etc.'—in other words is made up of an *agencement* (Callon 2005: 4–5).

There is a deliberate word-play in the notion of *agencement*. *Agencer* is to arrange or to fit together: in one sense, *un agencement* is thus an assemblage, arrangement, configuration, or layout. The referent in everyday French is often physical, such as the parts of a machine; indeed, in ordinary parlance, *les agencements* are fixtures and fittings, and to be *bien agencé* is to be well equipped

(Collin, Knox, Ledésert, and Ledésert 1982). The other side of the word-play, however, is *agence*: agency. (I retain the French *agencement* because this word-play does not carry over into the term's usual English rendering as 'assemblage', which thus has somewhat too passive a connotation.) As Callon and Caliskan (2005: 24–5) put it: '*Agencements* denote socio-technical arrangements when they are considered from the point [of] view of their capacity to act and to give meaning to action.'

The notion that actors are sociotechnical combinations—that they are *agencements*—has the virtue of implicitly highlighting the question of the attribution of agency, in the sense of the capacity for intentional action. (Note that this is a weaker sense of 'agency' than a common sociological use of the term to mean the capacity for intentional action that alters social structures.) Ordinarily, we think of agency in markets as residing in individual human beings, but that attribution is not inevitable. The law of contract, for example, often attributes aspects of agency not to individuals but to the organizations to which they belong. An intrinsic aspect of making a deal—a commonplace intentional action in financial markets—is the taking on of commitments, for example to deliver securities or money (at least the electronic traces thereof). While traders may speak or type the words that bring a deal into being, those words commit not those who have spoken or typed them but the organizations of which they are members. Should the individuals in question leave those organizations, these obligations do not depart with them.

Much of the sometimes fierce debate around actor-network theory that has taken place within the social studies of science and technology has concerned the attribution of agency to non-human entities (see, especially, Collins and Yearley 1992). At least equally interesting from the viewpoint of markets, however, is how the attribution of agency distributes it across human beings. Sometimes, for example, the agency of traders is denied. For instance, prior to the introduction of sufficiently small and portable computers, traders making use of option theory usually did so by consulting paper sheets of theoretical option values. In both Chicago and London, those who did this were frequently referred to by their peers as 'sheet monkeys': agency-less slaves of the physical sheets and of the mathematical model embodied in them. The present-day equivalent epithet is 'F9 monkey'. Pressing the F9 key when using a spreadsheet instructs the program to perform the calculations implemented in the spreadsheet, and an 'F9 monkey' is someone who allows the resultant number or numbers to determine their actions.

The attribution of agency is often interwoven with issues of gender. Thus one sheet-using options trader told me that others questioned the masculinity of the use of sheets. Fellow traders 'would laugh at you and try to intimidate you out of the [trading] pit, saying, "You're not a man if you're using those theoretical value sheets." They'd take your sheets and throw them down on the floor and say, "Be a man. Trade like a man.... You shouldn't be here. You're not a trader. You can't trade without those"' (MacKenzie and Millo 2003: 124). My colleague Lucia Siu has discovered that in at least two of China's commodity futures exchanges most traders are women. Although their roles as trading intermediaries are similar to those of many of their predominantly male Western counterparts, their jobs lack the prestige and high rewards of the latter. They are seen more as the tools of other actors, and the skill and initiative they bring to their trading are largely disregarded.

The notion of *agencement* thus has a virtue that is not amongst those standardly claimed for actor-network theory. Tracing the *agencement* making up an economic actor, rather than focusing exclusively on what one might call action's glamorous agential peaks, broadens the field of view of the social-science investigation of finance, not just towards things but towards less high-status human beings. There has, for example, been considerable attention to accountants, to their professionalization and regulation, and so on. The detailed content of the work of their lower-status counterparts, book-keepers, has in contrast almost never been studied by social scientists, yet— as emphasized in Chapter 6—it is book-keepers who typically perform the primary classificatory acts that are the foundation of corporate accounts.[16] Again, gender is involved. The bifurcation of the task of producing accounts that took place from the late nineteenth century onwards became a gendered bifurcation, a separation between the almost exclusively male professional and the clerk, who was increasingly likely to be female (Kirkham and Loft 1993).

Another virtue of the notion of *agencement* is that it suggests that actors should not be seen as having fixed natures or fixed characteristics. The equipment that makes an actor what it is, the particular material processes of calculation it engages in, the specifics of the distribution of cognition—all these shape the nature of actors, or so the social studies of finance postulates. Again, the point is fundamentally an actor-network theory one: 'actors are network effects. They take the attributes of the entities which they include' (Law 1999: 5).

Consider rationality, for example. The central divide in modern financial economics is between the orthodox view of actors as rational and the 'behavioural finance' view of actors as subject to systematic psychological biases of the kind identified in the experimental work of Daniel Kahneman and Amos Tversky (for example, Kahneman and Tversky 1979). Implicitly or explicitly, both views conceive of the actor as an individual human being or akin to such a human. Typically, neither view takes into account in any systematic fashion the ways, discussed above, in which individual human beings are embedded in *agencements* of multiple other human beings and technical and conceptual equipment.

Rather than endorsing either the rational-actor or behavioural-finance viewpoints, the social studies of finance investigates how the nature of actors is shaped by the *agencements* that constitute them. For example, the incorporation of concepts and procedures from economics into actors' conceptual equipment may make the behaviour of actors more rational, in the sense of becoming closer to the postulates of economic models. At its most basic, a human being equipped with a financial calculator is a different actor from one without one. I was amused, for example, to discover some years ago that colleagues who were using classroom experiments to illustrate behavioural finance insisted that their students (employees in the finance sector) not bring their financial calculators with them. The calculator made the student too rational!

The claim that the attributes of actors are not fixed can be extended beyond rationality to the other stereotyped attribute of the economic actor: selfishness. It is easy to assume that the individuals and organizations in financial markets are motivated uniformly by private monetary gain alone. However, significant aspects of those markets are gift economies. For example, those who make inputs into the LIBOR calculation are not paid to do so, and the data providers that disseminate LIBOR pay the British Bankers' Association only a modest fee. Furthermore, many aspects of financial markets rely on trust, for example that a deal made verbally between traders will be honoured even if subsequent price movements render it disadvantageous. It is not accidental that the coat of arms of the London Stock Exchange bears the motto *dictum meum pactum*: my word is my bond. Any pre-digital financial market would have been hamstrung if verbal commitments could not in practice be relied upon. Even in today's derivatives markets, deals are often struck informally and full confirmations by fax or electronically follow only days or weeks later.

Selfishness is perhaps most interesting in relation to collective-action problems. These are situations in which there is a course of action available that will be of net benefit to all those concerned, but in which the benefit cannot be restricted to those who have taken part in the action, and the benefit to each participant resulting from his or her individual contribution is outweighed by the cost of that contribution. In such situations, selfishly rational actors will free-ride, leaving it to others to take the necessary action, which will therefore not happen if all those involved are rational egoists. Typical examples are cases in which traders need to forgo private profit-making opportunities in order to benefit their market as a whole (for example, by preserving its reputation for orderliness or probity),[17] or in order to preserve a tacit price-fixing agreement from which they all gain.

Gifts, trust, and collective action are of course questions of status and of culture. As all social scientists know, gifts should not be thought of as arbitrary altruism: to be invited to join one of the British Bankers' Association's LIBOR Contribution Panels increases a bank's standing in the market in question. London's tradition of 'gentlemanly capitalism' (Thompson 1997) helped make *dictum meum pactum* not an entirely empty boast: to renege on a verbal promise would demonstrate that one was not a gentleman. Yet physical setting and technology may matter too. The experimental evidence on collective action suggests that it is easier to sustain in contexts of face-to-face interaction, and 'open-outcry' trading pits provided just such a context.[18] Free-riding and defection for private benefit from tacit 'sharing' agreements may be harder for other traders to detect when trading is conducted by telephone or electronically, and traders in those contexts may not be able to express their disapproval as effectively as they can in face-to-face interaction.

The issue of whether and how actors can be configured so that they will contribute to collective action, rather than free-ride, is particularly pressing in relation to environmental questions, many of which are collective-action and/or inter-generational problems. As noted above, sulphur-dioxide metrology was mobilized in the USA as the foundation of a market. In Europe, it became part of a sociotechnical system designed to promote international collective action by making both contributions and free-riding visible: 'tote-board diplomacy' as it has been called by the main study of it.[19] (A 'tote-board' is a public indicator of the level of contributions to a drive to raise funds for charity. The role of a similar 'technology of altruism' in 'Téléthon' television fund-raising is noted by Callon and Law 2005.) The United Kingdom's reputation in the 1980s and 1990s as the free-riding 'dirty man of Europe'—a reputation that was damaging to the then Conservative government—arose from the visibility of its apparent failure in this respect.[20]

It is also important that the course of action that is in an actor's interest is often not self-evident, and decision makers are at least sometimes influenced by calculations performed by economists and other professional cost–benefit analysts. (Again, actors sometimes seem to need economists to help them be rational!) Thus the Montreal Protocol, the international agreement phasing out ozone-depleting substances, was facilitated by a cost–benefit analysis by the Environmental Protection Agency that was accepted as in effect showing that for the United States the issue was *not* a collective-action problem: the costs to the USA of phasing out ozone depleters would be outweighed by the benefits of its own restraint, even if no other country exercised restraint (Barrett 2003: 227–30). A similar cost–benefit analysis from the President's Council of Economic Advisors had a significant influence in debates in Washington: it helped defeat opponents of the protocol and persuade key officials (Benedick 1991).

In contrast, international action to slow global warming may be being hampered at least to some degree by the absence of a similarly authoritative calculation. The UK Treasury's review, led by the economist Sir Nicholas Stern, was intended to provide it, and the review (Stern 2007) indeed concluded that the global costs of curbing emissions are outweighed by the global benefits of doing so. However, the review's methodology—particularly its approach to the numerically dominant factor in such calculations, the choice of the 'discount rate' used to calculate the present value of future costs and benefits— has proved controversial, and consensus has not emerged.

It would, of course, be hopelessly naive to imagine that political (or indeed managerial) decisions are simply the result of cost–benefit analyses. The point, rather, is this. If action is shaped by actors' interests (a plausible proposition shared by social science perspectives ranging from Marxism to rational-choice theory), then attention must be paid to the material calculation of those interests. Everyone I've met in financial markets wants to make money, but it hardly advances the study of such markets to note that this interest is pervasive. What one needs to examine is how beliefs about markets, physical and conceptual tools, the structure of the connections between actors (Burt 2005), and so on influence calculations. Interests are not given: they are calculated within *agencements*.

Precept 6: Classification and Rule Following Are Finitist Processes

As the above discussion indicates, actor-network theory has been an important inspiration for social studies of science. It would, however, be a mistake for the field to restrict itself to a single set of intellectual resources. A different intellectual tradition from the social studies of science and technology (and related fields) has much to offer too: finitism.[21]

From the viewpoint of this book, finitism is most easily introduced as a theory of the application of terms to instances or particulars. Consider a term 'A', which could be an everyday word such as 'walk' or 'red'; a mathematical term such as 'converge' or 'polyhedron' (Lakatos 1976); or—as discussed in Chapter 6—an accounting term such as 'depreciate', 'asset', or 'finance lease'.

One view of the application of terms to instances is to conceive of terms as having fixed meanings. Once we have decided, individually or collectively, what a term means, then the infinite universe of items, processes, activities, states of affairs, and other particulars is divided up into instances of A and of not-A: red items and items that are not red; walking and activities that are not walking, such as running; polyhedra and entities that are not polyhedra; purchases of capital assets and activities that are not purchases of capital assets; 'finance leases' and states of affairs, such as operating leases, that are not 'finance leases'; and so on.[22] On this view of meaning, which is sometimes called 'extensional semantics', a term's 'extension'—the 'set of things of which it is true' (Barnes 1982: 31)—is fixed in advance of usage of the term. It may sometimes be difficult to determine whether a newly encountered particular is an instance of A or not, but if extensional semantics is correct the difficulty is merely empirical.

In contrast, finitism denies that the universe of all the items and activities that may ever be encountered should be thought of as divided up in advance into instances of A and of not-A. All we ever have—as individuals or as an entire culture—is a finite set of past applications of 'A' to particulars. When a new particular is encountered, the difficulty is more than the empirical one of determining its properties: we need to decide whether it is sufficiently like the previous particulars we have classed as A to warrant that classification. No two directly observable entities or activities are ever entirely identical; there are always differences between them that could be pointed to as well as similarities; 'every situation is in detail different from every other' (Hesse 1974: 12).

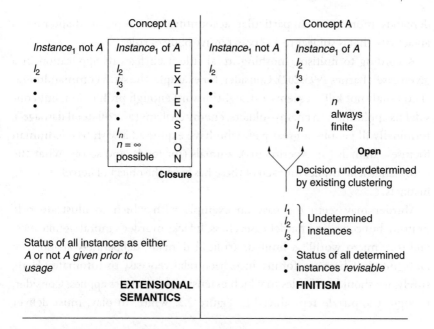

Figure 2.1. Extensional semantics and finitism

Source: Redrawn from figure in Barry Barnes, *T. S. Kuhn and Social Science*, 1982, The Macmillan Press Limited, reproduced with permission of Palgrave Macmillan.

Extensional semantics and finitism are neatly summarized by the sociologist of science Barry Barnes in the diagram I have reproduced as Figure 2.1. Note that finitism goes beyond the assertion that meanings are social conventions (Barnes, Bloor, and Henry 1996). That assertion is entirely compatible with the extensional-semantics view that once the meaning of 'A' is chosen, the instances to which it correctly applies are then fixed. Rather, in a finitist perspective every application of a term to an instance is implicitly a decision. Not only is the extent of similarity to previous particulars classed as A always in principle contestable, but those previous instances are always revisable: we may decide that one or more previous applications of 'A' were mistaken.

An area in which finitism is of particular importance is in understanding what it is to follow a rule, the classic discussion of which is in Wittgenstein (1967). Rule following matters for the understanding of financial markets because of the extent to which they are rule-governed. As Vogel (1996) suggests, although we think of the current epoch as one of 'deregulation' of markets, rules are proliferating. In apparent paradox, creating 'freer markets' demands 'more rules'. In particular, accounting—the topic of Chapter 6—is an activity that is subject to a very extensive body of rules.

According to finitism, 'nothing in [a] rule itself fixes its application in a given case' (Barnes 1995: 202). Consider, for example, the sixth commandment, 'Thou shalt not kill'. It seems a straightforward enough prohibition, but consider its application to enemy soldiers, enemy civilians (as 'collateral damage'), terminally ill people in great pain who have expressed a wish to die, human foetuses, animals (in experiments), animals (for food), and so on. What the commandment implies for each of these has been the object of fiercely varying instincts.

Murder may seem too easy an example with which to illustrate rule finitism, but consider a harder case: chess. It lacks murder's moral significance, and is a 'micro world': a limited, artificial domain, deliberately stripped of ambiguity.[23] (Chess has, for instance, been relatively easy to automate.) Here, surely, we should find rules to which extensional semantics applies. Consider, though, the puzzle reproduced in Figure 2.2. White, to play, must deliver

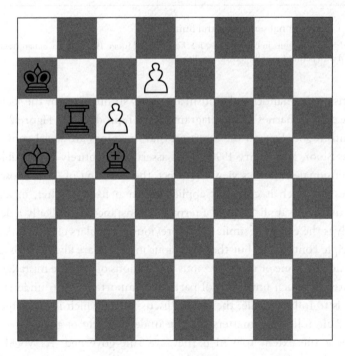

Figure 2.2. White to play and mate in a single move
Source: Puzzle composed by Richard Haddrell.

checkmate in a single move. The solution is that white moves his or her most advanced pawn to the eighth rank and replaces it with the rook that currently blocks the diagonal from the white bishop to the black king. The latter is thus exposed to check, and has no flight square because the rook now controls the eighth rank. It is checkmate.

Any chess player will respond that the 'solution' is not a legal move: it is contrary to the rules of chess. Consider, however, the pawn-promotion rule as it stood in the *Laws of Chess* in May 2005: 'When a pawn reaches the rank furthest from its starting position it must be exchanged as part of the same move for a queen, rook, bishop or knight of the same colour' (FIDE 2005a: rule 3.7.e). The solution to the puzzle could, in principle, surely be defended as a reasonable interpretation of what it is to 'exchange' the pawn for a rook. One could of course imagine a rule of interpretation being added to seek to specify what the pawn-promotion rule means, but if finitism is correct that is simply to enter a regress, since the rule of interpretation will itself contain terms that need to be interpreted.[24] (One explanation of the sheer volume of the rules governing financial markets, especially governing accounting in the USA, is precisely that this regress has been entered.)

The chief advantage of finitism as a resource for the analysis of financial markets is less the way in which it highlights the in-principle flexibility of classification and rule following (a point that many in the finance sector are already well aware of) than the way in which—precisely by highlighting that in-principle flexibility—it channels attention to the factors that in practice constrain it. As the philosopher and sociologist of science David Bloor puts it, in a passage of which I have already quoted part in Chapter 1:

According to meaning finitism, we create meaning as we move from case to case. We *could* take our concepts or rules anywhere, in any direction ... We are not prevented by 'logic' or by 'meanings' from doing this ... The real sources of constraint [are] our instincts, our biological nature, our sense experience, our interactions with other people, our immediate purposes, our training, our anticipation of and response to sanctions, and so on through the gamut of causes, starting with the psychological and ending with the sociological. (Bloor 1997: 19–20, emphasis in original)

An actor-network theorist—attuned to the ways in which technologies (walls, weapons, prisons, writing ...) contribute to the production of social order—would want to add 'things' or 'technologies' to Bloor's list. I think that's right. Consider the chess puzzle. If a similar position appeared in a chess tournament, and a player overcame his or her instincts sufficiently to play a move analogous to the 'solution', what would stop it being successful is indeed 'interactions with other people': the opponent and tournament controller would not accept it. But if one were playing a chess computer, the constraint is technological: the move could not be input into the machine (at least unless one had access to the source code of the chess program and the skills to alter it). As will be seen in Chapter 6, it's the same with accounting. Constraint comes not only from other people, but also from machines.

Precept 7: Economics *Does* Things

Researchers in the wider social sciences who study markets, for example economic sociologists, often see themselves as in competition with economics. There is no reason why that should be the case for social studies of finance. Modern financial economics, for example, offers an analysis of markets that is remarkably successful—more successful than any systematic alternative (behavioural finance included)—and the social studies of finance should not, in my view, see itself as committed to disputing that success.

 That attitude comes naturally to someone with a background in the social studies of science. No philosopher, historian, or sociologist of physics sees him- or herself as in competition with physics. (It's not that the knowledge produced by the natural sciences can't or shouldn't be contested, but that to contest it is to *do* science, not to analyse it sociologically.) However, the attitude should not become simply complacent acceptance of a hegemonic discipline. If a material sociology of markets is to talk about economics—and it needs to—it must have something interesting to say.

 A promising line of enquiry in regard to financial economics explores the hypothesis that the field's success is in part a 'performative' success, not simply a descriptive or analytical success. The term 'performative' was coined by the philosopher J. L. Austin, and a basic usage is to distinguish utterances that do things—'I apologize', which if one says it *is* an apology—from utterances that report on states of affairs separate from the utterance, such as 'It is raining' (see Austin 1962). An economic model, for example, is sometimes not simply a representation of a market as an entity entirely separate from the model, but a tool used by market participants, and sometimes the widespread use of such a tool can change markets in consequential ways (MacKenzie 2006). Applying the notion of 'performativity' to economics (as done influentially in Callon 1998) thus suggests the hypothesis that financial economics succeeds because it has been able to reshape the world. By being incorporated into regulatory structures, pricing software, trading strategies, and so on, it has created conditions of which it is a reasonably good empirical description.

Note that suggesting that economics is performative is not quite the same as saying that ideas from economics influence people. They do, in the sense that those who have taken an economics degree or an economics-influenced MBA do seem often to think differently from those who haven't. But as I've emphasized above, an economic model embodied in a system for pricing and risk management can have effects even if the users of the system don't believe the model, don't understand it, or even don't know that it exists. Economics is embodied in procedures and physical artefacts, not just in ideas.

Since I have discussed the performativity of financial economics at length elsewhere,[25] I give a different example of the precept that 'economics does things' in this book: the part played by economics and by economists in the establishment of the markets for emissions permits. It's actually a more clear-cut case of the precept, because unlike most of the markets analysed by financial economists emissions markets did not previously exist: they were invented by economists. They're thus not a challenging case from the viewpoint of establishing that economics does things, but the emergence of these markets is nonetheless worth attention because of the pivotal place that they now occupy in environmental policy and politics.

Precept 8: Innovation Isn't Linear

Part of what makes the role of economists in inventing emissions markets interesting is that invention is not the simple thing envisioned by a 'linear' view of technological innovation, and 'the performativity of economics' is misread if seen through the lens of a linear view, as it has been by some critics of the notion.[26] In such a view, to put matters very simply, the first step is when scientists discover features of the natural world. Next, the practical implications of those discoveries are deduced by technologists and become inventions. Those inventions then diffuse, and have effects on societies and economies.

All aspects of a linear view of innovation have been criticized for several decades—a still-useful account of many of its flaws can be found in Barnes and Edge (1982)—and indeed it's questionable just how widely it was ever believed, at least in the above simple, stark form (Edgerton 2004).[27] I have already touched upon the weakness of the notion of scientific 'discovery' when it is interpreted to mean stumbling over what is already there. Nor is technological innovation simply the deduction of the implications of scientific discovery. Technologists may or may not draw upon science, and when they do they use it creatively as a resource rather than simply deducing its implications. Much innovation takes place during diffusion: Fleck (1994) calls this 'innofusion'. The users of technologies are often an important source of innovation (Oudshoorn and Pinch 2003). Technologies are shaped to fit their 'contexts' (MacKenzie and Wajcman 1999), and 'contexts' are often deliberately reshaped to fit technologies (MacKenzie 1990), rather simply changing in response to adoption of those technologies.

As Callon (2007) suggests, a linear view of the performativity of economics would be no more valid than a linear view of technological innovation. New financial products and trading mechanisms can indeed be viewed as innovations (as Chapter 4 discusses), and economics is reasonably often drawn upon in these innovations. However, it is not the only source of them, and the outcome of processes of economic innovation is affected by many other factors. Financial innovation is shaped by matters such as legal structures, political processes, and even by broader cultural differences: the 'cultural geographies' discussed in Chapter 4. The markets in emissions permits are indeed economists' inventions, but as discussed in Chapter 7, they are shaped by much more than the intentions of their inventors.

Precept 9: Market Design Is a Political Matter

That linear views are invalid has an important consequence. If the process by which technologies or markets develop were as a linear model posits, the politics of technology (or the politics of markets) would be reduced to a simple but unattractive set of choices: to embrace innovation indiscriminately; to acquiesce passively; or to resist innovation. However, because linear views of innovation are false, a more discriminating and nuanced politics of technology, seeking actively to shape the innovation process and its outcomes, is possible, and the same is surely true of the politics of markets.

The desire to provide a straightforward illustration of the way in which market design is a political matter is the main reason why this book goes beyond financial markets to examine the new markets in carbon emissions. The detail of their design is enormously consequential, and it is being contested politically (although on nothing like the scale that the issue's importance deserves). The carbon markets are, however, no more than an illustration. That the design of markets—for example, the formal and informal rules that govern them—is a political matter is true more widely. Apparently minor matters— 'technicalities', often technicalities little understood by non-participants—can have big effects, for example, giving advantages to some actors and some strategies and disadvantaging others. (My favourite example, discussed in Chapter 5, is the 'uptick rule' in the USA, which translated into political terms made it harder to vote 'against' a corporation than 'for' it.) An effective politics of markets—whether 'left-wing' or 'right-wing' in inspiration—needs to engage with such apparent 'technicalities', not just with the overall virtues and demerits of markets.

Precept 10: Scales Aren't Stable

A prejudice that impedes the development of a politics of markets of the above kind is the tendency to divide phenomena into small, 'micro' phenomena (details, technicalities, interpersonal interactions, and so on) and big, 'macro' phenomena (globalization, neoliberalism, capitalism, the international system of states, and so on) and to think of only the latter as political.

A material sociology of markets should be suspicious of the assumption that scales are fixed: that 'micro' phenomena will remain small, and 'macro' phenomena stay big. In science and technology it is frequently the 'details' and the 'technicalities' that matter, separating a successful experiment or machine from a failure. An important emphasis in science and technology studies is the need to 'open the black box', to investigate the contents, normally hidden, of successful procedures and successful machines. (In engineers' terminology, a 'black box' is a device the internal structure of which is opaque or can be disregarded, and which can be treated simply as transforming given inputs into predictable, appropriate outputs.) So long as they 'work', black boxes are an important source of power: indeed, on an actor-network view they are the only source of power. 'A macro-actor', wrote Callon and Latour in the first exposition in English of actor-network theory, 'is a micro-actor seated on black boxes' (1981: 299).

The most vivid instances of changes in scale are those in which apparently 'micro' matters (patterns of social relations among small numbers of people, 'technicalities', and so on) become large. I've discussed elsewhere a vivid example of the first—the 'imitative' trading amongst arbitrageurs, many of whom knew each other personally, that led to the downfall of the hedge fund Long-Term Capital Management and to the near-paralysis of significant parts of the global financial markets (MacKenzie 2003)—so let me here offer an example of the second. It indeed concerns a small technicality: the arithmetic of security prices.

Until 1997, stock prices in the USA were denominated in eighths of a dollar, so a stock could cost $45^3/_8$ ($45.375), but was not allowed to have a price of, for example, $45.37, $45.38, or $45.40. Research by two financial economists, William Christie and Paul Schultz (1994), found that broker-dealers on NASDAQ (the National Association of Security Dealers Automated Quotation system) rarely posted price quotations that ended in an odd eighth ($^1/_8$, $^3/_8$, $^5/_8$, or $^7/_8$). Subsequent investigation by the Department of Justice and Securities and Exchange Commission of 4,500 hours of broker-dealers' tape-recorded telephone calls found that this was a market norm, not just a statistical quirk, with broker-dealers phoning each other about odd-eighth quotes:

Trader 1:   Who trades CMCAF [Comcast UK Cable Partners Ltd.] in your
            place without yelling it out?
Trader 2:   ...Sammy
Trader 1:   Sammy who?
Trader 2:   It may be the foreign department...

Trader 1:   What?
Trader 2:   The foreign didn't realize they had to trade it.
Trader 1:   Well, he's trading it in an eighth and he's embarrassing…
Trader 2:   …foreign department
Trader 1:   He's trading it in eighths and he's embarrassing your firm.
Trader 2:   I understand.
Trader 1:   You know. I would tell him to straighten up his [expletive deleted] act and stop being a moron.

(Department of Justice 1996: 25–6)

It is common in many markets for prices to cluster at round numbers, and there were possible innocent explanations, to do with the limited processing capacity of human brains, for the avoidance of odd eighths. Round numbers (in this case, zero, a quarter, a half, three-quarters) are cognitively salient to human beings (Yule 1927) and the use of coarse units—quarters, not eighths—as a market norm may reduce the risk of error and minimize negotiation (Harris 1991).[28] However, Christie and Schultz suspected implicit collusion to keep the spread between the highest 'bid' price at which a dealer would buy a stock and the lowest 'offer' price at which a dealer would sell it at least at 25 cents, not 12.5 cents.[29] An informal 'no odd eighths' rule would make defection from a tacit agreement of this kind instantly visible when NASDAQ broker-dealers scrutinized their peers' on-screen prices. (The norm is of interest in the light of the above discussion of collective action in that NASDAQ is not a face-to-face market. The collective action aspect arises because a broker-dealer using only even-eighth quotes was forgoing market share that would have been obtained by posting bids or offers that were an eighth better than his or her competitors'.)

The issue 'scaled up' in a literal sense. Twelve and a half cents per share becomes a huge sum when aggregated over transactions involving billions of shares: a class-action law suit by NASDAQ investors led to the payment of damages reported to be $910 million, then 'the largest civil antitrust settlement in history' (Ingebretsen 2002: 153). It also scaled up in a wider way. The crisis destabilized NASDAQ, arguably the world's second most important stock market (after the New York Stock Exchange). The Securities and Exchange Commission responded to the odd-eighths episode by insisting on changed access and order-handling rules, amongst the effects of which was to create opportunities for fast, low-cost stock trading by direct computerized matching of buy and sell orders, with no mediation by brokers. This made possible 'day trading' by lay people, which became widespread in the USA in the late 1990s and was, for example, a component of the dot.com boom. An apparent technicality of the arithmetic of stock prices helped shift the technological foundations and wider cultural economy of stock trading in the United States. Scales were indeed not stable.

3

Assembling an Economic Actor

with Iain Hardie

London: Wednesday, 5 January 2005. Hardie and MacKenzie are observing trading by a hedge fund. With traditional investment vehicles producing poor returns, hedge funds have been growing rapidly in number and in capital. They tend to cluster in particular places, notably in New York (some in midtown Manhattan, but mainly in the northern suburbs, especially Greenwich, Connecticut) and in the area in which we are: in and around Mayfair and St James's in London's West End.

The room we are sitting in is neither ostentatious nor large: even hedge funds managing hundreds or billions of dollars are small organizations, and this one is made up of only five people. The room faces off the street, and often the only noises to be heard are typing on keyboards and the hum of the fan cooling the fund's powerful computer server. Yet the world is continuously being brought into this quiet room.

At noon, Europe's three-minute silence to commemorate the victims of the Asian tsunami is observed. Electronic mail from other market participants, often at major investment banks, arrives almost continuously: it brings electronic traces of prices and other news; analyses of markets; confirmation of trades; and so on. Screens display numbers representing indicative prices in the markets in which the fund concentrates: emerging market bonds, the 'credit default swaps' that provide protection if a bond issuer defaults, and currencies. A scrolling on-screen 'ticker' lists major transactions in emerging-market bonds. Telephone conversations take place. Most are brief: often, the fund's main trader is seeking price quotations, and if the numbers he is quoted down the telephone line are attractive, a purchase or sale worth as much as $5 million is completed in a further few quick words. At one point, the speakerphone is switched on to listen to staff at an investment bank answering questions about their views on particular emerging markets.

The matters that attract attention, in the form either of conversations or of close scrutiny of computer screens, are heterogeneous: the minutes of the US Federal Reserve's Open Market Committee, released the previous evening in London time, which are taken as indicating that further interest-rate rises are on the way; the prices of the government bonds of the Philippines, which have defied a sharp global decrease following the release of the minutes; the soon-to-be-announced figure for US non-farm employment; the exchange rates of the Mexican peso and South African rand; politics in Ecuador; price quotation conventions in the Turkish bond market; and much else.

Economic actors are *agencements*, as discussed in Chapter 2: particular arrangements of embodied human beings, physical objects, technical systems, procedures, and so on. What we are observing is a modest *agencement*—a combination of only five people, some familiar technologies (the server, the keyboards, the screens, the network connections), and some specialized algorithms, procedures, and forms of knowledge—yet one that has to span the globe. It trades bonds, currencies, and derivatives originating in Africa, Asia, Europe, North America, and South America. The world it spans is infinitely complex, and even the attenuated information that flows into the room via the computer networks is in practice unlimited in quantity. For their fund to be an economic actor, these five people, along with their physical and conceptual equipment, have to turn this complexity into patterns that are simple enough to grasp, and then take appropriate action. How this happens is the topic of this chapter.

Studying a Hedge Fund

Hedge funds are, as noted above, actors of growing importance in the global financial markets, but have been the object of remarkably little social science attention outside of financial economics.[1] The distinction between a 'hedge fund' and market actors of other kinds was originally a creation of law and of regulation, especially of the wave of securities regulation in the USA that followed the Wall Street crash of 1929 and subsequent Great Depression. Some limited exceptions aside, the Investment Company Act of 1940 made it illegal for investment companies to short sell (to sell securities they do not own, for example by borrowing them in the expectation that by the time they need to be returned their prices will have fallen) or to use leverage (to buy securities using borrowed funds). In consequence, any economic actor in the USA desiring the capacity to act in those ways had to configure itself so that it was not an 'investment company' within the meaning of the act.[2]

Restrictions on short selling and leverage vary between countries, and have generally eased in recent decades. However, a 'hedge fund' can still be viewed as an economic actor set up in such a way that constraints of this kind on it are minimized. Although there is some variation internationally in legal require-ments, in the UK, USA, and most other countries hedge funds are allowed to accept only 'qualified investors'—individuals who are wealthy and/or deemed sophisticated—and direct investment by members of the general public is prohibited. Hedge funds are also not normally permitted to advertise (this is known as the 'non-solicitation' requirement). There is in addition sometimes a limitation on the number of investors permitted: for example, under section 3 of the 1940 Investment Company Act, no more than 100.

What is generally regarded as the first hedge fund was A. W. Jones & Co., set up in 1949. (Jones had a Ph.D. in sociology from Columbia University, but there seems to have been no connection between his academic work and his hedge fund.) Jones's striking success was made public by an article in *Fortune* (Loomis 1966), and it began to attract imitators, as, later, did the Quantum Fund led by the celebrated George Soros. The hedge-fund sector has not enjoyed entirely smooth growth—there have been well-publicized setbacks, such as the near-failure of Long-Term Capital Management (LTCM) in September 1998 (MacKenzie 2003)—but in recent years it has expanded sharply.

In 1990, there were fewer than 1,000 hedge funds, managing $25 billion in assets; by 2004, there were more than 8,000 funds, managing almost $1,000 billion.[3] The flow of capital into the hedge-fund sector since our observa-tions in January 2005 has continued to be substantial—for example, around $50 billion a month in the later part of 2006—and by July 2007 assets under management were estimate to have risen to over $2,000 billion (Mackintosh

2006; Thomas 2007). Hedge funds may be about to move into the retail investment mainstream for the first time. At the time of writing, the UK Financial
Services Authority has proposed rules that, if implemented, would add 'funds
of funds' (which, as the name suggests, invest in portfolios of hedge funds)
to its authorized product list and allow them to take investments from the
general public.

Hedge funds' annual management fees of 1 to 2 per cent are in line with
those of other actively managed investments, but they also charge a performance fee, typically 20 per cent of profits—that is, of increases in net asset
value. (Normally, net asset value has to rise above its 'high-water mark' in
previous periods before this fee applies.) To curb the incentive to excessive risk-
taking created by this fee structure, hedge-fund managers are conventionally
expected to have as much as half of their own personal net worth invested in
the fund that they manage, so that they suffer losses as well as benefit from
gains.

At times, hedge funds can become important owners of particular classes
of security: in early September 2005, for example, hedge funds were reckoned
to hold between a seventh and a quarter of the stock of Germany's leading
corporations, taken in aggregate (Jenkins and Milne 2005). Because nearly all
hedge funds are active traders rather than passive 'buy-and-hold' investors,
and because the use of leverage is common, their contribution to overall
trading volumes is much higher than the proportions of investors' capital that
they manage. In 2005, hedge funds were believed responsible for between a
quarter and a third of trading on the New York and London Stock Exchanges
(anon. 2005b), and for around half of total trading in the main market in which
the fund we studied operates, emerging-market government bonds (anon.
2005a). By 2007, a single fund, Citadel, was said 'to account for more than
5 per cent of all daily share trading volume on the NYSE and Tokyo Stock
Exchanges' (Gangahar 2007) and 'for more than 10 percent of trading in the
most liquid Treasuries': the sovereign bonds of the United States (Beales and
Tett 2007).

Research access to hedge funds is hard. The sector is a discreet one, partly
through necessity (the non-solicitation requirement) and partly through
choice, with many hedge-fund managers traditionally shunning personal pub-
licity, especially published photographs. As noted, the industry is highly concentrated geographically. Although New York has always dominated in terms
of assets under management (and still does), London—by far the leading

hedge-fund site in Europe—has been growing fast. In 2002, 28 of the world's 50 largest hedge funds were based in New York and only 3 in London. By January 2007, however, New York's share of the top 50 had fallen to 18, while London's had grown to 12 (Willman 2007).

The fund to which we (Hardie and MacKenzie) gained access was based physically in London, although its primary registration, like that of many other hedge funds, was in the Cayman Islands. It was of roughly average size in terms of assets managed. The category into which it fell at the time of our observations in 2005—$25–100 million—covered approximately a third of all hedge funds, with slightly less than a third being larger and slightly more than a third smaller.[4] The fund consisted in early 2005 of the two people, whom we call partners A and B, who set it up; a 'strategist' (partner C, a trained economist); an operating officer (partner D, who though based in the trading room is responsible for aspects of what in financial markets is called 'back-office' work); and a trader's assistant. (An intern was also present on one of the days of our observations.)

In a group as small as five, the presence of even a single researcher is intrusive, so we felt it unreasonable to ask for prolonged access, and our observations of the fund's trading are restricted to the first week of January 2005.[5] Because Monday, 3 January was a market holiday, those observations cover four days. Hardie was present throughout; MacKenzie (because of other commitments) for part of 4 January and all of 5 January. Mostly, we simply took notes, but the fund allowed us to tape-record the 'strategy' meetings it holds at 9.00 a.m. each morning, and as we began to develop a sense of which trading-room verbal interactions were interesting analytically, we sought and were granted permission to tape-record those too.

While noting as best we could what others did and said, we concentrated our observations on partner A, the trader. (Although partner B sometimes trades, partner A was responsible for all the trading during our observations, and references below to 'the trader' are always to partner A.) He allowed us to sit behind him, slightly to one side; we could observe all his actions and all the visible objects of his attention (see Figure 3.1). We could hear his part in all telephone conversations, and we were also able to listen to telephone conference calls. We occasionally asked the trader to explain actions he had just taken, trying to time such enquiries so as not to disturb the flow of his actions. (Heath, Jirotka, Luff, and Hindmarsh 1993 outline the cues participants in dealing rooms use to avoid disrupting others' action sequences.)

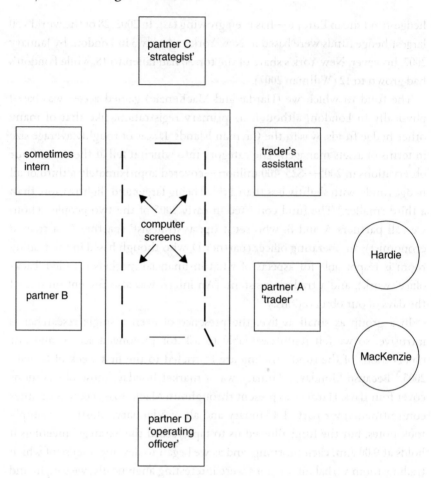

Figure 3.1. Layout of the hedge-fund trading room

The trader seemed remarkably unperturbed by this close observation, but plainly our presence could have affected what he or his colleagues did. However, it is worth noting that the focus of our observations was behaviour that is central to effective trading. Investors in hedge funds often judge them on their performance month to month, especially in the case of a relatively new fund (as this one was), and in that context four trading days are consequential. To depart from successful routines would have had a high cost, and the impression we have is that the trader and his colleagues did not allow our presence to disturb their actions in this respect.

We supplemented those observations with follow-up interviews with partners A, B, C, and D, and with several informal meetings between Hardie and partner A. Partner A also permitted us to forward to ourselves nearly all the electronic mail messages he received and sent during the period of our observation. (No selectivity on his part was involved: we simply ran out of time to forward the complete set of messages.) Printed out, these e-mails fill eight lever-arch files.

Our observations are of course very brief, and any one hedge fund is likely to have idiosyncratic features, so to place our study of this particular fund in context we have also drawn upon a wider snowball sample (so far involving fifty-one interviewees) of traders in other hedge funds and in investment banks, of those who manage such traders and provide them with other services, and of the 'funds of funds' that are now the dominant category of investor in hedge funds. When an interview is quoted without attribution to our fund's trader or one of his colleagues, the quotation comes from this wider set of interviews.

The Arrangement of Trading

Since an *agencement* is an arrangement, let us begin with layout. In January 2005, the hedge fund we studied leased two modest rooms in a shared office building. One room was used for the 9.00 a.m. and other meetings and for some conference calls. The other, where most of the action we observed took place, could have been mistaken for normal accommodation for clerical workers, except for two features (see Figure 3.1). First, rather than being distributed for privacy, desks formed a single rectangle in the middle of the room, and the occupants of chairs all normally faced inwards. Second, there were more computer screens than occupants of the room: in front of the trader, for example, were four screens. The plethora of screens interfered somewhat with lines of sight when seated—partner B would often stand to talk to the trader—but the centripetal layout of the room suggests a desire to facilitate communication and mutual visibility.

The fund specializes in 'emerging markets': countries such as Turkey, Lebanon, the Philippines, South Africa, Russia, Hungary, and the nations of Latin America that are outwith the heartlands of the global financial system but nevertheless have significant capital markets. (Sometimes countries such as Iceland, which are developed but on the periphery of the metropolitan heartlands, are also considered as emerging markets, although not by this hedge fund.)

The governments of all the countries in which the fund specializes issue bonds in their own or foreign currency. Bonds are tradeable debt securities that typically commit their issuer to repay the capital sum (the principal) on a given 'maturity' date and to pay 'coupons' (periodic, normally fixed, interest payments) until that date. They are the main means by which both developed and emerging-market governments bridge the shortfall between revenues and expenditures, a shortfall they nearly all encounter almost continuously. The capacity for successful bond issuance enhances a government's freedom of action: money can be spent now—on infrastructure, education, health, war fighting, and so on—and repaid only in the future, and governments frequently pay the principal on existing bonds that have reached their maturity by issuing new bonds. The prices and coupon rates at which investors are prepared to buy bonds have a direct effect on a government's debt-service costs, and thus on its budget balance and ultimately on the policy choices open to it (Hardie 2007).

The fund we studied also trades currencies, but the core of its trading is of bonds and bond-derivatives such as bond futures (a 'future' is a standardized exchange-traded contract which is close to equivalent economically to a commitment to a future purchase or sale of the asset in question at a set price) and credit default swaps (which, as noted, are contracts roughly analogous to insurance against a bond issuer defaulting). The bonds the fund trades are identified by country and maturity date (and sometimes also by coupon rate). When the trader telephones a salesperson at an investment bank and asks, 'Can you get me a level on Brazil 14s—one four?', what are being sought are 'bid' (purchase) and 'offer' (sale) price quotations for the Brazilian government US dollar bonds maturing in 2014. ('One four' is a wise precaution because the Brazilian government bonds maturing in 2040 are also actively traded, and a mistake between the two would be serious.) The further qualification— 'Can you ask him [the bank's trader] to show me a bid for [$]5 [million]?'— indicates something of the scale on which the fund trades. If the price quotation is attractive, a few further words on the telephone and a brief e-mail or Bloomberg message confirm the deal.

Such transactions can be conducted with apparent ease and informality because they mobilize entities not all of which are rendered evident simply by observing and listening to the trader. Here we encounter an aspect of *agencement* that the social studies of finance (with the exception of Lépinay 2004) has so far largely ignored: the 'back-office' infrastructure of trading. When the trader has struck a deal, he writes down its parameters on paper on a 'trade blotter' in a folder that lies on the desk between him and partner D. On one of her screens is the electronic 'blotter' of a trade-capture and portfolio-management system the fund leases. Like other such systems, it contains 'security masters', accessible on-screen via pull-down menus, which contain automatically updated electronic characterizations of all the securities their users are likely to trade. (An interviewee at a firm that provides technical systems to hedge funds told MacKenzie that as of January 2006 his firm's system contained 220,000 security masters, updated daily as coupons or principal are paid, and so on.) A small but critical part of partner D's role in ensuring the fund's smooth operation is to use the menus to call up the appropriate security master and enter into the electronic blotter whether the transaction was a sale or a purchase, the quantity and price, and some other details such as the identity of the counterparty.

Partner D's work aside, the fund's 'back office' is not physically present. The trade-capture system transmits the record of the fund's trading to its 'administrator', which is a separate firm, the relevant office of which is in Dublin. Amongst the services the adminstrator provides is 'reconciliation': ensuring that the fund and its counterparty have indeed made the same trade. Inconsistencies—'breaks' as they are called—are common in the world of trading. Sometimes the parties to a trade manually enter details that do not match; sometimes their two security masters, supposedly characterizing the same security, in fact differ. (Of the 1,300 employees of one firm that provides high-tech administration services, 680 are based in Mumbai, working through the London and New York nights, many of them identifying and, as far as possible, resolving breaks.) Crucially, too, the administrator's staff and technical systems employ the trade-capture data to check the trader's and his assistant's calculations of the changing daily values of the fund's assets, which are critical figures because they determine performance.

The fund is also linked electronically to its 'prime broker', a leading international investment bank. When the fund agrees a trade, the prime broker makes the necessary transfers of the electronic traces of money or of title to securities. (A bond, for example, is now almost never a paper certificate: it is an item in an electronic database.) The bank commits itself to make these transfers even if the fund is unable to pay for them, thus facilitating the fund's trading in an additional sense: the fund's counterparties know that not just its creditworthiness, but the bank's, stands behind the trades.

Data transfers from the fund's technical systems to the bank's make it possible for the latter to monitor the fund's risk-taking and its cash flow. At the end of every trading day, the bank's system 'sweeps' the dozens of trading positions that make up the fund's account, and places excess cash on overnight interest-bearing deposit. When the fund is short (has sold securities it does not own, the capacity to do which is, as noted above, almost a defining feature of a hedge fund as an economic actor), the bank will try hard to lend it the requisite securities, either from its own inventory or elsewhere, even if they are 'hard-to-borrow'.

Distributing Cognition

The fund's capacity to enact trades thus depends on people and technical systems not physically present in its trading room. So too its capacity to know which trades to enact. The fund deals in the currencies and government securities of far-flung countries with complex economies and intricate politics, securities that are entitlements to payments that are sometimes far in the future. Who, for example, can confidently know whether the fiscal situation of a country that has issued a thirty-year bond will be good enough for it to repay the principal when it finally falls due or whether its government then will be willing to make the payment?

The decisions to be made are difficult ones, and the amount of potentially relevant information is vast. Much of it is available in the trading room directly on-screen. Sitting at their desks, their attention on their screens in the manner described by Knorr Cetina and Bruegger (2002a), the trader and his colleagues almost continually sift this incoming flow of information. It comes from many countries. Some parts of it are quantitative: above all, data on price movements in the many markets in which the fund trades. Other parts are qualitative. On one of the trader's screens, for example, were titles of Reuters news stories. If he chooses (he seldom does, for reasons suggested below), the trader could click his mouse to open up Reuters' account of conditions in the rice market in Manila, or learn that 'after long languor Egyptian politics wakes up'.

Five people (the intern present on one day played no active part) thus confronted multiple appresentations of markets and innumerable representations of events in much of the globe. If human beings had unlimited powers of information processing, calculation, and memory, a single unaided human could perhaps turn the information flowing into the room into an optimal trading portfolio. Since human capacities are limited, as noted in Chapter 2 and as Herbert Simon emphasized long ago (Simon 1955), the necessary tasks are distributed across technical systems and multiple human beings: what goes on in the trading room is indeed 'distributed cognition' in Hutchins's sense (1995a; 1995b).

For example, a technical tool on which all bond traders depend is a yield calculator. The complicated diversity of bond prices frequently needs converting quickly to and from a more uniform metric. Thinking in terms of yields enables different bonds to be compared, and indeed it is common for bond prices to be quoted, or bond-auction bids to be priced, not as sums in dollars or other currencies, but as yields. In today's financial markets, the calculation of yields has become a routine, 'black-box' software feature. However, an incident on the second day of our observations suddenly rendered it visible.

The trader asked his assistant to produce a software-implemented calculator to enable price quotations for Turkish government bonds in the form of yields to be converted to and from lira prices. The assistant did so, employing the standard definition of 'yield' as the average annual rate of return offered by a bond over its entire remaining lifespan at its current market price, which is calculated by finding, by iteration, the discount rate at which the sum of the present values of the bond's coupons and principal equals its market price. The trader, however, quickly saw that his assistant's calculator was wrong. The assistant did not have a crucial piece of 'local knowledge'—the convention in the Turkish bond market is to employ not the standard definition of yield but the annual coupon payments expressed as a percentage of market price:

Trader: Turkish T-bills work on a simple yield and not a compound yield. Did you know that?
Assistant: No.

Once corrected, the Turkish yield calculator becomes part of the sociotechnical *agencement* that constitutes the hedge fund. The calculator's construction is itself heterogeneous. It mixes programming expertise, knowledge of market convention, and specialized factual knowledge: the coupon rates of Turkish government bonds with specific maturities. Two people produce it: the trader could in principle have written it himself, but in practice he needs to delegate the task, and also to assess whether it has been carried out to his satisfaction. In these aspects, the Turkish yield calculator is unusual only in that we were present as it was being constructed. What Hutchins (1995a: 374) says of navigation is true also of our hedge fund: 'The setting of...work evolves over time as partial solutions to frequently encountered problems are crystallized and saved in the material and conceptual tools of the trade and in the social organization of the work.'

The 'social organization of the work', in the sense of the distribution of cognition and action across the people in the room, was evident during our observations in many ways. For example, the trader frequently asks colleagues questions regarding information he has (possibly temporarily) forgotten: 'At what price did I do that trade?' or 'What was the [US] unemployment rate last month?' (As Hutchins 1995a: 134 puts it: 'remembering is jointly undertaken'.) When the trader is out of the office during office hours (which typically happens only briefly), he relies on his colleagues to observe market activity. When he returns, his first words often are 'What's happening?' or 'How is the market?'

Partner C also frequently takes the initiative in orienting the trader's attention to forthcoming data releases, and partner B often points him very directly to relevant market developments: 'Hey...you can put the trade on again at 110', or 'Wow. Phil [Philippine government bonds] is trading down. Don't you see these messages?' Implicit in pointers of the latter kind is often a view of an appropriate trade. If that view conflicts with the trader's, a brief discussion will often take place:

Partner B: ...have you seen the ZAR [South African rand]?
Trader: Yes, it's going my way. What is your problem? Do you want me to take it off now?

On other occasions, however, the trader will do no more than acknowledge the comment ('Yeah, I saw it'), or will not reply at all.

Although the trader has evident confidence in his views, he acknowledges that others have expertise that he does not: in particular the 'strategist', partner C. The latter's role is to follow economic and political developments in emerging-market countries but also (for reasons we explore below) economic developments in other countries: mainly, but not exclusively, the United States. The following exchange, for example, took place after the monthly release of the US employment figures, the data event during the period of our observations to which by far the most attention was devoted. The trader and partner C are looking at the same information screens during the exchange, and the trader is simultaneously trying to complete the purchase of some Brazilian bonds (the breaks in the text are mainly when he is talking on the telephone about this):

Partner C: Christmas sales have been kind of sluggish. By all accounts there was a lot of discounting and going out and ordering new merchandise and also this employment report, the reason why it is below expectations was because retail jobs cut by 20,000.

Trader: ...So the economy is weak, yeah...

Partner C: So the retailers are having a tough time. They're not hiring like they usually do in December and are probably discounting.

Trader: ...So the number. Based on this number, what do you think Treasuries [US government bonds] should do, overall? If you had to close everything else off and, based on this number, just on these numbers, what?

Partner C: Just Treasuries?

Trader: Yeah, what would you say Treasuries should do? Up, down, unchanged.

Partner C: In a word, I would say unchanged.

Trader: Right, thank you. But don't you think that market professionals will look through the numbers and they will imply something for inflation? Or that's not going to happen?

Partner C: You asked for one word say I gave you the, yeah, I'll embellish a bit more. Yeah, it's as I said. It appears that Christmas was kind of, overall it was okay for retailers. It was okay because they were discounting to move the merchandise. So that's positive for inflation, for December anyway...But you have to weigh that up against the fact that the average hourly earnings was a bit higher than expected.

Trader: Right.

Partner C: So?

Trader: That's what I meant about the, reading through those...

Partner C: Yeah, that's why I say unchanged because there are these cross-currents going through.

That was an exchange about the bearing of economic conditions on the US bond market. Other exchanges between the trader and partners B and C debate specific features of trades. They often begin quite casually and move gradually towards a collective decision:

Trader: Should we do, I mean I'd like to do the trade, the Taiwan dollar trade versus the [US] dollar. You don't think...

Partner B: He'll [partner C will] tell you to do it versus the euro.

Trader: But this is a big change. I mean you know, you can't change like that, like overnight. Let's think about it. Maybe we change it, okay, but ...

Partner B: Change what?

Trader: I mean, in a way, it's a trade that it says go long the dollar and short the euro, right? I mean...this trade, if you don't think the dollar/euro is going towards, let's say, in at 120 [an exchange rate of 1 euro = $1.20]. If you thought the dollar/euro was going to 135, you wouldn't propose this trade.

Partner C: Well, I would in the sense that, there's three scenarios, two of which, this Taiwan thing will work...in Europe. One is that US does the right thing.

Trader: Right.

Partner C: And the euro...more against the euro.

Trader: My proposal, which I've made on the Mexican peso as well, is that we do these trades against a basket of dollars and euros, at this point, rather than just go all short euros.

Partner C: Yeah, I mean I'm not proposing that I've changed my view on the dollar generally, just, I was thinking just through the Taiwan and the Asian, Taiwan but all the, it's one way or the other, if you believe that story is going to happen this year...

Partner B: I believe it.

Partner C: And I do too.

Partner B: But the issue we're discussing is not whether to buy the Asia. What we're discussing is what to short against it. ....

Partner C: ... if you're ambiguous about, if you're a little bit ambiguous about dollar's direction for the year, then it would be, I think, still a kind of a win/win against Taiwan versus the euro ...

Cognition is seldom entirely separate from emotion (Damasio 1995). After discussions such as the above have stabilized an interpretation and generated a decision, or even when the trader has taken a decision without consulting his colleagues, they frequently provide him with emotional support. His work is stressful, involving actions in which large amounts of money (his own and his colleagues', as well as the fund's investors') are at stake. Support for decisions that have already been taken was often restated explicitly: 'I really like that trade' or 'Yes, I would be pretty comfortable with that.' If prices do not move as predicted, colleagues' comments both support the trader and encourage him to maintain focus: 'Yeah, don't let it affect you'; 'You're going to make no money thinking about it. Just forget about it and move on.' Sometimes the encouragement to do this last is very explicit: 'What else would you buy? What else is there to sell?'

Multi-Site Cognition

The cognitive processes that inform the fund's decision-making are distributed more widely than over the people and technical systems in its trading room. The necessary sifting of potentially relevant information is also conducted elsewhere, often in different countries or continents. Sometimes, the results of this sifting arrive via telephone calls or via telephone or web-cast teleconferences organized by investment banks. Most commonly, however, the results of others' sifting arrives in the form of electronic mail messages. Into this category fall the vast majority of those e-mail messages received by the trader during our four days of observations that did not have a specific purpose such as to confirm a deal or to give a price quotation—and even messages giving price quotations often also contain a brief commentary on market developments.

Usually, these e-mails are not the bilateral messages on which Knorr Cetina and Bruegger (2002a) focus, but messages to multiple recipients. As the trader put it: 'In a way the e-mails that you get are like being ... in an area where, you know, there are twenty different people sharing information.' A sample of the e-mails follows (items marked with an asterisk are the titles of electronically attached pages from services such as Bloomberg News):

(sender 1) 4.1.05, 14:58: 'CHILE COURT SAYS PINOCHET CAN FACE KIDNAPPING, HOMICIDE CHARGE'* At last . . .

(sender 2) 5.1.05, 00:30: Today's highlights

Brazil: In terms of data releases, watch today for the December C[onsumer]P[rice]I[ndex]-Fipe ([Sender's bank's prediction]: 0.6%) and fx [foreign exchange] flows for December.

Mexico: The peso nearly reached our 11.45 recommendation target and we advocate closing long USD/MXD positions when the peso gets closer to that level.

(sender 3) 5.1.05, 02:34: ROP [Republic of the Philippines] flying despite EM [emerging market] sell off and rates. . . . !!!! technicals . . .

(sender 4) 5.1.05, 07:19: [Philippines' government bonds] holding in very well vs-rest of emg [emerging market] spreads tighter by 8–10 [basis points]

(sender 3) 5.1.05, 07:38: 'Philippine 10-Year Dollar Bonds Rise on Narrower Budg'*— market on fire despite overnight action in Latam [Latin American] credit. If this story is the sole driver the market participants are much more naive than even I gave them credit for. . . . after 11 months budget deficit was at 160, an annualised amount 175bn pesos. . . . of course the annual deficit was likely to come in at somewhere between 170–190 . . . this story is surely no surprise.

(sender 5) 5.1.05, 08:22: Still think Philli sells off more as it is only down 1/4 point

(sender 3) 5.1.05, 08:24: [Philippines' government bonds] Just on fire.

(sender 6) 5.1.05, 11:26: BRAZIL JUST GETTING WHACKED ON THE BROKERS, 27'S, 40, 34 [bond maturities]

These incoming electronic mail messages generally contain information already available to the trader via the screens in front of him. He has access to Reuters, Bloomberg News, and other services. He can easily find out when the level of the Consumer Price Index for Brazil is due to be announced, the exchange rate of the Mexican peso against the dollar, the prices of the bonds of the governments of Brazil or the Republic of the Philippines, and the extent of their reported budget deficits.

These electronic mail messages thus generally serve to draw the trader's attention to some of the data items available to him, and not to others of those items, and often explicitly or implicitly suggest 'framings': ways of interpreting data items (see Beunza and Garud 2004). For the trader and his colleagues to monitor all available data items would be infeasible. The constant arrival of 'pointers' reduces the need to attempt to do so, and sometimes feeds directly into action. After a flurry of e-mail on the morning of 5 January (including the messages from senders 3, 4, and 5 quoted above), at 8.30 the trader concludes that the prices of the government bonds of the Republic of the Philippines are about to fall, and short sells $5 million of such bonds (denominated in US dollars) to sender 3's bank, e-mailing to his counterparty (who is located in Hong Kong): 'You haven't moved [your prices]. London will sell it.'

Clearly, the messages quoted above differ. Sender 1 is drawing attention to a news item, and offering a personal opinion. Sender 2 draws attention to a forthcoming data announcement (many incoming messages do this), and, in respect to Mexico, offers his investment bank's explicit trading advice. The messages from senders 3, 4, 5, and 6 take the form of reports on or analyses of market developments: no advice is explicit, but only a brave recipient or one with a long-term orientation would receive sender 6's message and promptly buy Brazilian government bonds.

The sources of messages such as these are of course economic actors in their own right, who can be presumed often to have an interest in what others will do when they receive them. It is in effect expected that market participants will 'talk their book' when circulating ideas for trading—that they will already hold a position, the virtues of which they are propounding—and a certain amount of 'gilding' or exaggeration in so doing is discounted (less pardonable is what Biggs 2006 refers to as 'sandbagging': advocating a position while oneself unwinding it). It is important, however, that many of the exchanges we are discussing (such as the e-mails about Philippine bonds) are multilateral, so that opportunism that leads to an idiosyncratic viewpoint may be detectable. As the trader says, 'it's fairly obvious . . . because you can see if one person is saying A, and everybody else is saying the opposite'.

Furthermore, some sources of ideas or sifting are more credible and more authoritative than others. As the trader puts it: 'some people are more informed; . . . some people are more thoughtful, sophisticated; some people are simpler, you know they have sort of based their decisions on hunches and so forth . . . so there's a difference in style, and I don't like to pigeonhole this guy is always right, this guy is always wrong . . . but of course they have, you have some sort of a bias whether, you know, how they think, and their style . . . and you factor that into your decision.' Partner B likewise notes: 'as you talk to all those people day after day after day, you kind of develop a feel for who has the right mindset and who doesn't...you will feel that, yeah, this guy has a good call on the market and that guy not so much.'

Selectivity in Information Sifting

Fully to characterize the sifting of information that goes on within the fund's trading room and in other locations connected electronically to it is a task beyond this chapter. Here, we discuss only two aspects. The first is geographical: the surprising extent to which the attention of our fund, for example in the 9.00 a.m. strategy meetings, was actually directed to the USA. As already seen, although the fund trades the bonds of countries such as Brazil and the Philippines it nevertheless paid detailed attention to matters such as, for example, the pre-Christmas retail market in the USA. Our follow-up interviews confirmed that that was not unusual. Partner C reckoned that the weight given to international factors—'usually the US, really'—in the fund's decisions was around 30–40 per cent, with considerations specific to the emerging-market country in question accounting for around 60–70 per cent.

The metric of 'yield' allows the vast range of bonds issued worldwide quickly and easily to be compared. For example, the yield of the dollar-denominated bonds issued by Brazil or the Philippines can be compared with the yield of similar US Treasury bonds, and the perceived probabilities of default by Brazil or by the Philippines are condensed into 'credit spreads' of the yields of their bonds over Treasuries. Indeed, a price quotation for an emerging-market bond will often take the form of a spread of its yield over comparable Treasuries.

The valuation of emerging-market bonds as spreads over US or euro government bonds means that, *ceteris paribus*, the price of the former will move in line with movements in the latter. However, our fund 'hedged out' this direct connection, for example by taking offsetting positions in US and euro bond futures. A less direct link nevertheless remains. If domestic investments in the USA earn only low yields, emerging-market bonds (with the additional 'spreads' they offer) seem to become more attractive. Amongst the consequences can be an improvement in the perceived creditworthiness of emerging-market governments: more attractive bonds mean lowered debt-service costs and thus improved budget balances, and an increased possibility of selling bonds with longer maturities, which has the effect of reducing the risks intrinsic to frequent refinancing. In contrast, if US yields rise, emerging-market bonds lose some of their attractiveness, and this virtuous circle can reverse, with perceived government creditworthiness declining and credit spreads widening.[6]

In consequence, US interest rates and bond yields affect not just the overall levels of emerging-market bond yields but also the spread of those yields over Treasuries, a factor to which our fund *was* exposed. Much of the action in emerging-market bonds that we observed had to do with the release on the night of 4–5 January of the minutes of the December meeting of the US Federal Reserve's interest-rate-setting Open Market Committee, which as noted above indicated a clearly increased probability of interest-rate rises to come. Despite the protection offered by the trader's hedges, it is thus not surprising that on the morning of 5 January we observed him reading those minutes with great care. They were the key interpretative context for the emerging-market 'sell off', including the puzzling initial failure of the bonds of the Philippines to fall in concert, and the anomaly in the pricing of Brazilian bonds to be discussed in Chapter 5.

Such phenomena are, of course, part of the meaning of that most familiar of notions: 'globalization'. It is worth noting, however, that in this case globalization acts in part through an algorithm. Without the metric of 'yield', comparing the bonds issued by different governments, with all their particularities, would be slower and much harder. An *agencement* that includes a yield calculator (or its less mobile predecessors, the 'yield books' that banks used laboriously to produce) differs from one without such a resource (just as Chapter 1 suggests is the case for an *agencement* including an option pricing model). In particular, the metric of 'yield' helps to construct a *global* bond market.

A second issue concerning selectivity in cognition is the extent to which attention is paid to the politics of the emerging-market countries in whose bonds the fund invests. At one point, we noticed the trader carefully reading a news story about Abdalá Bucaram, the maverick, populist former President of Ecuador, styled (by himself, as well as by his enemies) *el loco*, the madman. This story had not arrived via an e-mail message, and it prompted us to ask the trader how important a consideration was the politics of the countries whose bonds he traded.

His answer was succinct and general: 'The weaker the credit, the more important the politics.' The higher the probability of a government defaulting on its bonds, the more salient is information on that country's politics. That Pinochet might finally stand trial was, as far as we could tell, simply political news about Chile, and a source of personal satisfaction (or otherwise). That *el loco* might return to Ecuador from his exile in Panama was, in contrast, news of a different kind. The credit of Ecuador, said the trader, 'is one of the weakest there is' (Ecuador defaulted on its bonds as recently as 1999). In such a case, 'one or two guys can change the way things are'.

A single trader spending a few minutes reading a news story is of course a weak datum, but the trader's explanation is consistent with the extensive study by Mosley (2003). A key bond-market divide is between governments that are reckoned reasonably likely to default, and those whose default is regarded as effectively inconceivable. Ecuador is in the first camp. The UK and USA are in the second camp, and Chile has made partial, sometimes painful progress towards joining them. Bond investors monitor both camps in respect to government deficits, inflation, and interest-rate decisions, but 'politics' in countries in the second camp tends to be of interest only to the extent to which it is likely to affect these factors. Only 58 per cent of Mosley's interviewees mentioned elections in such countries as a factor they took into account, and of those who mentioned them almost nine-tenths said they were not important (Mosley 2003: 56). In contrast, as one interviewee told her: 'Politics is huge for emerging markets' (Mosley 2003: 129). Our trader's explanation implied a further differentiation—for example, the politics of Ecuador is seen as demanding attention of a different kind from that of Chile—and in his attention to Ecuadorean politics the trader was not unique. In April 2005, Ecuador had to abandon an attempted bond issue 'because of rising political tension' (Weitzman 2005).

Conclusion

The notion of *agencement* does not displace the classic concerns of economic sociology. Social networks, for example, plainly still matter (indeed, are part of *agencements*), for example when securities are hard to borrow, but a prime broker with good connections to custody banks can still do so. Nevertheless, *agencement* is a potentially useful broadening of economic sociology's intellectual resources, in particular in its emphasis on 'technical' linkages as well as on 'social' ones.

The risk of broadening, however, is that it becomes indiscriminate. The task of tracing an *agencement* in an interconnected world is formally endless, and the notion could become simply a jargon into which to translate banal description and narrative, as happened to some degree when actor-network concepts first became fashionable in English-language science and technology studies some twenty years ago. It is thus essential to be selective: to focus, for example, on aspects of *agencements* that are not obvious and on ways in which the composition and configuration of *agencements* affect economic action.

At the most basic level, the notion of *agencement* helpfully directs us to the conditions of possibility of economic actors: the often-ignored infrastructure that enables them to be the actors they are. Why are there now over 8,000 hedge funds? The reasons of course include economic and political changes, but it is also important that setting up a hedge fund is much easier than it was twenty years ago. The real-time interconnection of trade-capture and other systems makes it possible to standardize, automate, and risk-manage administrative and prime-brokerage services, which can thus be supplied on an industrial (rather than 'cottage industry') scale and relatively cheaply.

It is worth noting that it is in the infrastructure of economic action— rather than in what Chapter 2 called action's glamorous agential peaks, such as trading—that employment is largely to be found. While we know of no precise breakdown of finance-sector employment in this respect, it is clear that traders are only a small minority. The vast bulk of jobs concern other roles in *agencements*. Their gender balance is different: trading is still mainly a male preserve, but more women are to be found in the infrastructure that underpins it. The geographical location of the infrastructural jobs also differs, at least potentially, from that of the glamorous ones. The Republic of Ireland, for instance, is not a prominent site of trading but has become perhaps the world's leading site of hedge-fund administration, providing not just 'offshore' legal status and a favourable tax regime, but also a robust communications infrastructure. ('Locating computers in a place with hurricanes, it's just not . . . a good plan', noted one interviewee from the world of administration, explaining why the Cayman Islands were unattractive in this respect despite their tax advantages.)

Ireland also offers trained English-speaking staff and responsive regulation: 'in Dublin, you can go and visit the regulator...have a cup of coffee', said the same interviewee.

A smoothly functioning infrastructure is normally invisible: we had deliberately to seek out the infrastructure of our fund's economic action, rather than it being drawn to our attention by events in the trading room. However, in the wider hedge-fund world there are ways in which apparently infrastructural issues can suddenly impinge on freedom of action. Thus one main means by which risk is controlled in that world is 'mark-to-market' collateralization of contracts. As market prices move in favour of one or other party to a contract, collateral assets are transferred between them. Such transfers now often take place daily.

In the words of one interviewee, it is logical to meet such 'mark-to-market calls' by pledging out 'the most illiquid collateral that you have that fits the collateral requirements'. So what remains in a hedge fund's easily grasped 'box' (the unlent and unpledged securities that it owns) will often tend to be its most liquid assets. Under normal circumstances this is unimportant, but when a fund suddenly needs cash (for example, because of investor withdrawals or of mark-to-market requirements that must be met in cash) it can be consequential, especially if combined with technical systems that have not been set up to include fields that allow the fund readily to determine matters such as how quickly assets pledged as collateral can be reclaimed and made available for sale. Financial assets may seem abstract—they are, as noted in Chapter 1, tokens of rights and obligations, normally in electronic form, not objects that can be consumed directly—but whether or not a hedge fund has a technical system that allows it quickly to ascertain the status of these assets can affect a key aspect of it as an economic agent, its freedom of action:

The market starts to go down, now you got to sell something, because you're getting calls all over the place on mark-to-market. So you just, you look and say, 'oh, what can we sell?' In a perfect world you'd sell a balance of your portfolio of liquidities so that you keep some sense of control over the balance of what's there. But if you don't know where that collateral is and when it's coming back you are just relying on the faith of people that you pledge it for a week and it will come back a week later, and you don't care' cos it's going to come back. In a normal market that would be fine but in a fast market you've got to sell now. So, you say, 'oh shit...it's going to take me a month to figure that out [which illiquid assets can be sold] so I'm just going to sell this [highly liquid] US two-year T-bill', or whatever it is. So ... a ... hedge fund ... if they're not prepared for it, will be left with their most illiquid collateral only, which is also the stuff that the Street already knows you own. Cos you created a lot of attention when you bought it ... And then you start selling it, and they go, 'shit, that guy owns 30 percent of that issue, we better start selling it too'.

As well as *agencement* constituting the conditions of possibility of economic action, the distribution of cognition and of action it involves may shape the properties of actors. For example, as noted above, an economic actor equipped with a yield calculator is different from one without any equivalently easy way of comparing bonds. More generally, as Chapter 2 points out, orthodox finance theory posits (for the purposes of modelling) an investor who is a completely rational individual with unlimited cognitive capacities, but this has been challenged by 'behavioural finance'. The latter field also views investors as individuals, but, as noted in Chapter 2, sees them as hampered by the systematic cognitive biases revealed by experiments of the kind conducted by Kahneman and Tversky (1979) and summarized in their 'prospect theory'. One such bias is a systematic tendency to behave differently in situations of perceived gain (in which many subjects become risk averse, unwilling to take the chance of losing what they have won) and perceived loss, in which the propensity is to gamble to recoup the loss. For traders, the temptation is thus to avoid making a loss 'real' by liquidating a loss-bearing position, but to continue doggedly to hold it—in the jargon of trading, to become 'married' to it—in the hope it recovers (Fenton-O'Creevy, Nicholson, Soane, and Willman 2005).

Hence the apparently commonplace matters of emotional support and assistance in focusing after a trading loss are of theoretical significance: amongst their effects may be to diminish the 'prospect theory' bias referred to above. Traders' culture is certainly reflexively aware of that bias. In the pits of the Chicago Board of Trade, for example, traders sometimes hummed Mendelssohn's wedding march to signal that a colleague appeared to have become 'married' to a position (Zaloom 2006), and our wider interviews confirm that traders (and especially those who manage traders) are alert to the possibility of 'marriage'. Note the form of the general point this suggests. That individual traders are affected by their colleagues and managers, that their culture is reflexive, and that cognition and action are distributed across people and technical systems may have the effect of making the economic actor more like the fully rational agent posited by orthodox finance theory.

However, also note that economically rational action may not always promote stability. Another possible effect of the composition and configuration of *agencements* is on the risk of contagion: the spread of a financial crisis in one country to others, including countries with few trade or other connections to the original site. With the technical infrastructures of modern markets making it easy for a hedge fund or other economic actor to invest in many countries simultaneously even if it has only modest assets, highly selective information-processing routines are likely to be optimal (Calvo and Mendoza 2000), and we certainly observed such selectivity. It would, for example, be most unlikely to be cost-effective for our fund to hire a Magyar-speaking economist to deepen its understanding of Hungary, one market amongst many in which it operates.

There may in consequence be situations in which the optimal strategy for actors who spread their investments over many countries involves imitation: if an actor observes other actors—especially those judged to have expert understanding of the country in question—buying or selling, it may be sensible to do the same as quickly as possible. We should emphasize that we did not witness our fund behaving in this way, but our observations (and the corpus of e-mails to the trader) contain ample evidence of the circulation of information about particular classes of actor buying and selling. What is, however, harder to observe is *why* an actor is buying or selling. A sale of assets in one country may, for instance, arise simply because losses have been incurred in other countries with minimal economic links to it. Such sales may not convey any information, superior or otherwise, about the country in question, but may be misinterpreted as conveying 'bad news' (Calvo and Mendoza 2000).

With technical systems facilitating ultra-rapid reactions to sales and price falls, such processes can create surprising interconnections. On 22 February 2006, for example, a pessimistic analysis of Iceland's prospects by the bond-rating agency Fitch triggered falls in currencies ranging from the South African rand to the Indonesian rupiah: the Brazilian real, for example, temporarily fell almost 3 per cent (Johnson and Simensen 2006). Particularly yoked together in February and March 2006 was the geographically diverse trio of Iceland, Hungary, and New Zealand. The crucial linkage was the 'carry trade', a hedge-fund staple (though not a strategy employed by our fund). In this, a fund borrows in a low-interest-rate currency, typically the yen, and invests in the bonds or other assets of a high-interest-rate country such as Iceland. A significant depreciation of the currency of the high-interest-rate country can cause a carry trade to become loss-bearing, and at one point on 22 February the Icelandic krona had fallen by 9 per cent from its dollar exchange rate on 20 February. What appears to have happened on 22 February is that 'the emerging market contagion [was] caused by investors cutting profitable positions in order to plug their Icelandic losses' (Johnson and Simensen 2006).

Finally, what of agency? An actor-network economic sociology does not itself attribute agency, but instead follows the way in which such attributions are shaped and channelled by factors including the composition and configuration of *agencements*. Let us set aside the notorious controversy concerning actor-network theory and the attribution of agency to non-human entities such as physical objects, and consider only its attribution to human beings.[7] Agency is of course commonly attributed to individuals such as the trader, but is also often attributed to 'higher-level' entities. Our hedge fund, for example, is a legal entity, and, as noted in Chapter 2, the law of contract attributes agency to it, not to the individuals who comprise it.

Under some circumstances, too, market configurations can be such that agency can seem to have left particular economic actors and to reside in a market as a whole: for example, in the credit crisis that began in summer 2007, hedge funds and other economic actors often had little or no choice as to their courses of action, and had to sell assets even when it was a bad time to try to do so. The attribution of agency to 'the market' is indeed common when it is an entity invoked in political discourse, both right- and left-wing. More exotically, the economic agency of human beings is also sometimes attributed to entities 'inside' them, such as specific brain structures. Successfully doing so requires an *agencement* including specialist technical equipment, in particular a magnetic-resonance brain scanner, and is the terrain of the fascinating new field of 'neuroeconomics' (see, for example, Sanfey et al. 2003).

The attribution of agency may seem an esoteric, academic issue, but for financial-market practitioners it is in fact a pervasive concern. Many of the rewards to traders and those immediately around them come in the form of bonuses that are supposed to reflect individual contributions to a firm's profits. Because *agencement* is collective, this 'singularization'—the attribution of agency to specific components—is problematic,[8] and, unsurprisingly, is often the object of bitter jealousy and intense conflict. Its richness as a sociological topic has been demonstrated brilliantly by Godechot (2004; 2007).

The example of the attribution of agency reflects the overall merits of the notion of *agencement*. Used in a selective way, it can help trace linkages that are crucial in constructing economic agents and framing contemporary economic life, thus throwing familiar phenomena into new light and uncovering surprising connections and underpinnings. *Agencements* constitute markets, and investigating how they are made up is a crucial task for the social studies of finance and the material sociology of markets more generally.

4

Derivatives: The Production of Virtuality

In Chapter 3, Hardie and I noted that the hedge fund we studied sought to hedge—reduce or cancel out—its direct exposure to changes in US dollar and euro interest rates. The fund's trader could do this by opening up a trading screen on his computer and clicking his mouse to buy or to sell the bond futures traded on the Chicago Board of Trade or its European counterparts. It is a simple operation that takes no more than a few seconds, but one that has a complex history, which is the topic of this chapter.

Forty years ago, interest-rate risk could be hedged, if at all, only with difficulty. Not only did trading screens lie in the future: the exchanges via which financial futures and other financial derivatives such as options are bought and sold today either did not exist, or traded, as did the Chicago Board of Trade, only futures on physical products such as grain. As recently as January 1970, no organized financial-derivatives exchange existed anywhere in the world.

Such financial-derivatives trading as took place at the start of the 1970s was tiny in volume by today's standards, and was ad hoc. It was conducted either in the interstices and/or on the fringes of stock markets, or else 'over the counter': by direct negotiation, especially between banks. The burgeoning since then of financial-derivatives exchanges has been one of the defining features of the massive transformation of the world's financial markets. At the end of June 2006, exchange-traded derivatives totalling $84.4 trillion (the equivalent of around $13,000 for every human being on earth) were outstanding worldwide,

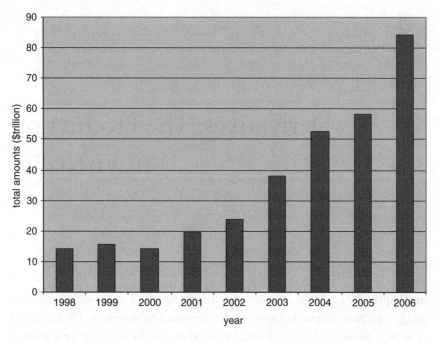

Figure 4.1. Total amounts of exchange-traded derivatives outstanding at end of June of each year from 1998 to 2006

Source: Half-yearly statistics from the Bank for International Settlements (<http://www.bis.org>), incorporating later data adjustments.

and the total was growing fast, having increased roughly sixfold over the previous eight years (Figure 4.1). Many of these contracts will have been entered into to offset the risks of other derivatives (so an unknown proportion of the total is thus in a sense self-cancelling), but the change from the early 1970s is nonetheless striking.

Most academic writing on derivatives is of course by economists, who have focused primarily on the pricing of derivatives (although there is a more 'institutional' literature on the economics of financial innovation and also useful work on why some derivatives succeed and others fail, both of which I will draw on below).[1] Recently, however, the attention paid to derivatives by human geographers, anthropologists, and sociologists has increased sharply.[2]

A common theme in this more sociological literature is 'the strangely imaginary ... or virtual character of derivatives' (Arnoldi 2004: 23). All financial securities are 'virtual' in the sense that their value lies not in their physical substance as paper certificates or entries in an electronic database but in the claims on future states of the world that they embody: rights to dividends from a corporation, to interest payments from a government, and so on. A derivative of such a security is thus an entity that derives its value from what is already an abstract claim, and so the development of derivatives markets can be seen as a further stage of the abstraction of monetary forms. Derivatives are 'money's "new imaginary" ', note Pryke and Allen (2000).

But how are 'abstract' or 'virtual' assets brought into being and made tradeable? As the developments in computer technology (above all, 'virtual memory')[3] that have given us the modern notion of 'virtuality' remind us, virtuality is always a material effect, indeed an elaborate, sophisticated, and expensive one. In this chapter, I explore three aspects of material production of virtuality. The first is the parallels (and also the dissimilarities) between financial and technological innovation. This theme *is* in the literature in economics (e.g. Silber 1981), but the view of technological innovation to be found there is too narrow, excluding for example its political dimension. Viewing derivatives as innovations offers a perspective on how 'economics does things' (Chapter 2's seventh precept) and highlights issues such as the intellectual property regime within which innovation takes place and the need, if innovation is to be successful, to take into account the interests of intended 'users' and to find a workable compromise between incompatible interests.

The second issue to be explored is the 'cultural geographies' (Thrift 2000) of derivatives. With the exception of Maurer's work on 'Islamic' derivatives (Maurer 2001; see also Maurer 2005), even the geographic and anthropological literature on derivatives is surprisingly homogenizing, seeming implicitly to posit a world in which, at least within its metropolitan core, 'place' no longer matters greatly. Spatial and cultural location is still significant, however, even in the metropolitan heartlands. The differing 'internal' cultures of financial markets have left their stamp, as have the different ways in which the relationship between investing and gambling (on which see de Goede 2005) is articulated legally. The relationship between a derivative and a wager is not just a general cultural issue. The exigencies of keeping derivatives separate from wagers (or, in some circumstances, making sure that they are wagers) have been critical aspects of their material production. They have affected which derivatives can be traded and which cannot, and the extent to which a derivative can be abstract and virtual.

The third issue to be discussed is facticity. The virtual character of a derivative contract is enhanced if, as is increasingly the case, it can be settled only by the transfer of cash, with neither party able to demand or impose delivery of an underlying asset. The measure used to determine the amounts to be paid must therefore be a 'fact': it must be an acceptable representation of the reality of which it speaks, and not be subject to manipulation. I focus on the most important set of facts of this kind (British Bankers' Association LIBOR, London Interbank Offered Rate, already touched on in Chapters 1 and 2), and note the fierce controversy over LIBOR that erupted in 2007–8.

The chapter's main empirical focus is the development of financial-derivatives exchanges in the USA and UK since 1970 and the emergence of the British financial spread-betting industry. The specificity of exchanges and of spread betting builds into the study a bias towards the discovery of heterogeneity: national differences in over-the-counter trading almost certainly exist, but would be harder to identify. That bias, however, is balanced by the choice of the USA and UK as comparator countries. Their overall financial systems have very similar contours, and in the literature on 'varieties of capitalism' (e.g. Hall and Soskice 2001) they are normally lumped together. The differences found between derivatives trading in the USA and UK are thus differences between two otherwise similar cases. Greater heterogeneity would probably have been found had the study encompassed the financial-derivatives exchanges now thriving in locations as diverse as Frankfurt, Stockholm, São Paulo, and Singapore, or those emerging in many other countries, such as Russia and the People's Republic of China.

Before turning to the main body of the chapter, it may be helpful to have a brief introduction to the main organizations covered, the relevant chronology, and the sources of information I have drawn on. The initial modern effort to begin organized financial-derivatives trading was the currency futures launched by the New York International Commercial Exchange in 1970. (A 'future' is a standardized, exchange-traded contract that is equivalent economically to one party committing itself to buy, and the other to sell, a set quantity of a given asset at a given price at a set future time.) That effort failed, but currency futures launched by the Chicago Mercantile Exchange's International Monetary Market in 1972 succeeded, as did the Chicago Board Options Exchange, spun off by the Chicago Board of Trade in 1973. (An option gives the right, but unlike a future does not impose the obligation, to buy—or in an alternative form of the contract, to sell—an asset at a set price on, or up to, a given date.) The Chicago Board of Trade itself, and a number of other US exchanges, also began trading financial derivatives in the mid-1970s.

The International Commercial Exchange, Chicago Mercantile Exchange, and Chicago Board of Trade had all originally been agricultural commodities exchanges. In the UK, the eventually most successful financial-derivatives exchange—LIFFE, the London International Financial Futures Exchange—was an entirely new development, established in 1982. In 1978, the London Stock Exchange set up a Traded Options Market, which merged into LIFFE in 1992. In 1991, the London Futures and Options Exchange, as the London Commodity Exchange was then known, launched property and housing derivatives; it too merged into LIFFE, in its case in 1996. (Property derivatives are of particular interest because housing, commercial property, and land account for wealth comparable in magnitude to the totality of stocks or bonds, yet the market in derivatives of them has been small, at least until very recently.[4] The failure of derivatives in the sphere of property throws their success in other spheres into an analytically interesting light.)

Financial spread betting began with bets on the FT(Financial Times)-30 share index offered by the bookmaker Joe Coral, and gained momentum with the establishment in 1974 by Stuart Wheeler of IG (Investors Gold) Index. In 1981, IG Index began to offer spread bets on the FTSE(Financial Times-Stock Exchange)-100 and Dow Jones indexes. Another firm, City Index, began offering financial spread bets in 1983, and others such as Cantor Index have joined the industry more recently. Spread bets are derivatives—they are contracts the value of which depends upon quantities such as stock-market indexes or exchange rates, just as an index future or currency future does—but they are deliberately constructed as wagers, for reasons discussed below.

The chapter draws upon four sets of sources. The first is existing histories of the Chicago Board of Trade (Falloon 1998), Chicago Mercantile Exchange (Tamarkin 1993; Melamed and Tamarkin 1996), and LIFFE (Kynaston 1997). The second is the trade press, which is often valuable in particular for revealing failed initiatives in derivatives trading. The third is a set of twenty-seven oral-history interviews conducted by the author with people central to the development of financial derivatives exchanges in the USA and UK and of financial spread betting in the UK. The fourth is a further set of twelve interviews which focused on the London interbank market, on the role of brokers in that market, and on LIBOR, and were accompanied by brief observation of brokers' offices, bank dealing rooms, and the process by which LIBOR is constructed. As elsewhere in this book, interviewees are anonymous except in the case of those who played the most important personal roles in the developments under discussion.

Innovation

The vast bulk of today's financial-derivatives trading is in products that did not exist in 1970. These products, especially those traded on organized exchanges, did not simply 'evolve'. They were *invented*. Indeed, today's financial-derivatives exchanges, especially the freshly established ones such as LIFFE, are the result of conscious, deliberate processes of design. Innovation in finance and in physical technology is not the same—three key differences are discussed below—but the comparison is analytically productive.

Let me begin with similarities between financial and technological innovation. Prior to the nineteenth century, what we now think of as 'science' played little role in technological innovation, but that role has now grown considerably. So too with finance. The academic discipline of economics had little effect on derivatives trading before 1970, but since then its role has been major (MacKenzie 2006).

As noted in Chapter 2, a widespread understanding of technological innovation is the 'linear model' in which science 'discovers' truths, technologists 'apply' science by working out its practical implications, and the resultant products 'diffuse' unchanged to users. Though still influential in public discussion, the linear model has been discredited by the modern literature on technological innovation (e.g., Barnes and Edge 1982; Fleck 1994; Sørensen and Williams 2002; Oudshoorn and Pinch 2003). Instead, that literature suggests that science and technology interact not as disembodied knowledge but as embodied expertise (often via the circulation of people); that science is a resource that engineers draw on creatively, rather than simply applying; that careful attention to users' needs and to 'local practical knowledge' (Fleck 1994) is necessary for successful innovation; and that much innovation—Fleck calls it 'innofusion'—takes place in what is conventionally regarded as 'diffusion'.

All of these aspects of technological innovation also characterize innovation in derivatives: as Callon now puts it, the 'performativity of economics' is a 'coperformance' involving 'economists in the wild'—lay as well as professional—rather than just 'confined' (laboratory or university) economists (Callon 2007). Academic economics has underpinned derivatives trading both technically and by providing legitimacy, especially against the charge of gambling (MacKenzie 2006). However, key innovations in exchange-traded derivatives have involved economists who left academia to work in the markets, such as Richard Sandor, who left the University of California at Berkeley for the Chicago Board of Trade, and his Mercantile Exchange counterparts Fred Arditti and Rick Kilcollin.

These economists in the wild did not simply 'apply' economics. They found themselves involved in processes of innovation that involved close interaction with the three main categories of users of derivatives: hedgers, who are concerned to protect their organizations against a risk such as currency or interest-rate fluctuations; speculators, who hope to profit by correctly anticipating those fluctuations; and market makers, who stand ready both to buy and to sell the product in question, earning the difference between the 'bid' and the 'ask' (the prices at which they are prepared to buy and to sell).

Hedging, speculating, and market making are categories of activity rather than of people and organizations: market makers, for example, often hedge their positions or deliberately take speculative positions, while some well-publicized derivatives fiascos have resulted from organizations starting out by hedging but slipping into speculating. Nevertheless, the categories of 'hedger' and 'speculator' are part of the 'lay sociology' that participants in derivatives exchanges deploy, and 'market maker' is a designated role with specific responsibilities.

Innovative exchange-traded derivatives need to be shaped in such a way as to be attractive to all three categories of user. For example, the International Commercial Exchange's currency-futures trading overlapped with the start of the break-up of the Bretton Woods system of fixed exchange rates, a favourable time because volatility encourages derivatives trading by giving hedgers, speculators, and market makers incentives to participate. However, insufficient effort seems to have been devoted to designing and marketing contracts that satisfied the needs of hedgers. '[T]he contract specifications had to be attractive to bank traders and corporate treasurers.... Successful futures contracts need, at a minimum, 20 to 25 percent commercial participation. You cannot have a market just for speculators' (Melamed and Tamarkin 1996: 174; see also Black 1986).

Exchange-traded derivatives are standardized products, so their specifications need deciding in advance. These include how big a single contract is to be; the 'tick size' (the minimum increment in price); the limits (if any) on daily price moves and on the size of position any one trader can accumulate;

the requirements for 'margin' (the sums participants in an exchange have to deposit with the exchange clearing house when they first buy or sell a derivative, and then have to adjust as prices fluctuate); the expiration dates of contracts; and the procedures for delivery of the underlying asset or for cash settlement.[5]

Successful choice of the specifications of derivatives contracts involves careful attention to sometimes conflicting interests: of hedgers and speculators; of exchange members and external customers; and of the 'longs' who have bought a derivative and the 'shorts' who have sold it. These interests are neither easy to determine—extensive research often seems to be necessary to elicit them, giving contract design something of the flavour of economic experimentation (see Muniesa and Callon 2007)—nor fixed. Indeed, a major entrepreneurial activity of financial-derivatives exchanges is to persuade both external customers and exchange members that it is in their interests to trade a new derivative (see MacKenzie 2006: 154–5 and 173–4 for examples from the history of the Chicago Mercantile Exchange and Chicago Board Options Exchange).

The potential for interests to conflict, even after they have been elicited and 'translated' (Latour 1987) in this way, makes contract design—like technological design (Winner 1980)—an inherently political problem. It is one that cannot be solved simply by fiat (overly favouring the interests of one group will probably be fatal, because others will then not participate in trading), but requires balance and compromise. Richard Sandor, for example, noted that the delivery procedure he designed for the Chicago Board of Trade's first financial derivative, futures on mortgage-backed bonds, 'is complicated and cumbersome. It appears to cause difficulties for both the longs and the shorts. It is in that sense fair, and may be the reason it has been successful' (Sandor and Sosin 1983: 267).

Design, marketing, and the encouragement (often via face-to-face meetings) of participation in trading are pressing matters, especially in the early days of a new contract, because exchange-traded derivatives are subject to 'virtuous' and 'vicious' circles akin to those identified in technological innovation by Arthur (1984) and David (1992). The archetypal example of the effects of these circles is the dominance of the QWERTY keyboard. It is not demonstrably optimal for electronic word-processing—its original motivation was to reduce the chances of the levers of a mechanical typewriter sticking together by minimizing the frequency with which adjacent keys were struck in succession—but QWERTY is 'locked in' to the English-speaking world's keyboards, and its rivals 'locked out': none has a realistic chance of displacing it.

Lock-in results from the advantages that sometimes flow to an incumbent technology or derivatives exchange simply by virtue of being incumbent. QWERTY's advantages are the familiarity of millions of users with that key-lay and the difficulties they would face in the first few weeks of using a different layout. The internal combustion engine's advantages include the century of intensive research and development effort that has been devoted to it (and not to its rivals), and the huge infrastructure of fuel supply and maintenance that a rival would have to create afresh.

In the case of derivatives exchanges, business tends to flow to where existing volumes of trading are high, because high volumes mean liquidity (even large transactions can be conducted quickly, easily, and without a large impact on price), low transaction costs, and a robust market price. Conversely, low volumes mean illiquidity, high costs, and unreliable prices. So an exchange that gains an established position in a particular derivative becomes, like QWERTY, hard to challenge (Silber 1981: 132). LIFFE, for example, found that the currency futures it launched in competition with those of Chicago Mercantile Exchange were not successful, despite London's overall prominent role in foreign exchange (Kynaston 1997: 95–6 and 126–7; Leslie and Wyatt 1992: 91). Instead, LIFFE's survival and success came to rest on derivatives that had no well-established rivals, notably FTSE-100 futures and UK and German bond futures.

There are, however, also differences between financial and most technological innovation. The tax treatment of derivatives is more critical to their success than in the case of most physical technologies. For example, the appeal of the London Traded Options Market to customers was initially limited by the way in which options were treated until September 1980 in UK tax law as 'wasting assets', which had the consequence that capital gains tax liabilities could be incurred on loss-making as well as on profitable trading (Steen 1982). In contrast, a large part of the appeal of financial spread betting is that in the UK customers' winnings are free from tax. Spread-betting firms incur tax liabilities as bookmakers, but these are modest and absorbed into the spread between the prices at which the firms buy and sell contracts.

Financial innovations are easier to 'reverse engineer' than most technologies (Tufano 1989: 230; Allen and Gale 1994: 53). To minimize the risk of dispute and litigation, the specification of derivatives has to be made as explicit as possible. Trading derivatives, pricing them, and hedging their risks may require tacit knowledge, but their design is easy to copy. Innovative technologies (especially those that *are* easily copied, such as pharmaceuticals) are protected from imitation by intellectual property law, particularly patenting. In contrast, the legal protection of innovative financial products (and, for example, of derivatives pricing models) has been limited, at least until very recently. In the USA, for example, financial products and models were presumed to fall within the 'business method' and/or 'mathematical algorithm' exemptions from the possibility of patenting. The general shift of intellectual property law from a presumption of open access—to which *patents* were the exception—towards a presumption in favour of private property (Merges 2000) has only quite recently encompassed financial innovations.

A pivotal case was *State Street Bank & Trust Co.* v. *Signature Financial Group*.[6] It concerned US Patent 5,193,056 (9 March 1993), assigned to Signature, which covered a data-processing system for calculating asset values and allocating expenses in a 'Hub and Spoke'™ system in which mutual funds share the ownership of a common investment portfolio. State Street had sought to have the patent ruled invalid, but in July 1998 the Court of Appeals for the Federal Circuit, which enjoys 'nationwide jurisdiction' over patent cases,[7] found in favour of Signature. State Street sought to appeal to the Supreme Court, but in January 1999 the latter denied it leave to do so (Lerner 2002: 903).

It is remarkable that, at least until *State Street*, financial derivatives, central as they are to the global capitalist system, developed in a legal regime with only limited intellectual property rights. Did that regime (a) slow innovation by reducing incentives, or (b) enhance innovation by facilitating copying and adaptation in a context in which QWERTY-like 'first-mover' advantages were an adequate incentive? That question points to a familiar debate about patenting that cannot be entered into here, but the extraordinary pace of derivatives innovation might incline one to (b). What is, however, clear is that copying was indeed easy. Specific derivatives have frequently been imitated without, at least until recently, fear of litigation. IG Index would, likewise, have been unable to prevent other firms offering analogous spread-betting contracts. Indeed, there is a sense in which entire exchanges have been imitated. LIFFE, for example, was more closely modelled on the Chicago exchanges, particularly the Mercantile Exchange, than on any British precedent (Kynaston 1997; Leslie and Wyatt 1992: 91).

Cultural Geography

The establishment of LIFFE highlights a theme prominent in ethnographies such as Abolafia (1996): trading is a cultural as well as an economic activity. The Chicago financial-derivatives markets inherited from their parent agricultural futures exchanges a tradition of often frenzied, open-outcry, face-to-face trading in 'pits'. Chicago's was a trading culture quite different from that of the New York Stock Exchange. There was no equivalent amongst Chicago's competing market makers of New York's 'specialists', who enjoyed what in Chicago was often perceived to be unfairly privileged access to the 'book' of unfilled orders (in return for an obligation to maintain an orderly market, in particular to trade with their own capital if there was a temporary imbalance between orders to buy and to sell).

There was an even greater gulf between Chicago's rough and tumble and the 'gentlemanly capitalism' (Thompson 1997) that played a dominant role in London until the early 1980s (the 'Big Bang' deregulation of 1986 was a key moment in its demise). It is easy to stereotype—to forget that an urbane self-presentation is perfectly compatible with dedication, financial acumen, and even hard-edged dealing—but nevertheless the elite of London's financial sector formed something of a 'status group' in Weberian terms (see Weber 1970; 2000a; 2000b). David Steen, a key figure in the development of the London Traded Options Market, nicely expressed in my interview with him (21 June 2001) the difference that he saw between London's ethos and that prevalent in the USA:

They [Americans] are much keener to make money than [we] are here ... When I was young, if you'd been to a public school, and particularly if you'd been to Oxford or Cambridge, you really didn't need to worry much more about anything else as far as social status was concerned. You could go anywhere and you'd be accepted anywhere. You knew where you were.

Established social standing made it possible to disdain small-minded pursuit of pecuniary advantage, which was sometimes called 'tizzy snatching' ('tizzy' was nineteenth-century English slang for sixpence): as Steen put it, 'people trading and taking a snatch at profit of sixpence a share'. In Chicago, in contrast, the equivalent of a tizzy was considered well worth snatching energetically.

LIFFE plumped unequivocally for Chicago culture over gentlemanly capitalism, opting symbolically for Chicago's brightly coloured trading jackets rather than the dark suits and black shoes traditional in the City. (LIFFE drew the line only at Union Jack jackets, fearing they 'would be seen on television selling the pound down the river' (Kynaston 1997: 73).) LIFFE's traders were often defiantly East End or 'Essex boys' (Zaloom 2003; 2006) rather than gentlemen.

The London Traded Options Market (LTOM) was far more ambivalently placed than LIFFE. Its inspiration too was Chicago (in its case, the success of the Chicago Board Options Exchange, although the immediate spur to its establishment was the threat that options on London shares might be traded in Amsterdam), but LTOM's London Stock Exchange parentage was too strong for it fully to embrace the more flamboyant aspects of Chicago trading culture. One market maker who moved from Chicago to LTOM in 1986 recalls that he 'was booed off the floor first day because I had brown shoes on'. His colleagues were no doubt teasing, but he found the attempt to translate Chicago attitudes and practices to London sometimes uncomfortable.

Tracing the economic consequences of differences of this kind is difficult. The spreads between LTOM's market makers' 'bid' and 'ask' prices in the late 1970s and early 1980s were large (Gemmill and Dickins 1986), far bigger than those in Chicago, and it is tempting to attribute this to the way in which Chicago's ethos of fierce competition between market makers failed to survive the translation to what was in some respects still a gentlemanly world. However, that may not be correct, for there are other possible explanations of large spreads.[8] For example, there were economically consequential tensions between LTOM and its parent, the London Stock Exchange. In particular, stock-exchange 'jobbers' (market makers) valued their right under exchange rules not to disclose large transactions for ninety minutes, because it made it easier to handle big blocks of shares. Delayed disclosure caused difficulties to London's options market makers (no equivalent right to delayed disclosure existed in the USA), because it meant they could never be entirely confident of the price at which they could hedge an options position. Wide bid-ask spreads can thus be seen as helping insulate them from the risks attendant on the difficulty of hedging.

More clear-cut is the effect upon derivatives markets of one aspect of the wider culture in which they are embedded: the trace left in the legal system of hostility to gambling. Section 18 of the UK Gaming Act of 1845 laid down 'That all Contracts or Agreements...by way of gaming or wagering, shall be null and void', rendering gambling debts unrecoverable in law. The USA went further, with most states (including, crucially from the viewpoint of the Chicago derivatives markets, Illinois) outlawing gambling.

Although organized exchanges dedicated to the trading of derivatives of financial assets are recent, such derivatives have long been traded in ad hoc ways, and exchanges dedicated to derivatives of agricultural commodities (grain futures, for example) have existed since the nineteenth century. The issue of how to draw the legal distinction between a legitimate derivatives contract and a wager is thus long-standing, and it is not straightforward: a derivative can indeed seem to resemble a bet on the movement of the price of the underlying asset. If it were ruled that a derivative was a wager, a derivative contract would have been illegal in the USA and unenforceable in the UK.

In eighteenth-century English legal doctrine, the overall distinction between a legitimate contract and a wager was informed by what O'Malley calls a 'materialist theory of exchange', in which 'the act of exchange must include some element of material value or title to [material] value' (2003: 239–40). The 'abstract' or 'virtual' nature of derivatives—which, as noted, is a main theme of recent theoretical discussion of them—is thus in fact their most long-standing legal drawback. A doctrine according to which legitimate exchange has to involve the transfer of title to material value endangers the legality of options on securities, which are at two removes from material value, being at best a claim on a title of ownership or other right. Nor was the problem restricted to derivatives of securities. A grain future might seem unequivocally to involve eventual transfer of ownership of a material asset, but in practice futures contracts on grain or other commodities were normally settled by cash payments. Delivery of grain (or even of the elevator receipts that were the main form of token of ownership of grain: see Cronon 1991) was rare.

For reasons that scholars have yet to explore in detail, nineteenth-century legal doctrine, in both England and the USA, became less 'materialist' and more favourable to derivatives. The distinction between a legitimate contract and a wager was redrawn around what became known as the 'intent test' (Swan 2000: 212–13): if the parties to a contract intended the delivery of the asset in question, then the contract was not a wager and was legal and enforceable, even if delivery did not actually take place. To agrarian critics of agricultural futures exchanges, 'intent' could seem 'an empty legal fiction' (O'Malley 2003: 243), since it was easy for futures traders to claim that they had intended to deliver the commodity involved, and had failed to do so simply because circumstances had changed. Nevertheless, critics' efforts to restore 'the eighteenth-century principle of material exchange' failed (O'Malley 2003: 244).

Trading of futures on physical commodities and of stock options passed the intent test (stock options could be settled by handing over share certificates, and that had come to count as delivery). However, the test created problems for more sophisticated financial derivatives precisely because of their more abstract nature. A stock index, for example, is a mathematical abstraction (it is not the price of any single entity, but is an average of prices), so by far the simplest way to construct a future on an index is to make it settleable by cash payment alone. But claiming intent to deliver would then be impossible, and the contract would as a result be liable to be ruled to be a wager. In consequence, although the Chicago exchanges had wished to introduce futures on stock indexes from the late 1960s onwards, they were unable to do so until 1982. (How the necessary legal and regulatory changes were brought about is discussed in MacKenzie 2006.)

In England, LIFFE faced the intent test and the 1845 Gaming Act (still on the statute book), initially in regard to interest-rate futures based upon LIBOR. Again, the issue was that LIBOR, being an average interest rate, was not deliverable. LIFFE devised what it hoped was a legally adequate hybrid: cash settlement, but with the 'long' having the right to demand delivery of a deposit similar to a loan in the interbank market (the market that LIBOR 'summarizes' in the way discussed below). In July 1982, LIFFE obtained Counsel's opinion that 'such a contract is not a wager in law' (Kynaston 1997: 58). In 1984, a similar hybrid was devised for LIFFE's new FTSE-100 futures, with 'buyers and sellers [able to] nominate shares they might wish to receive or deliver', again because of the fear that 'Gaming Act implications might preclude cash-only settlement' (Kynaston 1997: 131).

The issue of gambling was resolved decisively in the UK only in 1986, when, Kynaston reports, LIFFE's 'traditionally good relationship' (1997: 155) with the Department of Trade and Industry led to the inclusion in the Financial

Services Act of a provision (section 63 of the Act) laying down that no contract that constituted investment business within the meaning of the Act could be rendered 'void or unenforceable' on the grounds that it was a wager. The provision removed the barrier to derivatives that could be settled only in cash. They might still fail the intent test and thus be classed as bets, but they were now legally enforceable.

The 1986 provision had, however, an inadvertent consequence: it rescued the nascent British spread-betting industry (which has subsequently grown to compete with LIFFE for the business of individual customers) from the consequences of the 1987 stock-market crash. Because gambling remained legal in the UK, IG Index had been able to turn the analogy between derivatives trading and gambling from a problem (as it had been in the USA and for LIFFE) into a resource: making a derivative into a bet confers the tax advantage noted above.

The most common of the standardized contracts that IG Index and its competitors offer their customers are analogous to futures (the main difference is that the contracts are directly with the spread-betting firm, rather than between customers). In the case of FTSE-100 contracts, for example, firms quote a price at which customers can 'buy' the index from the firm, and a lower price at which they can 'sell' it to the firm. (As with market makers on exchanges, the firms' profits come mainly from the spread between the two prices.) A customer who believes the index will rise will buy the index, staking a certain amount (typically of the order of £5) per index point, hoping that the index will have risen by more than the spread by the time he or she sells the index back to the firm. A customer who believes the index will fall will begin by selling the index, and close the bet by buying (see, e.g., Vintcent 2002).

As with exchange-traded futures, spread bets thus offer the potential that a limited initial 'margin' deposit can become a much larger gain or loss. Spread-betting firms hedge any large resultant exposure to market movements by taking a position similar to that taken by the aggregate of their customers (often using futures on LIFFE or other exchanges). Until 1986, however, it was impossible legally to recover sums customers owed the firm. IG Index controlled that risk by requiring a deposit large enough to cover likely losses, but calculating that deposit involved estimating the size of plausible market movements; demanding too big a deposit would put customers off.

As noted in MacKenzie (2004), the 1987 crash involved a market move far greater than seemed likely, and it left many of IG Index's customers with liabilities exceeding their deposits. At that time, the firm was nowhere near as well financed as it is today and it could easily have become insolvent. Because its customers were in aggregate 'long'—had bet that prices would rise—its hedging meant that it too was long, and huge price declines meant it owed large sums to its brokers, which had to be paid immediately. However, many of its customers (who thought they knew gambling debts to be unenforceable) refused, or were unable, to pay what they owed IG Index. Fortunately from its viewpoint, IG Index was able to point them to section 63 of the Financial Services Act, which meant they had to pay (interview with Stuart Wheeler, 1 March 2005).

Facticity

'Culture' is thus not simply 'the context' within which derivatives trading takes place. Via matters such as the law of gambling, it shapes and is intermeshed with the detailed mechanics of this trading. Another crucial aspect of those mechanics is the nature of the asset, rate, or other quantity underlying a derivative.

For agricultural futures exchanges—which were, as noted, the sites from which modern financial-derivatives exchanges sprang—the most pressing issue in this respect was standardizing the underlying asset to an extent sufficient for claims on it to be tradeable without reference to any *specific* physical entities. In Chicago grain trading, standardization seems to have been an emergent property, co-evolving with futures trading (Cronon 1991). Later, standardization was an explicit part of the planning for a new contract, such as the Chicago Board of Trade's futures on mortgage-backed bonds or its futures on Treasury bonds, introduced in August 1977 and 'the exchange's most successful contract ever' (Falloon 1998: 251; the fine ethnography by Zaloom 2006 is of the Board of Trade's bond-futures trading). Bonds themselves could not plausibly be standardized, so in both cases the tricky problem of making different issues of bonds commensurable had to be tackled. The solutions found were a little elaborate but robust, though sudden shortages of the 'cheapest-to-deliver' bond (sometimes the result of a deliberate 'squeeze') are a recurrent problem of which all bond-derivatives traders must be wary.

A derivatives contract that can be settled only in cash avoids such problems, and cash settlement also facilitates the development of derivatives on entities that cannot straightforwardly be delivered: first of all stock indexes, and now a much wider range of quantities including, for example, weather and human longevity.[9] However, cash settlement raises a difficulty of a different sort (one quite distinct from the legal vulnerability arising from the 'intent test'). The measure used to determine cash settlement sums—whether it be a price, an index level, an interest rate, or a measure of weather, longevity, or other quantity—must be a *fact*.

One aspect of facticity—that is, of status as a fact—is adequacy of representation. The measure used for cash settlement must be believed genuinely to express conditions in the market or process underlying the derivative, so that someone using the derivative to hedge risk can be sure that (if conditions are unfavourable) the gain they will make from the derivative will cancel out the losses they will incur in the underlying market or from the underlying process.

Problems of adequacy of representation may, for example, have been one factor in the failure of the London Futures and Options Exchange's property futures (Patel 1994). The measure used for its housing futures was the Nationwide Anglia house price index, but that was based only on transactions in which Nationwide Anglia was the lender. It was only one of several candidate measures of the overall state of the UK housing market (even today, different indexes often offer markedly different estimates of the rate of change in house prices). Furthermore, the average countrywide condition of the housing market was less relevant to hedgers—such as developers concerned that the houses they were building would not fetch the anticipated prices—than local conditions, which in the housing market can often vary markedly. (In 2006, the Chicago Mercantile Exchange launched housing futures and options, using indexes that are specific to particular cities and based on identifying repeat sales of the same properties, but it is too early to tell how successful these contracts will be in the long term.)

In contrast, LIBOR is an example of a measure that *has* usually been taken as an adequate representation of the underlying market. It is the basis both of important exchange-traded derivatives contracts, such as the Chicago Mercantile Exchange's Eurodollar contract or LIFFE's Short Sterling interest-rate contract, and also plays the central role in the over-the-counter interest-rate swaps market. (In a typical swap, party A pays party B a rate of interest that is fixed for the contract's duration, while B pays A a floating rate, most commonly LIBOR.) The swaps market is the largest of all derivatives markets—it dwarfs even the huge markets in exchange-traded derivatives—with the consequence that, as noted in Chapter 1, by 2006 contracts totalling over $170 trillion (around $26,000 for every human being on earth) were indexed to LIBOR. Given that, it is surprising that LIBOR has never, to my knowledge, been the object of a social science study (the only detailed source on it is unpublished: Mason 1999).

LIBOR is the interest rate at which major banks can borrow funds from other banks in the London interbank market in a particular currency for a given period of time. (Because a range of currencies and time periods are involved, LIBOR is a set of numbers—six-month US dollar LIBOR, for instance—not a single number. Why the most crucial facts are a set of 'London' rates, not 'New York' rates, is an intriguing question in the cultural and political geography of financial markets that unfortunately cannot be discussed here.)

To understand how LIBOR is constructed requires a brief discussion of the interbank market. A key role in it is played by the 'voice brokers' discussed in Chapter 2. Such brokers sit at desks in rooms that resemble banks' trading rooms, but are more crowded, noisier, and more raucous. On each broker's desk is a 'voicebox' (consisting of a microphone, loudspeaker, and switches), which is connected by dedicated telephone lines to similar voiceboxes at the desks of each of the broker's clients in bank dealing rooms.

Sometimes interbank deals are struck directly, but more often a bank's dealer who wishes to place or to receive an interbank deposit will use his or her voicebox to tell a broker, who will then do one of three things: (a) use his or her voicebox to try to find a counterparty; (b) shout out the order to his or her colleagues; or (c) ask a 'board boy' (as they are still called) to write the order on one of the large whiteboards that surround the brokers' desks.

Brokers supply their bank dealing-room clients with screens that indicate current bid and offer rates for interbank deposits, and those screens are the most important minute-by-minute representation of the interbank market. There is, however, an element of judgement in the rates that brokers display on the screens. Not all banks are equal: their credit ratings differ, and a bank's credit risk department will typically impose a limit on the amount of money that can be on deposit with any particular counterparty bank. So a broker may, for example, choose not to display the most attractive interest rate that he or she knows of, if its source is a bank with a poor credit rating to which many of his or her clients would be unable to lend.

Dealers in banks also exercise judgement in interpreting the rates the screens display. Asked how he estimates LIBOR, one dealer told me:

within say the pool of sixteen [banks on a LIBOR Panel: see below]...you'll probably have three aggressive lenders, so the run-through you get from the broker is where you're going to get the first three lots of money. After that you have to move your price up until it becomes attractive enough for the people that don't want to lend to suddenly think, 'well, this is becoming attractive enough to do it', and that's where this spread...comes from [A LIBOR estimate is] not going to be a mid-market rate, it's going to be the point at which you are likely to get the money.

The judgement thus involved in estimating LIBOR raises another aspect of the facticity of the measure used to cash-settle a derivative: its robustness in respect to attempts to manipulate it. Those with no direct involvement in the market of which LIBOR is a representation might be guaranteed to be unbiased, but they would lack the detailed knowledge needed to exercise informed judgement, so there is no practical alternative to reliance on those whose involvement means they may have 'interests' in the outcome.

When the Chicago Mercantile Exchange launched LIBOR-settled Eurodollar futures in December 1981, it thus set up its own daily poll, designed by its chief economist, Fred Arditti. Each of a designated set of banks was asked to give an estimate of LIBOR, but before the average was taken the highest and lowest estimates were eliminated, so no one bank could influence the result by giving a very high or a very low estimate. '[I]n the beginning there [was] some minor grousing', Leo Melamed, then chair of the exchange, told me, but 'the beauty of the [LIBOR] "fixing" was that it was so overwhelmingly accepted as the "true" price for interest rates'.[10]

In 1985, the British Bankers' Association, membership of which is open to international banks trading in Britain as well as British-domiciled banks, introduced a centralized daily LIBOR 'fixing' (similar in outline to Arditti's) that eventually replaced all other fixings, although other 'LIBORs' are still sometimes quoted. The Foreign Exchange and Money Markets Advisory Panel of the Association selects panels of eight, twelve, or sixteen banks for each currency on the basis of those banks' 'reputation', 'scale of activity in the London market', and 'perceived expertise in the currency concerned', while 'giving due consideration to credit standing' (Mason 1999: 3–4).

By 11.10 a.m. each business day, each bank on a LIBOR panel reports to Telerate (now part of Reuters) 'the rate at which it could borrow funds ["unsecured", and "governed by the laws of England and Wales"] were it to do so by asking for and then accepting inter-bank offers in reasonable market size just prior to 11.00' (Mason 1999: slides 8 and 9) in the currency and for the time period in question. The rates are then ranked in order, the top and bottom quartiles are ignored, and the mean of the second and third quartiles is calculated. That mean is British Bankers' Association LIBOR, and by around 11.45 a.m. it is disseminated worldwide via all the main market networks.

The fixing takes inputs that may seem imprecise—'we ask *them* [the banks on the panel] to tell us what *other people* are offering'; there is no requirement that any loan actually be taken out at that rate; and what constitutes 'reasonable market size' is deliberately not defined exactly (Mason 1999: 4–5, emphases in original)—and from those inputs it produces facts. The fixing is designed to be *sociologically* robust, so to speak. The banks that produce the inputs will very likely have large derivatives portfolios indexed to British Bankers' Association LIBOR, the value of which will be affected by the final figure, but as well as the latter their inputs are also disseminated. One interviewee showed me that day's inputs into three-month sterling LIBOR, pointing with suspicion to a bank that had reduced its input—by a single basis point (that is, a hundredth of a percentage point)—from the previous day's, while all others had either increased theirs or left them unchanged. An idiosyncratic, manipulative input is thus on public display to the market. Furthermore, the exclusion of the top and bottom quartiles means that an overly idiosyncratic input would in any case be thrown out of the calculation. Finally, an advisory panel to the British Bankers' Association selects the members of Contributor Panels, and a bank that regularly made dubious inputs could face embarrassing removal. This sanction, one interviewee told me, has been used, albeit not recently.

During 2007–8, however, confidence in LIBOR came under unprecedented strain. The exclusion of the top and bottom quartiles cannot by itself protect LIBOR from issues that affect all banks. With first Northern Rock and then Bear Stearns needing to be rescued, almost any bank could seem at risk. Suspicions emerged that banks on LIBOR panels were reluctant to report that they could borrow only at high rates, because of fear of rumours that the bank in question was in trouble. This led to concerns that banks were 'herding'—keeping their inputs close to others' anticipated inputs—and that there was a downward bias to LIBOR. The *Wall Street Journal* became a prominent critic, for example reporting on 16 April 2008 a claim that three-month dollar LIBOR was thirty basis points below what it 'should' be. The British Bankers'

Association vigorously defended LIBOR, and though there were suggestions for alterations to it (such as asking each bank to report not the rates at which it can borrow but those at which others can borrow)' the Association rightly rejected knee-jerk changes. Nevertheless, there was growing interest in basing new derivatives on other indexes: in June 2008, for example, LIFFE launched a futures contract based on EONIA, a weighted average of the rates on overnight euro loan deals between banks.

Conclusion

The more theoretically oriented of the contributions to the geographical, anthropological, and sociological literature on financial derivatives have had a tendency inadvertently to replicate the appearance of the products they discuss: they have formed a rather abstract literature on apparently abstract products. However, a market in these products 'is more than a bright idea', says Leo Melamed, who led the Chicago Mercantile Exchange's move into financial derivatives. 'It takes planning, calculation, arm-twisting, and tenacity to get a market up and going. Even when it's chugging along, it has to be cranked and pushed' (Melamed and Tamarkin 1996: 295).

That calculation, cranking, and pushing (for some insight into arm-twisting, see MacKenzie 2006) is a key part of the material production of virtuality, as are issues such as the design of derivatives contracts, the legal boundary between legitimate trading and gambling, local cultures of trading, and how the facticity essential to cash-settled derivatives is generated. Such issues should matter to those who are interested in the 'big questions' of the theoretical literature—such as the extent and distribution of risk or the scope of globalization and commodification—because well-grounded answers to those big questions inevitably must involve the apparent detail of material sociology.

The question of spatiality, for example, demands a nuanced answer. Yes, global financial integration is a very real phenomenon; but no, it has not brought about 'the end of geography' (O'Brien 1992). LIBOR, for instance, is a global fact; but it is also *London* Interbank Offered Rate. Spread betting, to take another example, permits rapidly increasing numbers of residents of the UK to use the screens and key-pads of their mobile phones to enter into inexpensive derivatives contracts on thousands of global assets: the Nikkei index, Brent crude, gold, carbon-emissions permits, and so on.[11] The simple operation involved takes less than ten seconds and the contracts are usually confirmed in as little as five seconds. No fully equivalent experience has been available to residents of the USA, and such lived experiences of markets are surely consequential: by 2006, some 400,000 people in the UK had spread-betting accounts (Brady and Ramyar 2006). Currently, there is an attempt to repeat in the USA the success of financial spread betting in the UK in the form of 'hedgelets'—similar to spread bets, but formulated in such a way as to stop them being classed as wagers—but how successful that will be remains to be seen.

The material sociology of derivatives has many facets not discussed in this chapter. One that will be discussed in Chapter 5 is how arbitrage ties the prices of derivatives to their underlying asset (but also how it sometimes fails). Also important, but either not discussed in this book or touched on only very briefly, are the roles in derivatives trading of bodies, which are material entities par excellence, and of technologies (the sometimes traumatic shift from open-outcry to electronic trading is discussed by Zaloom 2006); the crucial functions of clearing houses (Millo, Muniesa, Panourgias, and Scott 2005); the structuring role of systems of regulation; and so on. It is clearly important to extend the analysis beyond the USA and UK to the world's many other derivatives exchanges, whether established or nascent. The issues of innovation, cultural geography, and facticity need addressing also in the context of the over-the-counter (direct institution-to-institution) market, not just exchange-traded derivatives. Nevertheless, I hope that this preliminary analysis indicates at least that we should not simply be fascinated by the virtual character of derivatives, but need to investigate in depth how that virtuality is materially produced.

5

The Material Sociology of Arbitrage

with Daniel Beunza and Iain Hardie

The derivatives discussed in the previous chapter, which now play such a central role in global finance, are contracts or securities whose value depends on the price of an 'underlying' asset, on the level of an index, or on an exchange rate, interest rate, or other quantity. Here, as elsewhere in finance, factual status is important. For a derivatives market to be credible, the price of derivatives must not be seen as arbitrary, or as subject to manipulation, but must adequately reflect conditions in the market for the underlying asset, in particular the price of the asset or the level of the index, rate, or other quantity involved.

Crucial to the functioning of derivatives markets is that a specific material process can tie the price of a future, option, or other derivative to the underlying asset or rate: arbitrage. In this chapter, we seek to develop a material sociology of arbitrage. As discussed below, 'arbitrage' is a term with different meanings, but this chapter follows market practitioners in defining it as trading that aims to make low-risk profits by exploiting discrepancies in the price of the same asset or in the relative prices of similar assets. For example, if the price of a derivative drifts too far away from that implied by conditions in the market for the underlying asset or rate, then arbitrageurs can step in and exploit the price discrepancy. They buy the 'cheap' instrument and sell the 'expensive' one, so limiting or reducing the discrepancy, reconnecting the market for the derivative with that for the underlying asset or rate.

Important though the role of arbitrage in derivatives markets is, it is found in many other contexts as well. A classic example historically was gold arbitrage. If the price of gold in Saudi Arabia exceeds its price in New York by more than the cost of transportation, arbitrageurs can profit by buying gold in New York and selling it in Saudi Arabia (or vice versa if gold is cheaper in Saudi Arabia). By buying and selling as close to simultaneously as possible, arbitrageurs avoid the risks of 'directional' trading: they profit irrespective of whether the price of gold goes on to rise or to fall.

Arbitrage requires technological resources, sustained effort, and expertise beyond the capacity of nearly all lay investors in financial markets. It is the preserve of market professionals, and is a crucial form of trading. (To bring the topic close to home for academic readers in the USA, we would note that the most successful of large university endowment funds, such as Harvard's, are often skilled practitioners of arbitrage.) Indeed, arbitrage *constitutes* markets, for example helping to determine their scope and the extent to which they are global: that international gold arbitrage is possible creates a world market in gold with a 'world price', rather than geographically separate markets with different prices.

In constituting markets, arbitrage has wider consequences for economies and political systems. For example, in the late 1990s arbitrageurs in hedge funds and investment banks began to perceive growing similarity between the bonds issued by the government of Italy and those issued by other European countries, notably Germany. For a variety of reasons (including distrust of the fiscal efficiency of the Italian state and consequent fears of it defaulting on its bonds), the prices of Italian government bonds had traditionally been low relative to those of countries such as Germany, thus imposing high debt-service charges on Italy. As arbitrageurs began to buy Italian bonds, their relative prices rose and the proportion of Italy's government expenditure devoted to debt service fell. The process—which was assisted by the liquidity created by the MTS electronic bond-trading system, set up by the Italian treasury in 1988 and discussed below—helped Italy meet the Maastricht criteria for European Economic and Monetary Union (EMU). Arbitrageurs' beliefs thus had a self-validating aspect—they prompted trading that made more likely the event, Italy's qualification for EMU, on which the beliefs were predicated—and arbitrage helped to create a European government bond market, rather than separate national markets.

The failures of arbitrage can be as consequential as its successes. Such failures were at the heart of two of the most serious crises of the post-war financial system: the 1987 stock-market crash and the 1998 turmoil surrounding the hedge fund Long-Term Capital Management (LTCM). A crucial aspect of the former was the breakdown of the link—normally imposed by arbitrage in the way sketched above—between the stock market and a key derivatives market: stock-index futures. In the case of LTCM, the forced unwinding of arbitrage positions caused huge, sudden, highly correlated price movements across the globe in apparently unrelated assets, bringing some markets close to paralysis.

There is an enormous disciplinary imbalance in regard to arbitrage. It has received almost no sustained attention in economic sociology, in economic anthropology, in economic geography, or in the strand of political science known as international political economy, even in the subsets of those specialities that deal with financial markets (the limited exceptions include Miyazaki 2003; Robotti n.d.; Beunza and Stark 2004; Hardie 2004; and MacKenzie 2003). In contrast, the central theoretical mechanism invoked by modern financial economics is 'arbitrage proof'. The field posits that the only patterns of prices that can be stable are those that permit no opportunities for arbitrage. Particular patterns of prices are then shown to be necessary by demonstrating that if prices deviate from that pattern, arbitrage is possible. The entire modern theory of asset pricing—especially the theory of the pricing of derivatives such as options—relies on 'arbitrage proof' of this kind. Paradigmatic is the Nobel-Prize-winning theory of options developed by Fischer Black, Myron Scholes, and Robert C. Merton (Black and Scholes 1973; Merton 1973). In their model, the price of an option is determined by the fact that it can be replicated exactly: it is possible to construct a continuously adjusted portfolio of holdings or borrowings of the underlying asset and cash that will have the same pay-off as the option in all states of the world. The price of the option must equal the cost of this replicating portfolio, for otherwise arbitrage is possible.

The conceptualization of 'arbitrage' in the work of Black, Scholes, and Merton, and in mainstream financial economics more generally, differs from the arbitrage as market practice that is the focus of this chapter. Orthodox economists define arbitrage as demanding no capital and involving no risk, while in market practice arbitrage seems always to require some capital and involves some risk, even if the risk is only that a counterparty to a transaction will not fulfil its obligations (Hardie 2004). Indeed, a purist would argue that the trading we consider in this chapter should not be considered 'arbitrage'.[1]

Purism, however, has its costs—a purist definition of 'arbitrage' excludes the real-world counterparts of the canonical arbitrages of finance theory, such as the arbitrage that imposes Black–Scholes–Merton option pricing—and purism is not the only possible response. Financial economists—especially 'behavioural' economists such as Andrei Shleifer—have begun to investigate the consequences of making the definition of arbitrage more realistic (see, for example, Shleifer and Vishny 1997). These economists rightly see the topic as a crucial one. Since, in orthodox views, it is above all arbitrage that makes markets efficient, the existence of limits to arbitrage casts into doubt the full validity of the central tenet of modern financial economics: the efficient market hypothesis, according to which prices in mature capital markets fully reflect, effectively instantaneously, all available price-relevant information.

We shall suggest below that there are potentially productive linkages between the emerging literature in economics on the limits of arbitrage and the 'material sociology' of arbitrage that we advocate. As noted in Chapter 2, material sociology pays attention to, amongst other things, the role played in social relations by technological systems and other physical objects and entities (including human bodies viewed as material entities). Since that role is of course pervasive, all sociology should be material sociology, yet social theory frequently abstracts away from physical objects and empirical enquiry often does not focus on them. As we shall argue, a proper understanding of arbitrage requires us to take into account both its 'physical' and 'social' aspects, and the two are ultimately inseparable. Arbitrage is *simultaneously* a 'physical' and a 'social' process.

In developing a material sociology of arbitrage, this chapter draws upon three data sources. One is fieldwork conducted by Beunza, in collaboration with David Stark, and reported previously in Beunza and Stark (2003; 2004; 2005). Beunza and Stark conducted a participant-observation study of the Lower Manhattan arbitrage trading room of a global, non-American investment bank with 128 offices in 26 countries across the USA, Europe, and Asia. The study comprised 65 half-day visits to the trading room over the course of 34 months. During those months, Beunza and Stark undertook detailed observation at four of the ten trading desks in the room (merger arbitrage desk, statistical arbitrage, special situations, and customer arbitrage), sitting in the tight space between traders, following trades as they unfolded, and sharing lunch and jokes with the traders. They complemented this data with in-depth interviews of a selected group of traders in a more private setting, typically a small conference room just off the trading room. In the final year of the investigation, Beunza and Stark were integrated more formally into the trading room—provided with a place at a trading desk, a computer, and a telephone.

The second source is a study of arbitrage by MacKenzie, which focused (a) on LTCM, where the main purpose was to understand the fund's crisis and what it implied for the limits to arbitrage, and (b) on forms of arbitrage, especially options arbitrage, that draw heavily upon finance theory, where the goal was to understanding the extent to which such arbitrage 'performs' finance theory in the fashion posited by Callon (1998). The study was based on semi-structured interviews with a 'snowball' sample of 26 arbitrageurs whose trading was relevant to these questions, on an analysis of the price movements in the crisis months in the markets in which LTCM operated, and on existing econometric analyses of options pricing (see MacKenzie 2003; 2006).

The third source is a study by Hardie and MacKenzie which focuses on several of the issues discussed in this chapter, including information flow between competing traders, relations between traders and managers, and circumstances in which trades that will almost certainly be profitable if held for long enough nevertheless have to be unwound. Its snowball sample (of traders in hedge funds and investment banks, of those who manage these traders, of those who provide administrative services, and of the 'funds of funds' that channel capital to hedge funds) comprises 51 interviews,[2] and the study also involves the brief period of observation of a hedge fund drawn on in Chapter 3.

It was during this period of observation that we witnessed the arbitrage trade that we describe in the next section of the chapter. However, the example is chosen for its simplicity, not because it encapsulates all the issues we wish to discuss—no single example does. Indeed, our goal here is not to report systematically on the three underlying studies, which have many aspects beyond those discussed here. Rather, our aim is to outline a material sociology of arbitrage consistent with our observations, interviews, and other sources of data, and also with the results of others in the social studies of finance who have touched upon arbitrage.

Brazil 14s and 40s

5 January 2005: Hardie and MacKenzie are observing trading in the hedge fund described in Chapter 3. Just after the fund's morning meeting, partner B notices an oddity in the Brazilian government bond market. The minutes of the US Federal Reserve's Open Market Committee, released the previous evening in London time, have been taken by market participants as indicating that further interest-rate rises are on the way, and have led to general price falls in the Brazilian bond market. However, the '14s' (an issue of dollar-denominated bonds that mature in 2014) are 'trading up': their price is high relative to other bonds. 'Hit the bid' (sell them), suggests partner B.

The trader does not respond immediately, but he goes on to ask his assistant to produce a chart of the prices over the last three months of the '14s' and the '40s' (Brazilian government dollar-denominated bonds that mature in November 2040). As the day proceeds, the trader takes a position in the 14s and the 40s, short selling the former and buying the latter. He also sends a contact in an investment bank the Excel file containing the price chart produced by his assistant, encouraging his contact to circulate it to others. (Later in this chapter we discuss why he does this.)

A bond maturing in 2040 seems very different from one maturing in 2014: much could happen in the quarter-century between the two dates. But the bond maturing in 2040 is 'callable': the Brazilian government has the right to recall the bond by repaying the principal early, in 2015. If Brazilian bonds continue to trade at anything like their current prices, it will be in the government's interest to do so, since it will be able to replace the borrowing more cheaply. The '40s' thus in effect mature in 2015 and so, despite appearances, a '14' and a '40' are quite similar.

On the morning of 5 January, none of this is said explicitly: it is part of what the trader and partner B, like all sophisticated participants in the Brazilian bond market, simply 'know'. (Hardie was an investment banker before returning to academia, and was involved in the initial sale of the '40s' on behalf of the government of Brazil, so he knows it too, though he needs to whisper an explanation to MacKenzie.) Nevertheless, the chart produced by the trader's assistant is a material representation that makes visible the reasoning underpinning the trade. Once he has configured the chart according to the trader's wishes—initially, it shows the prices of the 14s and the prices of the

40s, when the trader wants it to display the *difference* in prices—the prices of the two bonds can be seen to follow each other closely, as would be expected, but with the 40s almost always slightly more expensive than the 14s. Again, the reason is common knowledge amongst aficionados. The 40s are the most liquid of Brazilian government bonds, the ones most readily bought and sold, and thus the most attractive, for example to those who wish to create and to exit positions quickly. Indeed, in a later interview partner C describes the Brazil 40s as the 'asset-class benchmark' for emerging-market government bonds as a whole: 'if people are negative/positive on emerging markets, they buy or sell that specific issue.'

In order to read the trader's assistant's chart correctly, one needs to realize that on it 'time' flows from right to left (the earliest dates are on the right). Once that is grasped, however, someone viewing it can clearly see what the trader has seen: in recent trading days the 14s have become more expensive than the 40s, with the difference increasing sharply the previous day (4 January). The trader knows his market well enough to infer a cause that is confirmed only later in the day in a telephone conversation with the above-mentioned investment bank contact. The sell-off triggered by US Federal Reserve's minutes has concentrated in Brazil's liquid 40s. Indeed, as the contact tells the trader, unusually 'the real money guys [traders not in hedge funds but in bigger institutions] shorted 40s'.

The trader thus confidently assumes—and makes explicit in a telephone conversation with his contact—that the fact that 14s are more expensive than 40s is a price discrepancy that will be temporary. By short selling 14s and buying 40s, he—and indeed others—can perform an arbitrage (in market practitioners' sense of the term). The discrepancy would be expected to vanish in the normal course of events, but especially if others choose also to exploit it (perhaps because the investment bank contact circulates the assistant's chart to them), the process will be hastened, maybe considerably. By early afternoon, the trader has accumulated some $13 million of short sales of 14s and another $13 million of purchases of 40s. By mid-afternoon, he is able to say 'it's moved in my favour'—the discrepancy has started to reduce—'but not enough to unwind': he keeps the position on, expecting further reductions in the discrepancy. Only at the end of the week does he liquidate his position, earning a healthy profit.

Note what the trader is *not* doing in this trade. Like the gold arbitrageur, he is not taking a 'directional' view. He is not attempting to predict the policies of the Brazilian government, to estimate the probability of bond default by Brazil, or to anticipate the future courses of interest rates or inflation: because the 14s and the 40s are so similar, changes in factors such as these will affect the prices of each bond roughly equally, and with the trader's matched 'long' and 'short' positions the effects will cancel out. As the trader puts it in a telephone call to his contact in the investment bank, 'there is zero market risk' in the trade: its profitability ('there is at least half a point in that trade') should not be affected by overall rises and falls in the prices of Brazilian government bonds. In fact, as he acknowledges to us, the trader's position is not entirely free from risk—see below—but in its insulation from the major risk factors in his market, it is low risk.

Asked by the third author about the rationale of the trade, the trader says (just as a financial economist would) that the fact 'that this trade has presented [itself] indicates [an] inefficiency'. Temporarily, prices are reflecting something other than merely available information such as the relative liquidity of the two bonds. Although the trader's motivation may simply be to earn money for his hedge fund, his actions are helping to eliminate a discrepancy and correct the effects of an 'inefficiency'. In that respect, his trading, even if not free of risk, resembles arbitrage as conceived by financial economics.

The Materiality of Arbitrage

A price is a thing. Like all prices, those to which the trader was responding (and circulating in the form of the chart prepared by his assistant) were physical entities—patterns on computer screens and spoken numbers transmitted by telephone. The forms of embodiment of prices are various—the sound waves that constitute speech; pen or pencil marks on paper; the electrical impulses that represent binary digits in a computerized system or encode sound over a telephone line; hand signals in 'open-outcry' trading pits that are too noisy for voices to be heard; and so on—but are always material. If a price is to be communicated from one human being to another, or from one computerized trading system to another, it must take a physical form.

The materiality of prices matters to arbitrage because their physical embodiment affects the extent and speed of their transmission. Classical forms of arbitrage exploited the differences between prices in different places. The commodities and currency arbitrageur J. Aron & Company, for example, used to keep telephone lines to Saudi Arabia open constantly so it could as quickly as possible detect and exploit the emergence of discrepancies in gold or silver prices (Rubin and Weisberg 2003: 90–1).

The development of electronic price dissemination systems (especially the 'Monitor' system, introduced by Reuters in 1973) largely undermined the time-space advantages that firms such as Aron had achieved by the use of social networks and older communication technologies, notably the telegraph and then the telephone. It was much less likely, for example, that a trader could perform arbitrage by having two telephone lines open, selling an asset to one counterparty while buying it at a lower price from another. 'After the introduction of Monitor, prices [initially currency exchange rates, and later many other prices as well] suddenly became available globally to everyone connected to the system' (Knorr Cetina and Bruegger 2002b: 395).

Electronic price dissemination does not, however, entirely eliminate differences in the speed of transmission of prices, and those differences remain consequential, even if they are now measured in seconds or even microseconds, not the minutes or hours of traditional arbitrage. For instance, a price delay of as little as two seconds made the index arbitrage desk of a bank that competed with the bank studied by Beunza lose millions of dollars. Index arbitrage (the form of arbitrage at the heart of the 1987 crash, for example) exploits differences between the prices of index futures, for instance on the S&P500 index, and the prices of the stocks making up the index. On the day in question—described in Beunza and Stark (2004)—the numbers representing stock prices were being transmitted by the competitor's Reuters server with small delays, while futures prices were arriving normally, giving the appearance (on a day on which the market rose consistently) of persistent, attractive mispricing. Seeing apparent opportunities, the competitor's arbitrageurs traded in huge volumes and incurred large losses. As a trader explained, 'while they were buying, we were selling...the traders here were writing tickets until their fingers were bleeding. We made $2 million in an hour, until they realized what was happening.'

The way in which one of the traders in the bank studied by Beunza configured his two Unix workstations and Bloomberg terminal indicates the importance of speeds of transmission and precise times. Every day, the clocks in his Unix workstations are synchronized to an atomic clock. Across the top of one of his three screens, he has a slash sign that rotates and moves from side to side.

It is a 'pulse meter', used to gauge the 'price feed'—the speed with which information on prices is arriving—which stops moving when prices stop arriving. On his other Unix workstation, the trader has five coloured squares that work as 'speedometers', indicating how quickly orders are getting through network servers: if they are green, everything is fine; if they are yellow, the network is congested and deals are delayed; if they are red, servers are clogged. Two 'CPU-meters' also measure congestion in the bank's order flow (Beunza and Stark 2004).

The speed with which the physical entities that embody prices move is not dictated by physical and technological considerations alone. For instance, in the early days of connection by modem to the New York Stock Exchange, member firms tried to obtain an advantage by investing in faster modems. To prevent costly competition in ever-faster hardware, a 'speed limit' of 9.6 Kbaud was put in place. During Beunza's observations, this limit became a problem for some of the banks affected by the terrorist attack of 11 September 2001. Those banks' existing 9.6 Kbaud communication systems were inoperable, but sufficiently slow modems were no longer commercially available (Beunza and Stark 2003).

Such deliberate barriers to competition, however, have been eroding fast, and an 'arms race' has been under way for some time amongst arbitrageurs, and also those using automated order-placing systems to optimize their trading in other ways, in respect to transmission delays in computer networks (Bear, Hod, Enness, and Graham 2006). In this arms race, the physical placement of the relevant hardware matters. In particular, it is crucial to minimize even microseconds of delay between a trader initiating the purchase or sale of securities and the trade being implemented on an exchange's order-matching system. Firms are thus prepared to pay a premium to have their computer systems physically close to the exchange's system and connected to it as directly as possible. The end of face-to-face trading on exchange floors has meant that the human bodies participating in such trading need no longer be located in one place, but a recentralization of technological systems is running alongside the decentralization of bodies.[3]

Also sometimes important to the conduct of arbitrage, and simultaneously both physical and social, are the allowable forms that prices can take. In economic theory, prices are typically represented as real numbers—the equivalent of the points on a continuous line—while the physical embodiment of prices in market practice requires prices to be a subset of the rational numbers, the numbers expressible as a ratio of integers (see Mirowski 2002: 543). Furthermore, the allowable subset has often differed from that in the everyday usage of money.

For example, as noted in Chapter 2, until June 1997 stock prices in the USA were denominated in eighths of a dollar. The size of minimum units of price such as this affects the magnitude of the discrepancy at which arbitrage becomes feasible. After June 1997, when the New York Stock Exchange reduced the unit of price to a sixteenth of a dollar, the typical discrepancy that triggered index arbitrage decreased, and there were larger numbers of index arbitrage trades (Henker and Martens 2005). When in 2001 the Securities and Exchange Commission required the further shift from binary fractions to decimals (dollars and cents), the additional facilitation of arbitrage meant that index arbitrageurs faced enhanced competition—as one put it, 'We used to make our money by getting in between the sixteenth increments'—and some incurred losses.

Amongst the material entities involved in the performance of arbitrage are arbitrageurs' bodies. Concluding a transaction over the telephone with one party to buy gold, a currency, or other asset, while at the same time telling a colleague to sell it to another party at a higher price, is unlikely to succeed if one's conversation with the colleague can be heard. It is thus important in this (and in many other uses of the telephone in financial markets) that one switches off the telephone or voicebox microphone when talking to colleagues. The telephones used in dealing rooms often have thumb-operated switches behind the earpiece that make it easy to do this, and many people always use them to switch off the microphone when the party at the other end of the line is speaking, even if there is no parallel conversation for them to overhear. That way, it becomes a bodily habit that will not desert one in situations of excitement or stress.

Electronically conducted arbitrage can also involve bodily skills. Such trading involves placing 'bids' (offers to buy) or 'asks' (offers to sell) for the asset in question. This is generally done by using a computer mouse to click on a screen that, at least in the case of electronically traded futures, shows for each price level the numbers of bids (often in blue) and of asks (often in red). At busy times, these numbers and levels change from second to second, with blue and red bars seeming to dance up and down. If an arbitrage opportunity persists only for seconds (as is often the case), constant attention and rapid physical execution are needed. The anthropologist Caitlin Zaloom reports that as trainee futures traders she and her colleagues were made repeatedly to practise with a computerized gold-price arbitrage simulation, so that the disciplined attention and fast, accurate action they would need became bodily habits. They were encouraged 'to play commercial video games on our own time to increase our reaction speeds and hand-eye coordination'. A particular danger they were trained to avoid was 'fat fingering', in which, for example, instead of left-clicking the mouse to 'join the bid' (putting in an offer to buy at a set price) they accidentally right-clicked, inadvertently buying the asset in question at its current market price. The managers' aim was to 'train our bodies to operate as uninterrupted conduits between the dealing room and the on-line world, allowing our fingers to become seamless extensions of our economic intentions' (Zaloom, personal communication; see Zaloom 2006).

The bodily aspects of arbitrage are most prominent when it is performed in open-outcry trading 'pits': stepped amphitheatres, traditionally octagonal. Dozens or hundreds of traders stand on the rungs of a pit, making deals by voice or by eye contact and an elaborate system of hand signals. In Chicago (the prime site of open-outcry trading), the hand-signal language that is used is called 'arb' because its speed was essential to arbitrage. For example, when a trading firm spotted an arbitrage opportunity, canonically between the prices of gold futures traded in Chicago and in New York, it was quicker to 'arb' (hand-signal) instructions from the firm's booth to the trading pit than to send a clerk running to the pit with a written order (Lynn 2004: 57–9; see also Zaloom 2006).

Where bodies are positioned with respect to each other can be of considerable significance to arbitrage in open-outcry trading. For example, the two main forms of option are calls (options to buy at a set 'exercise price') and puts (options to sell at a set price), and discrepancies between call and put prices can be exploited by arbitrages such as 'conversion'. (In conversion, a trader sells a call option and simultaneously buys a put option with the same exercise price and expiration plus the stock or other underlying asset in question.) Options arbitrageurs on the American Stock Exchange found it advantageous to stand in between the 'specialist' (designated main trader) responsible for calls and the specialist responsible for puts on the same stock. That was the optimum bodily position for detecting and exploiting opportunities for conversion and similar arbitrages.

That the physical location of bodies is of such importance to open-outcry trading is one reason why, as noted in Chapter 2, pits and trading floors are bodily places in an especially strong sense: the extensive jostling and occasional fist fights are often over the right to occupy a particular spatial location in a pit. Not only are height and a loud voice advantages, but even mundane artefacts such as shoes are consequential: Chicago traders often wear platform heels to increase their height. Over the last ten years, however, open-outcry trading has declined rapidly, and it may soon become extinct. Nevertheless, bodily location still matters in the screen-based trading that has replaced it. Because arbitrage involves trading pairs (or larger sets) of securities, the expertise it demands is often distributed across more than one person. The physical placement of traders and other members of staff in the investment-bank trading room studied by Beunza was designed quite consciously to facilitate the necessary interaction, and also to inhibit interactions that might be detrimental (Beunza and Stark 2004).

For example, the bank's customer desk executes orders for clients while the 'special situations' desk trades complex, hybrid strategies for the bank and is not in direct contact with clients. The two sets of traders sit facing each other, separated only by their keyboards and computer monitors. One way in which the customer desk generates ideas is by considering why customers might be doing what they are doing: for example, as the head of the customer desk put it, if someone pays a lot for a stock, it can be interpreted as 'what does he know that I don't?' The physical proximity of the situations desk meant that possible interpretations of puzzling client orders could quickly and informally be discussed between desks:

I [the head of the customer desk] looked at it and said, 'why does he do that?' I talked to Josh [a proprietary trader] and it didn't make any sense. 'That guy's crazy,' we thought. That was the tip-off. We structured what we thought was a better trade . . .

'It is like brainstorming', the head of the desk said: 'we really don't know what we're gonna think in the end. I could have told "buy" to those guys, and conclude five minutes later that it was "sell".'

In contrast, the four 'statistical arbitrageurs' in the bank's trading room were deliberately kept at some distance from each other. 'Statistical arbitrage' involves the detection of patterns in the ever-changing flux of security prices. (It is of theoretical significance because by detecting, exploiting, and eliminating predictable statistical structure in price movements, it may leave behind only unpredictable randomness, making markets, in the terminology of financial economics, 'weak form' efficient. Statistical arbitrageurs, however, deny that structure is entirely eliminated in this way.) The structure exploited by statistical arbitrageurs is seldom or never deterministic: they hope only to do better than pure chance. In consequence, the risks of the activity are minimized if different statistical arbitrageurs are exploiting different patterns, and increased if—perhaps because they have shared ideas—their trading becomes too similar. As a senior trader put it: 'We don't encourage [statistical arbitrageurs] to talk to each other. They sit apart' (see Beunza and Stark 2004).

The Sociality of Arbitrage

A price is a thing, but it is also social. All forms of arbitrage depend for their success on what others will do. Even in the classic forms of arbitrage that exploit differences in the prices of the 'same' asset in different places, others must be depended upon to fulfil their obligations: for example, to deliver gold if the arbitrageur has struck a deal to buy it, or to deliver money if the arbitrageur has sold gold. Procedures carried out by others must also be relied upon to ensure that gold in Riyadh is 'the same' as gold in Manhattan. Others yet again may be needed to transport gold from one place to another. (When securities were paper certificates, their transportation from place to place and the risk of loss of them during such transportation were issues that arbitrageurs had to consider.)

The 'sameness' of gold is established by assay procedures 'external' to the market that can be treated by market practitioners as a 'black box'—a reliable process whose details they do not need to consider—and nowadays 'transportation' of securities is also usually treated by traders as a black-box matter. However, many—probably most—current forms of arbitrage exploit discrepancies in the prices not of the 'same' asset but of 'similar' assets: Brazil 14s and 40s; stocks and stock-index futures; stocks and options on those stocks; Italian and German government bonds; newly issued ('on-the-run') government bonds and previously issued ('off-the-run') bonds; government bonds and bonds carrying implicit government guarantees but backed by pools of mortgages; the shares of the two legally distinct but economically integrated corporations that until 2005 made up the Royal Dutch-Shell group; and so on. However, the similarity of assets such as the Brazil 14s and 40s, or of shares in Royal Dutch and in Shell, depends, at least over the short and medium term, on others within the market treating them as similar, and the arbitrageur can seldom afford to treat this as a black box.

The 'similarity' of financial assets is always in a sense theory-dependent. Sometimes, the theory in question is a sophisticated mathematical model, such as Black–Scholes–Merton option pricing. At other times, the theory is vernacular and down to earth: for example, that the 40s will remain Brazil's most liquid government bonds, or that the intended Eurozone would converge, making Italian bonds similar to German bonds.

To embark upon arbitrage, traders thus have to convince themselves that the theory on which the arbitrage rests is correct, or at least plausible enough to be the basis of practical action. They will often also want to or need to convince others. In our observations both of the investment bank and the hedge fund, there was much discussion of possible trades and of the theories underlying them, both inside the organization and in the form of analyses coming in from outside (and occasionally flowing in the opposite direction). Critical roles in these discussions are often played by material representations of value, such as the chart showing the recent history of the difference in prices between the 40s and the 14s, or a 'spread plot', showing the relative prices of Hewlett Packard and Compaq, which Beunza observed being closely followed in 2001–2 by 'risk arbitrageurs' hoping to exploit the probable—but not certain—merger between the two corporations (Beunza and Muniesa 2005). But material representations are often not on their own conclusive: information about what other traders are doing—for instance, about the behaviour of 'real money' in the Brazilian bond market—can also be important in allowing the plausibility of theories to be judged.

The need to convince others does not necessarily cease once a trader takes on an arbitrage position. Often, the price discrepancy that is being exploited will increase further before it decreases, which means that the arbitrageur will incur apparent losses. (For example, in September 1998, the Harvard endowment, whose arbitrage activities were caught up in the crisis surrounding LTCM, had racked up temporary losses that the *Wall Street Journal* (Sandler 1998) reported to be in excess of $1 billion.) Sometimes, apparent losses are actual outflows of money or securities (or, at least, the electronic traces thereof), for example as a result of the daily process in which exchange clearing houses adjust the 'margin' deposits that participants must maintain in order to be allowed to continue to hold their positions. At other times, there are no actual outflows, but as banks and hedge funds 'mark to market' (revalue their trading positions, which is now also normally done at least daily), a position shows a loss. In either case, the losses will be temporary (the outflow will be replaced by an inflow, a 'paper' loss will turn into a realizable profit) *if* the theory underpinning the arbitrage is correct, but others may need to be convinced of this to allow the arbitrageur to continue holding the position.

In a large institution such as a bank, the immediately important audience for arbitrage is an arbitrageur's manager or managers, who will normally be closely attentive to the 'P&L' (profit and loss) figures of those they supervise. 'There's a saying in trading circles', one trader and manager told us: 'the white sheet [P&L sheet] doesn't lie'—losses are real, and should be acted upon as if they are real. The arbitrageur's problem, however, is that from his or her viewpoint the white sheet does sometimes lie, at least temporarily. A common complaint amongst arbitrageurs is of being instructed by managers to liquidate loss-bearing positions that they were certain would become profitable. Even 'textbook' arbitrages can be subject to this risk: the traders in the Japanese securities firm studied by Miyazaki (2003) reported being forced to abandon index-arbitrage positions because of the apparent losses incurred when they had to deposit additional futures margin. Such management behaviour may seem incomprehensible until one realizes that the boundary between arbitrage and speculation is porous, and it can be hard for managers to be certain that arbitrageurs have not in fact started to speculate on the rise or fall of prices. Two of the most celebrated 'rogue traders'—Nick Leeson of Barings Bank and Jérôme Kerviel of Société Générale—were arbitrageurs who covertly became very large-scale speculators.

In hedge funds, the manager/arbitrageur divide seems typically to be much less marked: even in large funds such as LTCM the two roles are not distinct. Investors, however, form a more immediate audience than they do in the case of banks. Hedge funds report changes in net asset values to their investors monthly, while banks report quarterly or less frequently (depending on the jurisdiction in which they are incorporated), and losses in a hedge fund's trading are not masked by the profitability of other lines of business as they often are in banks. The increasingly important 'funds of funds', which allocate their investors' capital to hedge funds that they select (and also frequently withdraw it), are able to demand reports more often than monthly: sometimes even daily. So a large loss by a hedge fund conducting arbitrage—even a 'paper' loss—quickly becomes visible. One hedge-fund manager (and former investment banker) told us that in a bank 'you can justify why you want to hold on to those positions', while hedge fund investors 'don't care. They just look at the number [change in net asset value]'. The threat of investors withdrawing their capital from the fund is thus almost continuous: 'there is very small tolerance to losing money.... [W]e cannot have a losing month.'

The risk of arbitrageurs in a bank having to abandon their positions because of temporary losses is reduced if managers understand and accept the theory underpinning a trade, and thus believe that losses will indeed be temporary. One advantage of investment banks with long experience of arbitrage over newcomers such as the Japanese firm studied by Miyazaki is that this understanding is much more likely. Often, though, the technical details of arbitrage trading are daunting even to those with extensive market experience. For example, arbitrage between US government bonds and mortgage-backed bonds issued by bodies with implicit government guarantees involves (a) adjusting the spread between their yields to take account of the consequences of the fact that most mortgage contracts allow borrowers to take advantage of falls in interest rates by repaying a mortgage with funds borrowed more cheaply from another lender, and (b) offsetting those consequences, for example by appropriate purchases of interest-rate options. Neither the adjustment nor the offsetting is an elementary matter.

In such cases, trust in arbitrage often in practice has to be trust in the arbitrageur or arbitrageurs *as particular people*, just as in many cases trust in science comes down to trust in the scientist (see Shapin 1994). A hedge fund, a university endowment manager, or an individual trader or trading desk at a bank who or which has built up a good reputation is more likely to be trusted. LTCM's founder John W. Meriwether had led Wall Street's premier arbitrage desk (at Salomon Brothers), and his colleagues included other traders with high personal reputations. They were able to have LTCM's investors accept a three-year 'lock-in' in which they were not allowed to withdraw capital, and even after the near bankruptcy in 1998 they successfully recruited investors to a successor fund, JWM Partners. During the 1998 crisis, the overseers of the Harvard endowment appear to have trusted its management, and rather than insisting that loss-bearing positions be liquidated, they tolerated the apparent huge loss—thus making it possible for it to be temporary (as indeed it was).

Losses, even temporary, can in addition be avoided if other arbitrageurs and professional traders also come to view the price difference that an arbitrageur is exploiting as a discrepancy. In our observations and interviews, we were struck by the extent of the circulation amongst traders in different funds and banks, mainly by electronic mail, of ideas for trading and by the attention most professional traders pay to what others seem to be doing. If that discussion and attention leads others also to seek to exploit a discrepancy, then their purchases and sales will narrow the discrepancy, or at least reduce the risk of it widening. That, for example, was why the trader discussed in this chapter's second section wanted the chart displaying the 14s/40s anomaly circulated to others. 'All I want is people even to talk about it,' the trader told us. If others also took action on the pricing anomaly, they would prevent it widening. Should it widen, the trader explained, he might even come to doubt his belief (the 'theory' behind the trade) that the anomaly was a discrepancy that would close. 'There might be a reason [for the anomaly] I don't understand. I might have to reconsider the decision [to construct a trading position predicated on it narrowing].'

Another way of minimizing the risk of premature capital withdrawal is diversification. If a fund, trading desk, or bank holds a wide variety of arbitrage positions—for example, in different parts of the world and in different asset classes—then, on the face of it, there is little likelihood of enough of those positions losing money simultaneously to create a serious overall loss. (The matched 'long' and 'short' positions characteristic of arbitrage mean that common factors such as global economic conditions, the levels of interest rates, and the buoyancy of stock markets should have little or no effect.) Diversification of this kind was, for instance, a core aspect of LTCM's strategy.

However, the constant attention of many professional traders to what others are doing may undercut the benefits of diversification. If large numbers of traders are all led to take similar positions, then arbitrages that 'ought' to be uncorrelated can suddenly become linked. This, for example, was what caused LTCM's diversification to fail. LTCM tried hard to keep its positions private: as a very large market participant with a largely locked-in capital base, it was concerned less with the benefits of others preventing discrepancies widening than with their trading causing the opportunities it was exploiting to diminish or vanish. However, others did frequently take on similar positions, either because they were following the same general strategy (in part, in emulation of LTCM's success) or because they learned specifics of LTCM's trading directly or indirectly from those who took the other side of those trades. 'I can't believe how many times I was told to do a trade because the boys at Long-Term deemed it a winner', says one hedge-fund manager (Cramer 2002: 179).

The resultant overlapping set of arbitrage positions made it possible for an event to which LTCM itself had only a limited exposure—the Russian government's default on its rouble-denominated bonds on 17 August 1998— suddenly to cause highly correlated adverse price movements across the globe and in apparently unrelated asset classes. Arbitrageurs who incurred losses in Russia had to liquidate positions (even in apparently unrelated assets) to meet margin calls, withdrawals by investors, and other demands on their capital. In aggregate, the positions they sought to liquidate overlapped considerably with each other and with LTCM's portfolio. These liquidations in turn caused more losses, leading to further liquidations, and so on in a disastrous, market-paralysing spiral.

The sociality of arbitrage goes beyond relations to particular others such as managers, hedge-fund investors, and other arbitrageurs: the conduct of arbitrage is affected deeply by the forms of action in financial markets that are seen as permissible and to be encouraged or as impermissible and to be discouraged. One persistent issue is the difference in this respect between the two standard 'legs' of an arbitrage trade. Typically, a price discrepancy is exploited by buying (or in other ways taking a 'long' position) in an undervalued asset, and short selling a similar overvalued counterpart.

Long positions are almost always regarded as unproblematic, but short positions have historically often been the object of suspicion. Short sellers are frequently blamed for falls in price, and the activity is seen as morally reprehensible for other reasons: for instance, in current interpretations, the securities borrowing involved in short selling is contrary to *Sharia*, creating a problem for those who wish to set up 'Islamic' hedge funds. In some markets (for example, Mexican government bonds), only specific, trusted market participants are allowed by regulators to sell short. In other markets, short selling by a wide range of participants is permitted but is constrained in other ways. Until 2007, for example, short sales of stock in the USA were subject to the 'uptick rule' (see, for example, Robotti n.d.)—they were prohibited unless the last price change had been upwards—which could cause substantial delays in short selling if prices are falling consistently. Not all the problems of short selling are the result of deliberate policy (other constraints include the availability of securities to borrow, the cost of such borrowing, and sometimes the vulnerability of short sellers to predatory trading by those who hope to profit by forcing them to unwind their short positions), but the resultant difficulties can be crucial. Accordingly, for example, the 'stock loan' desk (which arranges stock borrowing) occupies a pivotal position on the bank trading floor studied by Beunza.

Because the extent of the problems of short selling varies from asset to asset, systematic effects of these problems can be detected. Thus Dow Jones futures and other stock-index futures seem to tend more often to be below the value implied by the level of underlying index than above it (Shalen n.d.). The trading required to exploit 'overpricing' of futures is straightforward: the arbitrageur has to establish a short position in futures (which means simply selling futures, and involves no particular difficulties), while buying the stocks that make up the index (also straightforward). In contrast, exploiting 'underpricing' of futures requires the arbitrageur to buy futures (again straightforward), but it also involves short selling the underlying stocks, which is, as noted, often more problematic.

Arbitrage can sometimes also raise more specific questions of proper conduct in markets. An interesting case of this was huge trades in Eurozone government bonds and bond futures undertaken by Citigroup Global Markets Ltd. on the morning of 2 August 2004. Like conventional arbitrage between futures and the underlying asset, Citigroup's trading intended to exploit a discrepancy, but in this case it was not a pre-existing price discrepancy but one resulting from differences in the liquidity of the bond and bond futures markets.

In the words of a Citigroup internal memo (quoted in Skorecki and Munter 2005), Citigroup's traders had noticed that 'the liquidity being offered in the bonds is far greater than that offered in the bund [German government bond] future'. (Bund futures are the benchmark European government bond future.) In consequence, a standard 'market neutral' position of the kind often constructed by arbitrageurs (in this case, short futures and long bonds) could be unwound profitably, even in the absence of a pre-existing price discrepancy, if the position was very large. Buying futures on a large scale to unwind the short futures position would lead to losses through 'slippage' (the price of futures would rise as the purchases were being made), but the arbitrage-imposed link between futures and bond prices would then cause the latter also to rise correspondingly. At that point, the greater liquidity of the bond market meant that the long position in bonds could be unwound by selling bonds at these favourable prices, and crucially the sales would not lead to slippage:

they could be completed before prices were forced down. The asymmetry in liquidity would mean that the profit from being able to sell bonds at these elevated prices, without slippage, would more than compensate for the losses caused by slippage in the futures purchases.

The bond-market liquidity on which the profitability of Citigroup's trade depended had not arisen spontaneously, but was the result of a conscious 'liquidity pact' between the banks and continental European governments using the MTS bond-trading system, which has now expanded far beyond Italy. The goal of the pact is to ensure that the euro-denominated government bonds of even the smaller European countries remain liquid. On most price-dissemination systems, prices are indicative: one can conclude a deal only by directly contacting the participant that has posted a price, and it is not obliged to trade at that price. On MTS, in contrast, the banks using the system have to commit themselves to trade up to a set quantity of bonds at posted prices. This exposes them to trading losses, but it makes the Eurozone government bond market, despite its fragmentation, more liquid and thus more attractive to investors. The *Financial Times* claims that 'banks were prepared to subsidise their MTS business' because governments often select banks at the 'top of the list in terms of MTS trading volumes' when awarding 'lucrative business such as derivatives transactions or syndicated bond sales' (van Duyn and Munter 2004).

Critical to Citigroup's trade was its materiality: it required 'hitting' all the bids (offers to buy bonds) on the MTS system nearly simultaneously, a task that was impossible manually. So Citigroup's traders developed software—which they referred to as the 'spreadsheet'—to do this. From 9.12 to 10.29 a.m. on 2 August 2004, they made the planned bond futures purchases, and the price of these futures and of European government bonds rose as anticipated. At 10.28 a.m., they launched the 'spreadsheet', with the intention of selling bonds to the value of €8 billion to €9 billion (Financial Services Authority 2005).

Although the 'spreadsheet' had been tested in simulated trading, and had been operated on a small scale in the actual market, it had been impossible to try it out on anything like the scale required on 2 August, so how it would operate in material reality was not known with full certainty. Some twenty seconds after launching the 'spreadsheet', the traders became concerned that it had not functioned properly, so they activated it a second time. In fact, it had worked even better than anticipated. In consequence of the second activation and of the unanticipated success of the first activation, instead of the bond sales cancelling out earlier purchases, Citigroup was left with a net short position in European government bonds of €3.8 billion. The 'spreadsheet' (designed to sell bonds) was hurriedly reconfigured to buy them, and reactivated at 11.25 a.m. (Financial Services Authority 2005).

Although Citigroup's trading had not gone as planned, it made a profit of almost £10 million, much more than the trade was expected to yield, because after Citigroup's huge bond sales other participants in MTS sharply reduced the prices they were quoting, and the 'spreadsheet' was thus able to buy bonds back at prices significantly lower than those at which it had sold them. What is of interest, however, is the reaction to the trade. Citigroup had not traded on inside information, nor had it spread false rumours. Yet '[m]any traders on the day Citigroup did its deal thought the bank was breaking a "gentleman's agreement" ' by taking advantage on such a huge scale of the 'forced liquidity' required of participants in MTS. A leading banker said that: 'By some European government treasuries, this trade was perceived as open warfare.' The sentiment was not universal—another senior banker said, 'Citigroup spotted a way to make a quick buck. I guess we just have to say well done to them' (van Duyn and Munter 2004)—but Citigroup was widely condemned, and the UK Financial Services Authority (FSA) forced it to relinquish the profits from the trade and to pay a further penalty of £4 million.

The FSA did not accuse Citigroup of having broken the law, but nevertheless held that its trading had violated two of the authority's 'Principles for Business'. In particular, the FSA ruled that Citigroup Global Markets Ltd. 'did not have due regard to . . . the likely consequences the execution of the trading strategy could have for the efficient and orderly operation of the MTS platform' (Financial Services Authority 2005: 2). Precisely as Abolafia (1996) posits in his classic ethnography of financial markets, behaviour in such markets is in practice governed by more than the pursuit of self-interest and the constraints of the law: less explicit norms matter too.

Conclusion

Our argument in this chapter has been that arbitrage—how it is practised, its risks, its uncertainties, its limits, and its capacities to weld markets together into a financial system—can properly be understood only if it is grasped in its full materiality and sociality. That kind of rich, qualitative understanding is of course different from the more abstract but quantitatively more precise understanding typically sought by economists, even 'behavioural finance' specialists. Nevertheless, there are areas of overlap between a 'social studies of finance' perspective and financial economists' recent investigation of the consequences of relaxing their discipline's traditional purist definition of arbitrage.

For example, Shleifer and Vishny (1997) model the risk that those who provide arbitrageurs with capital will withdraw it prematurely in the face of temporarily adverse price movements. Brav and Heaton (2002) address what in our terms is the difficulty that arbitrageurs can have convincing themselves and their audiences that a price pattern is indeed a discrepancy that can be the object of arbitrage. In circulating the chart of the price history of the Brazil 14s and 40s, the trader we observed was seeking to solve in practice the problem modelled by Abreu and Brunnermeier: the limit to arbitrage that can arise when 'rational traders face uncertainty about when their peers will exploit a common arbitrage opportunity' (2002: 341). Attari, Mello, and Ruckes (2005) model a risk that became very pertinent for LTCM after the fund's difficulties became known to others at the start of September 1998, but of which all large arbitrageurs need to be wary: that the combination of capital constraints and positions known to other traders can make arbitrageurs' actions predictable and exploitable.

Shleifer and Vishny, Brav and Heaton, Abreu and Brunnermeier, and Attari, Mello, and Ruckes put forward four separate models, each capturing one of the aspects that we posit as intrinsic to arbitrage as market practice. No integrated model has yet emerged from the literature in economics on the limits of arbitrage, but our fieldwork suggests that it is in the *interaction* of arbitrage's aspects that its crucial limits may reside. Thus the crisis surrounding LTCM arose from the way in which capital constraints akin to those modelled by Shleifer and Vishny interacted with the consequences of others imitating a single prominent arbitrageur, and LTCM's crisis was worsened (to a degree that is hard to determine) by other traders 'arbitraging the arbitrageur' in the manner modelled by Attari, Mello, and Ruckes.

We would therefore be hopeful that the study of arbitrage could be a productive area of collaboration between financial economists and those in the wider social sciences prepared to tackle financial markets in their full materiality and sociality. We are in addition certain that arbitrage is a pivotal topic for social studies of finance. The details of arbitrage may seem to be little things, but they are little things connected to big issues: as, for instance, the materiality of Citigroup's 'spreadsheet' connects to the 'forced liquidity' of MTS and thus to government budgets, Economic and Monetary Union, and even the overall project of European unification. The powers and limits of arbitrage are critical to global financial markets, and the material sociology we advocate is needed to understand them.

6

Measuring Profit

Clinton, Mississippi, Friday, 20 April 2001. The Deep South: during the Civil War, Sherman based himself here when besieging the city of Jackson. Clinton's streets are lined with historic buildings and shaded with old trees. Yet Clinton is also the New South, the site of the ultramodern corporate headquarters of a leading telecom company—a building that in the words of one reporter rises 'like a dark steel mother ship' (Ripley 2002).

In the mother ship, an accounting manager is at work, and part of her job is to produce facts. The telecom company is building the physical infrastructure of the information age: the optical-fibre networks for synchronized, high-speed, high-capacity transmission of data. But it also leases capacity on other companies' networks, primarily so as to link its own network to those of local carriers. Although all of this capacity has had to be paid for under its lease agreements, not all of it has been used. With a few key strokes and mouse clicks, she allocates the costs of the unused portion to two accounts: 'Other Long Term Assets' and 'Construction in Progress'. What she has thereby done is to classify a set of transactions as creation of assets, and the classification will ultimately feed through into her company's published accounts.

A common prejudice about accounting sees acts of classification of this kind as boring; certainly, few social scientists outside of academic accountancy have ever studied them in detail. Yet scales aren't stable. The company is WorldCom, with 20 million customers and 60,000 employees. It carries more Internet traffic and more international telephone calls than any other company in the world (Jeter 2003: xx–xxii). Over the months to come, WorldCom will unravel, and that Friday's classificatory act—dictated by the accountant's superiors—is at the heart of the process. As it unravels, it undoes much of what little confidence remains in the United States in corporate financial reporting. That confidence has already been damaged badly by the bankruptcy of Enron in December 2001. WorldCom's announcement on 25 June 2002 that it has identified accounting irregularities amounting to $3.9 billion adds to growing fears that Enron is not unique.

On 21 July 2002, WorldCom's unravelling culminates in the world's largest ever corporate bankruptcy. Whatever doubts political elites in the United States have felt about the Sarbanes–Oxley Bill, with its draconian measures to regulate financial reporting and punish dubious practices, vanish. Four days later, the House approves Sarbanes–Oxley 423 : 3, and the Senate votes 99 : 0 in its favour. On 30 July, George W. Bush signs the Act onto the statute book. Over the years that follow, international companies seeking stock-market listings start to choose London, in part to avoid Sarbanes–Oxley's costs of compliance and heavy penalties. A few key strokes on a Friday in Mississippi have contributed to a shift in the centre of gravity of the world's financial markets.

The Measurement of Financial Performance

The consequences of that Friday's actions were unusual in their scale, but the actions themselves were not. Today's societies are saturated with measurement, to such an extent that it has often become invisible. (If, for example, a part in your bicycle or car fails, its replacement will fit exactly, with no filing or reshaping needed. It's a mundane achievement, but one that rests on a huge, hidden infrastructure of measurement and precision engineering.[1]) Amongst the things we measure is financial performance, especially profit, and it is perfectly conceivable that there are more specialists (book-keepers, accountants) in that form of measurement than in any other.

The measurement of profit has become a gigantic enterprise because it is central to economic governance. As enterprises become bigger, whether they are profitable or loss-making ceases to be apparent to even the most experienced proprietorial eye: record keeping and calculation are required. When they become public, listed companies, their shares can be bought and sold by investors with no direct personal contact with the companies they own.

An audience thus emerges for public financial facts about companies, not just internal measures of performance. The desire that those facts be trustworthy—and repeated scandals in which they turn out not to be—mean that their production is not just a private matter. Auditors, regulators, tax authorities, governments—all those now have a part to play. The top firms specializing in the measurement of profit—the 'big four': Deloitte Touche Tohmatsu, Ernst & Young, KPMG, and PricewaterhouseCoopers—are amongst the leading global companies. Financial performance generally, and profit specifically, are crucial signals in a free-enterprise, capitalist system. If an activity is profitable, it attracts resources, and in terms of the logic of such a system it *should* do so, because profit indicates that the value of an activity's output is greater than that of its inputs. Conversely, if an activity makes a loss, resources flow away from it.

A company's financial reporting now typically takes three main forms. Its 'income statement' (in the UK, its 'profit and loss account') records, for a given time period such as three months or a year, the company's revenues and the expenses incurred in earning them. Its 'balance sheet' records the amounts of its assets and liabilities at the end of the time period being reported on. Finally, its 'cash flow statement' records the cash it paid and received over the time period.

The need for three forms of report arises because measuring profit is not simply counting cash. Modern financial reporting is 'accruals based', which means that there is no simple correspondence between a corporation's cash flow in a given time period and its revenues and expenses in that period. For example, the cost of the electricity consumed by a company in the current quarter is counted as an expense in that quarter, even if the bill has yet to arrive. If an item is sold to a customer in the current quarter, that is recognized as revenue, even if the customer has not yet paid. As any textbook of accounting (e.g. Perks 2004: 173–4) notes, a company's profits under 'accruals-based' accounting is thus not the difference between the cash it has received and paid out. Instead, profit is the difference between revenues earned in a given period and the expenses incurred in earning them, even if the corresponding cash receipts or payments took place in an earlier period or will not take place until a later one.

If a manufacturing company buys a machine, or an airline an aeroplane, only a portion—often quite a small portion—of the costs involved will normally be classified as an expense in the period of the purchase, because the machine or aeroplane can be expected to continue to generate revenue years into the future. Instead, the costs of the purchase will appear not on the company's profit and loss account, but on its balance sheet—as an 'asset'. As the asset ages, its balance-sheet value will typically be reduced, and it is the loss of value in a given time period—the 'depreciation'—that is treated as the expense and set against revenue for that period.

That is the significance of what the WorldCom accountant did. The costs of leasing unused network capacity could have been classified as an expense analogous to the consumption of electricity. Along with some other smaller adjustments, 'capitalizing' those costs—classifying them not as an expense but as purchase of an asset, more like a machine or an aeroplane than the cost of electricity—reduced WorldCom's expenses in the second quarter of 2001 by $610 million (Beresford, Katzenbach, and Rogers 2003: 108), enough to turn what would otherwise have an overall loss into a profit.

Accounting Classification

Acts of classification are fundamental to the measurement of profit. All book-keepers and accountants, and many lay people, have to decide—often dozens of times a day—which accounting category best fits a transaction or other economic item. In an age in which most accounting in developed countries is computerized, this typically takes the material form of assigning to the record of the transaction a numerical code from the organization's 'chart of accounts', so permitting the automated processing and aggregation of items by the organization's accounting system.

For instance, when I incurred a cost chargeable to the main grant that supported the research reported in this book, I had to decide which of the codes listed in Figure 6.1 (a subset of Edinburgh University's chart of accounts) to assign to it. Sometimes I found the task straightforward. If I went by train within the UK to interview someone, that struck me as unequivocally '3202'. But I confess that as a purely amateur book-keeper I was often a little puzzled. If I paid someone's expenses to come to talk to a workshop I was running, was that still 3202? Was it maybe 3102? When I bought a conference phone to do telephone interviews, was that 3102 or 3512? Given a bit of imagination, I could even envisage classifying the phone purchase as 3202 or 3206, because it was a substitute for physical travel.

```
3004   Research Teaching (At)
3006   Research Assistants (Ar)
3032   Research Fellows (Af)
3102   Research Other Costs
3138   Research Consumables
3202   Travel/Subs – Within UK only
3206   Travel/Subs – Outside UK/EC
3438   Insurance Cover
3512   Exceptional Items
3712   Research UoE O'heads Recovered
```

Figure 6.1. Examples of codes from the University of Edinburgh's chart of accounts

Such decisions are pervasive. They include the following:[2]

1. Is an item an accounting item? Consider, for example, a brand. The right
    to call your company's sweet fizzy drinks 'Coca Cola™' is clearly valuable.
    In a broad sense of the term, that right is as much an 'asset' as the
    machinery used to produce and to bottle the drinks; indeed, it may be
    worth vastly more than that machinery. The right seems clearly to meet
    formal definitions of 'asset' such as 'Assets are probable future economic
    benefits obtained or controlled by a particular entity as a result of past
    transactions or events' (FASB 1985: 16). Accountants have, however, wor-
    ried that brands lack a characteristic that they believe accounting items
    must have: measurability. As International Accounting Standard 38 puts
    it, 'An intangible asset shall be recognised ... only if ... the cost of the asset
    can be measured reliably' (IASB 2005: 1599). How can one put a figure on
    the value of the right to call a liquid Coca Cola? How can one tell whether
    that right has got more valuable over the past year, or less? A change in
    value would affect not just a corporation's balance sheet but its income
    statement, from which its earnings or 'profits' are calculated. If a brand is
    treated as an accounting item, would its owner's profits become a mere
    opinion? There are methodologies for measuring the value of a brand,
    and firms that specialize in the task, but the credibility of the results is
    contested (Power 1992).
2. If an item is an accounting item, what kind of an item is it? Is it an
    'expense', an 'asset', a 'liability', 'income', 'reserve', or 'capital'? As already
    noted, such classifications can have substantial consequences, for exam-
    ple for a corporation's earnings.
3. What overall 'scale' shall we use to measure an item? In terms of the
    measurement of assets, for example, a key issue is whether to use 'historic

cost' or 'fair value'.[3] The former is the traditional approach: an asset is recorded at what it originally cost, minus the extent of its subsequent depreciation. 'Fair value', in contrast, is 'The amount for which an asset could be exchanged, or a liability settled, between knowledgeable, willing parties in an arm's length transaction' (IASB 2005: 2217). Both approaches have their advocates, often passionate advocates (the supporters of fair value are currently in the ascendancy in standard setting). Fair value has the virtue that what a firm's assets are currently worth will usually be more relevant than what they once cost. Historic cost measurement is complicated by inflation and by the need to estimate depreciation, and it can seem inappropriate in the case of assets such as land and buildings whose value often rises through time. Historic cost, though, has the advantage that it will usually be easier to establish and to document what an item originally cost than what it is currently worth. To its critics, 'fair value' achieves relevance at an undue price in terms of objectivity.

4. How will measurement actually be done? Take costs, for example. If a corporation manufactures items or sells services, how is their cost to be determined? Few production or service-provision activities are entirely bounded off from other such activities. A factory, for example, will usually produce multiple items, often of different kinds. How are the costs of labour, machinery, heat, light, and other common services to be allocated amongst them? Nor do all problems vanish even if a firm buys in ready-made all the items it sells. Suppose such a firm sells an item from its inventory of similar items. What is the corresponding cost? Is it what it paid for the most recently acquired such item ('last in, first out'), or for the oldest such item ('first in, first out'), or some kind of weighted average? If prices are changing, the difference between the answers may be consequential.

Similarly, how is revenue to be measured? In accruals-based accounting, a firm's revenue in a given period is, as already noted, not identical to the cash it receives in that period. The revenue from a sale, for example, is 'recognized' when an item is sold, not when it is paid for. Items can, however, subsequently be returned, and sometimes customers will fail to pay. Because returns and the extent of 'bad debts' lie in the future, they need to be estimated if appropriate 'provisions' for them are to be made when measuring revenues.

5. To which time period does an item belong? *When*, for instance, is an item 'sold'?[4] When a customer says verbally that he or she will buy it? When a contract is signed or a purchase order received? When the item leaves the warehouse? When the invoice is issued? When payment is received? Furthermore, many items are manufactured over a time period that begins only after they are ordered, and many services are provided not at a single point in time but over an extended time period. Is the corresponding revenue earned at the start of the time period, at its end, at an intermediate point or points, or gradually throughout the period? If the last of these, what proportion of the revenue is to be regarded as earned at any given point in time?

The allocation of costs across time periods presents similar issues. Take advertising, for example. Is it generating sales in the current period (in which case, it should be recorded as an expense in that period), or will it lead to sales in future time periods (in which case, its recognition as an expense should be deferred to those time periods)?

6. Is an item 'current' or 'long-term'? A company's debts, for example, are conventionally divided between 'current liabilities', which are expected to fall due within a year or less, and 'long-term liabilities', which are not expected to need honouring within that period. Similarly, 'current assets'—those that can be realized within a year or less—also form a distinct subcategory. The classification is consequential because current assets and liabilities are prominent components of the ratios used to assess a company's financial health.[5] Traditionally, a 'current ratio' (current assets : current liabilities) of 2 : 1 was regarded as an indicator of health, while a ratio of 1 : 1 or lower could be read as a signal that a company was close to insolvency. The classification of an item as 'current' or not is thus consequential.

7. Where are the boundaries of an organization?[6] Which transactions fall within those boundaries, and which outside them? A prominent feature of Enron's practices, for example, was the creation of 'special purpose entities' that could, the firm's senior managers and auditors believed, legitimately be treated in accounting terms as separate from it. There are several entirely proper reasons for creating such entities (they are, for example, a foundation of the entire field of 'structured finance', including much of the credit-derivatives market touched on in Chapter 2),

but they can also be used to avoid classifying items as liabilities of a corporation on the grounds that they are liabilities of the special purpose entity, not of its parent. How, then, is the 'separateness' of an entity from its parent to be defined? Outside investment? If so, how much (at the time of Enron, 3 per cent was regarded as sufficient)? Outside control? If so, how is control to be measured?

8. Is a corporation a 'going concern': that is, is its survival reasonably assured? The answer makes a huge difference to how its assets are valued. Machinery, for instance, will normally be worth a lot more if the firm that owns it can be expected to continue using it to generate revenues, by comparison with a valuation of what it would fetch if sold second-hand or for scrap. A firm's directors thus have to certify explicitly whether or not they are employing a 'going concern' assumption and auditors must consider whether the assumption is appropriate. Their decision to contest that assumption is normally catastrophic for the firm in question. With its assets valued only at the proceeds of liquidation, they will usually be dwarfed by its liabilities, and bankruptcy ensues.

Accounting for Economic Reality

What factors might structure the multiple explicit and implicit choices involved in accounting classification and measurement? In the remainder of this chapter, I explore various possible answers to this question: first, 'economic reality'; second, the rules of accounting; and third, a range of other social and technological factors. Let me begin with 'economic reality'. The purpose of financial reporting, it would widely be agreed, is to represent accurately the economic situation of a corporation, so that its existing investors, its creditors, and other stakeholders can assess matters such as whether their money is being well used or whether they will be paid, and potential investors can decide whether or not to entrust the corporation with their capital.

An obvious complication is the strong feedback from 'report' to 'reality'. Financial reporting directly affects the economic health of corporations. A corporation that appears sound and profitable is attractive to investors and to lenders, while a bank that appears unsound is vulnerable to a bank run.[7] To withdraw the 'going concern' assumption will normally cause a firm to cease to be a going concern (Hines 1988: 256). Nevertheless, economic health is not simply a matter of accountants' reports. All readers will be aware that there are some purchases they cannot make, and some patterns of expenditure they could not sustain without increasing their income; and something similar holds for corporations. A corporation can become unable to meet its financial obligations just as an individual can, and financial reporting—however optimistic—may not prevent this happening. Indeed, accounting scandals frequently take the form of the sudden insolvency of an apparently profitable corporation.

However, the goal of capturing economic reality is insufficient to determine the practice of accounting, even if no other considerations intrude. For example, accounting has its local cultures and traditions. Not only have formal rules and standards varied considerably between countries, but practice sometimes varies even when rules seem similar. Thus even prior to recent European harmonization, the rules governing the depreciation of fixed assets were similar in the UK and France, but the typical implementation of the rules was quite different (Walton, Haller, and Raffournier 2003: 23). As a consequence of national differences, when the assets and profits of a corporation are calculated according to the practices of more than one country, the resultant figures can differ considerably. In 1993, for example, Daimler-Benz AG listed on the New York Stock Exchange, and until 1996 (when it started using exclusively US rules) it prepared two sets of accounts, US and German. The value of its shareholders' equity (the difference between the valuations of Daimler-Benz's assets and its liabilities) was 40 to 45 per cent higher in its US accounts. Its earnings also differed, and the most dramatic difference (in 1993, Daimler-Benz's German accounts showed profits of 615 million DM, when its US accounts recorded a loss equivalent to 1,839 million DM) seems to have been caused mainly by revaluations designed to reduce discrepancies in asset values (Bay and Bruns 2003: 397–9).

Members of different local cultures of financial reporting may believe strongly that their practices best capture reality. For example, a continental European corporation's accountants may have felt they were taking proper account of a rapidly changing and uncertain world, when to their British and American counterparts they seemed to be salting away large undeclared profits. That such convictions can be passionate means that the harmonization of international accounting standards across the European Union and the ongoing harmonization between Europe and the USA have been fraught. Such harmonization is intended to make it easier for global investors to compare corporations that report in different jurisdictions, but the key figure in these efforts forecast 'blood all over the streets' as they came to fruition (Sir David Tweedie, quoted by Tricks and Hargreaves 2004).

Particularly controversial was International Accounting Standard 39 (IAS 39), governing the valuation of financial instruments such as derivatives.[8] The key issue was the bearing of the standard upon situations in which derivatives are used to hedge a risk, for example when a bank offers its customers fixed-rate mortgages or guaranteed interest rates on their deposits, and uses derivatives (often LIBOR based) to offset its consequent exposure to changes in interest rates. Banks typically take the view that in such situations the economically realistic accounting treatment is what is called 'hedge accounting', in which fluctuations in the market value of hedging instruments are not recognized in their balance sheets and income statements, on the grounds that those gains and losses are offset by fluctuations in the value of the items being hedged. Opponents of IAS 39 argue that its rules governing the permissibility of hedge accounting are too restrictive, for example in failing adequately to take into account the way in which banks hedge risks such as interest-rate exposure in aggregate, not item by item. The danger, they argue, is that what in economic reality are risk-reducing hedging transactions will be made to appear risky by injecting spurious, artificial volatility into their earnings. (For example, an interviewee who was an accountant for a bank complained that the items being hedged—for example, a portfolio of fixed-rate mortgages—are often not 'marked to market'—revalued as market prices change—but the instrument used to hedge them has to be.) In 2004, concerted lobbying by banks led the European Commission to endorse the standard only in part, a decision condemned sharply by the UK Accounting Standards Board, which was reported as suggesting that UK companies 'should ignore it' (Tricks and Buck 2004).

It might be imagined that disputes over whether accounting rules reflect 'economic reality' could be settled by turning to the acknowledged experts on the latter: economists. In fact, the small minority of economists who have taken research in accounting seriously have rarely been able decisively to settle the issues at stake. As already suggested, perhaps the single most important overall question in financial reporting is how to define and measure 'income' (or 'earnings' or 'profits'). The great British economist John Hicks provided what has become perhaps the canonical definition of 'income',[9] but he admitted it was not precise. Making it precise—in particular, separating income unequivocally from capital—might be 'chasing a will-o'-the wisp', said Hicks. Economists, he wrote, 'shall be well advised to eschew *income*'. The concept was a 'bad tool…which break[s] in our hands' (Hicks 1946: 176–7, emphasis in original). Accountants, however, have never been in a position to duck what is perhaps their central classificatory responsibility. As Dennis Robertson put it, 'The jails and workhouses of the world are filled with those who gave up as a bad job the admittedly difficult task of distinguishing between capital and income' (quoted by Kay 2004).

The Rules of Accounting

If 'reality' is not sufficient to structure the practice of accounting, perhaps rules are? The extent of formal, written rules of accounting has varied with time and place, and there has sometimes been strong opposition amongst accountants to such rules. In Britain (and perhaps especially in Scotland, the original home of an organized profession of accounting), there has often been a conviction that the requirement to capture economic reality—to give 'true and correct view' or 'a true and fair view' of the financial situation of companies, as successive UK Companies Acts have required—necessitates 'a custom-built document' requiring 'the exercise of an informed judgment' with which others, even accountants' own organizations, should not 'interfere' (Slimmings 1981: 14). Such a perspective emphasizes professional status: one of the hallmarks of a 'professional'—as distinct, say, from a 'bookkeeper' or other 'clerk'—has been taken to be the exercise of 'judgement' (see, for example, Porter 1995).

Nevertheless, the direction of historical change, driven above all by accounting scandals, has been towards rules and principles that are spelled out rather than implicit. The Great Crash of 1929 raised huge question marks over whether the financial reporting of many US corporations reflected their economic situations. In part to ward off government intervention (possibly even compulsory government auditing of corporate accounts), the American Institute of Accountants made at least a symbolic sacrifice of some of the accountant's individual discretion, and began to promulgate formal accounting standards (Zeff 1984). The effort did indeed help to keep accountants in charge of formulating standards—in 1938, the Securities and Exchange Commission delegated its standard-setting powers to the Institute's Committee on Accounting Procedure—but it marked the beginning of a proliferation of formal standards. The episode serves as one of the prime examples of the rise of the 'ideal of mechanical objectivity, knowledge based completely on explicit rules' (Porter 1995: 7). The six brief 'rules or principles' formulated by the American Institute of Accountants in 1934 had by 2008 become the Financial Accounting Standards Board's 163 standards, some of which exceed a hundred pages.[10] The equivalent set of standards promulgated by the International Accounting Standards Board—which govern accounting in the European Union, and have also been adopted widely outside of Europe—is slimmer, but even it (e.g. IASB 2005) is already over 2,000 pages long in total, and growing.

Here, the finitist perspective sketched in Chapter 2 leads to a clear-cut prediction: that even the most detailed rulebook will on its own be insufficient to determine the practice of bookkeeping and accounting. Indeed, the very size of the rulebooks—especially of the rulebook of American accounting, which has tended to be more explicitly prescriptive than other national traditions, especially that of the UK—and their tendency to grow inexorably in length year after year could be seen as an exemplification of the Wittgensteinian regress outlined in Chapter 2. If one attempts to remedy the underdetermination of actions by rules by adding rules of interpretation, one is embarked on what is in principle an endless task.

Indeed, the International Accounting Standards Board has spawned a body specifically entrusted with the task of interpretation, the International Financial Reporting Interpretations Committee (IFRIC). Its task is, however, not straightforward. Determining what standards 'imply' is not a simple exercise in deductive logic. As noted in Chapter 7, for example, IFRIC's proposed Interpretation ('IFRIC 3') of how standards should be applied to 'emission rights' proved immensely controversial, and had to be withdrawn.

An 'emission right' is a novel accounting item, but it should not be imagined that the underdetermination of actions by rules is to be found only in the case of new items. Consider, for example, a set of accounting items of a very old kind, 'inventories': companies' stocks of unsold items. There is, to my knowledge, no disagreement whatsoever over the principle that the International Accounting Standards Board lays down for valuing inventories: 'Inventories shall be measured at the lower of cost and net realisable value' (IASB 2005:

662).[11] Implementing this agreed principle, however, involves measuring both 'cost' and 'net realisable value'. As suggested above, the cost of a manufactured item is not simply the cost of the raw materials directly used in it. Workers' wages are also part of the cost, but in most situations those workers will be producing many items, sometimes of different kinds, not just the item in question, so a decision needs to be taken about what proportion of their wages (and associated employer's costs) should be counted in the cost of the item in question. Machinery, too, is normally used to produce many items, thus raising similar issues concerning how to apportion its depreciation. Because of these and the other contingencies alluded to above—apportionment of the cost of heat, light, buildings, administrative services, etc.—many firms do not attempt to measure the costs of individual items of inventory, but instead estimate a 'standard cost'. Although the aggregate of such standard costs can be checked against the record of actual expenditures—as was done, for example, in the firm studied in MacKenzie (2008)—they are certainly not self-evident empirical facts.

Similarly with measuring 'net realisable value'. That involves determining whether the item or items can be sold, and if so for how much. That in turn involves judgements about both market conditions and the item or items: have they, for example, been superseded by superior alternatives? Unsurprisingly, such questions can sometimes be hard to answer unequivocally, and it is difficult to imagine even the most detailed set of rules making the satisfactory determination of 'net realisable value' entirely algorithmic. Measuring the value of inventories is thus far less straightforward than might be suggested by the apparently simple principle—'the lower of cost and net realisable value'—laid down in the 'rulebook' of international accounting: indeed, inventories are often seen by auditors as a matter that demands their special attention because of the large effects different valuations can have on a firm's balance-sheet situation and profits.

To take another example of the way in which agreement over a rule or definition does not prevent dispute over how it is to be applied, consider the accounting classification with which this chapter began: WorldCom's classification of the costs of unused portions of line leases as 'assets'. Because World-Com has come to be seen as a straightforward case of accounting fraud, it is easy to imagine that the classification was unequivocally 'against the rules'. Matters are, however, not quite as clear-cut as that. When WorldCom's Chief Financial Officer, Scott Sullivan, was called upon by its Board to justify the classification he did so, citing US accounting's canonical definition (already quoted above, and as far as I'm aware entirely uncontested): 'Assets are probable future economic benefits obtained or controlled by a particular entity as a result of past transactions or events' (FASB 1985: 16).

In his paper to WorldCom's Board, Sullivan argued that the costs of leasing large amounts of network capacity—larger than might actually be needed—were costs of acquiring customers (which can legitimately be classed as an asset); that the classification of those costs as an asset 'does not contradict' the above definition of 'asset'; and that it met the requirements of the relevant more detailed rules:

The lease commitments were entered into to obtain access to large amounts of capacity under the theory that revenue would follow and fully absorb these costs and to expedite 'time to market'. We believe that this provided an advantage over our competitors and created the leader in Internet backbone at OC 192-c.[12] The commitments were entered into with the knowledge that we would incur an expense prematurely and the revenues would be earned subsequent to that date. The Company was willing to absorb this cost prior to recognizing the revenue stream because it believed that the future revenues would be matched up with these costs. These commitments were entered into as the result of customers for which services would be rendered and the lease commitments were entered into to expedite the customer provisioning and revenue stream in accordance with SAB 101[13] and as further supplemented by FASB 91,[14] direct and indirect costs associated with obtaining a customer may be deferred and amortized over the revenue stream associated with that contract.

(Sullivan 2002: 1–2)

Sullivan's argument was not a priori outrageous. WorldCom hoped that the customers it attracted would stay with the firm for years, and the costs of acquiring them would thus indeed give rise to the 'probable future economic benefits' crucial to the definition of an 'asset'. The practice of treating 'customer relationships' as an asset—and thus 'capitalizing' the costs of acquiring those relationships, rather than treating those costs as expenses—seems reasonably widespread: a colleague of mine in accounting, Yannis Tsalavoutas, was able quickly to provide me with a sample list of UK companies which do just that.[15] Often, for example, companies such as lawyers or consultancies are bought specifically to gain access to their clientele, and the costs of doing so treated as an asset.[16]

Sullivan can thus be seen as attempting to construct an analogy: that leasing large amounts of network capacity (even if it turned out not to be needed) was like other ways of acquiring customers, the costs of which could legitimately be treated as assets. As we shall see below, his argument persuaded one audience but failed to persuade another, more crucial one. The point, however, is that 'persuade' is the right term. The costs involved did not self-evidently meet the formal definition of 'assets', but nor did they self-evidently fail to meet it. The definition did not carry with it instructions sufficient to determine how it should correctly be applied in a specific case. Unfortunately from the viewpoint of this chapter, Sullivan's argument was never tested in court. Sullivan pleaded guilty to securities fraud, testified in court against WorldCom's chief executive, Bernard Ebbers, and received a jail sentence of only four years, prosecutors having entered a plea in mitigation for him on the grounds that he had been a cooperative witness. Ebbers's—unsuccessful—defence was that he was ignorant of 'detailed' matters such as the classification of the costs of leases as assets, not that the classification was legitimate. He was jailed for twenty-five years.

Earnings Management

What WorldCom had been seeking to achieve was, of course, a favourable portrayal of its financial performance. Just how widespread are efforts of this kind? Clearly, there is no unequivocal, direct way to answer this question. Researchers and other outsiders have no privileged access to the reality of companies' economic situations that could serve as a benchmark.

Fortunately, however, there is a considerable body of quantitative research within academic accounting that enables us indirectly to address the question of the extent of efforts at favourable portrayal. This research concerns 'earnings management', the canonical definition of which is given by Schipper (1989: 92): 'purposeful intervention in the external financial reporting process, with the intent of obtaining some private gain (as opposed to, say, merely facilitating the neutral operation of the process)'. Schipper's definition does not say so explicitly, but earnings management is usually taken to be permissible, legal forms of this intervention. ('Fabricating invoices to create fictitious sales revenue'—Schipper 1989: 93—is fraud, not earnings management.) The prevalence of earnings management is thus of interest, not just as an indicator of the extent of efforts at favourable portrayal, but precisely because it is behaviour 'within the rules'. The extent of earnings management is thus a measure, albeit a very crude one, of the degree to which discretion can in practice be exercised even when, as in the USA (the site of most research on the topic), the financial reporting process is governed by extensive, formal rules.

What 'private gain' might induce managements to engage in earnings management? Probably most important is what appears to be a widespread belief amongst corporate managers that stock analysts and investors prefer corporations whose earnings rise predictably to corporations whose earnings fluctuate substantially, even if around the same underlying trend. (The belief in the pervasiveness of this preference seems to have informed the opposition, discussed above, to the standard governing accounting for derivatives, IAS 39.) If the rewards enjoyed by corporate senior managers reflect stock prices, as in recent decades they increasingly have, there is thus an incentive for 'income smoothing', in other words for exploiting permissible discretion to reduce the volatility of earnings. Clearly, too, there is usually, though not always, an incentive to avoid reporting losses, and it is often very important to meet or to surpass stock analysts' predictions of corporate earnings. (The main exception to the need to avoid reporting losses is that one of the techniques of earnings management is the 'big bath', in which a corporation reports a large loss, portraying it to analysts and investors as 'one-off' and the result, for example, of restructuring. A pessimistically calculated big-bath loss—involving, for example, large provisions for liabilities and for bad debts—enhances future profits, which are boosted as the provisions are unwound.)

One approach taken in research on earnings management is to identify situations in which there is a clear, temporary incentive to manage earnings; to scrutinize corporate accounts for patterns consistent with earnings management; and to examine whether those patterns correlate with incentive situations. A pioneering study of this kind was Jennifer Jones's (1991) examination of the financial reporting of firms in industries that were petitioning the US International Trade Commission to recommend tariffs and import restrictions. Such petitions stood a chance of being granted only if there was evidence that domestic industry was being 'hurt' by overseas competition. Jones focused on accruals: balance-sheet changes for which there is no immediate cash-flow counterpart such as depreciation, changes in the valuation of property, plant, and inventory, and estimates of accounts payable and receivable. She estimated the discretionary component of such accruals by subtracting from total accruals a regression-based estimate of 'normal', 'non-discretionary' accruals. Aggregating results for five industries (automobiles, carbon steel, stainless and alloy tool steel, copper, and footwear), she showed statistically significant negative discretionary accruals in the years of International Trade Commission investigations.

Initial public offerings of stock (IPOs) are another situation in which there is a temporarily strong incentive to 'window-dress' accounts (in this case to portray financial strength). A comparison of the 'unexpected' accruals of companies engaged in IPOs with a matched control group of similar companies found that 62 per cent of the IPO firms had higher accruals than the corresponding control (Teoh, Wong, and Rao 1998: 187, table 3). Since chance processes would suggest a 50 per cent figure, 'this implies that roughly 12 percent of the issuing firms manage earnings' (Healy and Wahlen 1999: 373).

A different approach to the detection of earnings management is to examine the statistical distribution of earnings, looking for discontinuities or 'kinks' at earnings levels that correspond to particularly strong incentives to earnings management: zero earnings (and thus the divide between making a profit and registering a loss); earnings in the previous year or previous quarter; and corporations' or analysts' earnings predictions. Such kinks turn out to be substantial (see, for example, Figure 6.2). For instance, analysis of US corporate earnings for 1976–94 suggests that '30% to 44% of the firms with slightly negative pre-managed earnings exercise discretion to report positive earnings' (Burgstahler and Dichev 1997: 124).

The detection of earnings management abounds with conceptual and methodological difficulties (see, for example, McNichols 2000). Analyses based on 'discretionary' or 'unexpected' accruals are extremely sensitive to the model of 'normal', non-discretionary accruals that is employed (if, for example, earnings management is widespread, 'normal' levels of accruals may already reflect such management) and they cannot detect techniques of earnings management that do not involve accruals. Nor are distributional analyses unequivocal. A distributional 'kink' is not in itself evidence of earnings management. It may be, for example, that anticipated small losses are turned into small profits not by changes in accounting classifications but by 'real' interventions (sales drives, cuts in expenditure on maintenance or on research and development, and so on). Burgstahler and Dichev (1997) attempt to

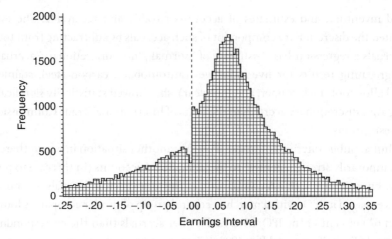

Figure 6.2. Frequency distribution of reports of net annual income by US corporations, 1976–1994

Source: Reprinted from *Journal of Accounting and Economics*, 24 (David Burgstahler and Ilia Dichev,' Earnings Management to Avoid Earnings Decreases and Losses', 99–126), copyright 1997, with permission from Elsevier. Burgstahler and Dichev draw their data from Computstat, and the population of corporations excludes the financial sector and regulated industries. Income is scaled by division by the corporation's market value at the start of the year; interval width is 0.005. The dashed line is the zero-earnings point.

overcome this problem by investigating cash flow from operations and levels of accruals around reference points such as zero earnings, but this kind of analysis may not be entirely robust (Dechow, Richardson, and Tuna 2003). There are even potential issues of reflexivity. Some sophisticated investors are already employing academic earnings-management detection models (Henry 2004), and it would be surprising if regulators were not doing so too, so there is now an incentive to manage earnings in ways that the models cannot detect.

Nevertheless, the overall thrust of the literature on earnings management is consistent with pervasive anecdotal evidence (most authoritative is Levitt 1998) of extensive earnings management by US corporations, at least in the 1980s and 1990s. (Empirical study of periods prior to the 1980s is too sparse to allow any definitive conclusions, and it is not yet clear whether the prevalence of the practice has declined since the scandals of the early 2000s and the subsequent high-profile criminal trials.) Attempts to achieve favourable portrayals appear to have been widespread, and—just as a finitist analysis would predict—the world's most rule-intensive system of financial reporting did not eliminate discretion from corporate accounting.

Contesting Classification

It would, however, be quite mistaken to conclude that accounting is practised free from constraint. For example, again consider the case of the WorldCom accounting classification with which this chapter began. The most interesting character in the WorldCom episode is, ultimately, not the chief executive Ebbers (an understandable figure, given the temptations and pressures of the months in which the dot.com and telecom boom turned to bust), nor Sullivan (despite the fact that his actions serve as an almost textbook example of the logical gap between rules and definitions and their applications), but World-Com manager Cynthia Cooper, who headed an internal audit team including two key colleagues, Gene Morse and Glyn Smith. Cooper was a career accountant, brought up in Clinton, Mississippi, site of WorldCom's headquarters. She first learned accounting at Clinton High School (it is a small-town story: she was taught the subject by Glyn Smith's mother), and went on to take an undergraduate degree in it at Mississippi State University and a postgraduate qualification from the University of Alabama. Her roommate at Mississippi State remembers her sitting in accounting classes 'in the front row, dead center ... she would pepper the professor with questions' (Ripley 2002).

Cooper and her division were responsible for internal matters such as budgets, performance evaluation, and identifying inefficiencies, not for checking WorldCom's financial reporting: that was the role of its external auditors, Arthur Andersen. In March 2002, however, her interest in the data underpinning WorldCom's income statement and balance sheet was piqued by a visit from the manager of WorldCom's wireless division, John Stupka. In 2001, Stupka had made provision for customer bad debts totalling $400 million. Sullivan had unwound the provision, thus boosting WorldCom's reported income, and Stupka was unhappy, because the bad debts, no longer provided for, were about to damage his division's financial performance figures (Pulliam and Solomon 2002).

To Cooper, Stupka had been right to create a reserve when he could reasonably foresee a proportion of customers failing to pay, and Sullivan's reversal of the provision 'smelled funny'. She queried it with an Andersen auditor responsible for WorldCom, who 'brushed her off' (Pulliam and Solomon 2002). Cooper then turned to Gene Morse: 'She came back to me and said, "Go dig" ' (Pulliam and Solomon 2002). She also took the issue of the reversal of the provision to WorldCom's audit committee, where she presented the arguments against it. Sullivan justified it, but eventually conceded.

Cooper's choice of Morse to 'dig' was astute: he had both determination and computer skills. Blocking his enquiries was the access-control matrix of WorldCom's computerized accounting system. He would need high-level approval for the 'read' permissions he needed, and that request would make clear that the internal audit team was straying beyond its remit. Instead, Morse offered to help test a program that a member of the WorldCom information-technology staff was checking. The program gave Morse access to the records of huge numbers of transactions, indeed such large numbers that he had to begin to work late at night after his downloading of giant files—such as the 350,000 monthly records that made up 'intercompany accounts receivables'— began to be blocked because of their effects on system performance. (Such records typically include scanned versions of documentation such as invoices, hence the size of such files.) Knowing Cooper, Morse, and others were working late, Cooper's father would sometimes take in sandwiches for them to have at midnight (Jeter 2003: 169).

Morse began to focus on 'journal entries' such as the one described at the start of this chapter, via which costs were classified as purchases of assets. His instinctual response to some of these was that they were wrong. 'This stinks', he remembers thinking in one case (Pulliam and Solomon 2002). By the start of June 2002, Morse had found accounting classifications totalling $2 billion that seemed dubious to him and to Cooper. She and Smith began to raise them with Max Bobbitt, who chaired WorldCom's audit committee, with Ferrell Malone, the WorldCom 'engagement partner' of KPMG (which had taken over from Andersen as the company's auditors), and with senior colleagues in WorldCom's Clinton headquarters, such as Controller David Myers. Eventually, the disputed classifications reached WorldCom's full audit committee on 20 June. Sullivan justified them verbally to the committee, and over the following weekend he prepared the written justification quoted above.

The case made by Sullivan in defence of classifying the costs of unused portions of network leases as assets divided accountants from lay people. At least some of the latter found it convincing: 'To some non-accountants [on WorldCom's Board], Sullivan's justifications seemed reasonable, and some thought KPMG did not sufficiently understand the Company or the industry' (Beresford, Katzenbach, and Rogers 2003: 128). As that quotation indicates, however, KPMG's accountants sided with Cooper's case. Even Myers, who as World Com's Controller had been heavily involved in its high-level accounting processes and decisions, conceded to Cooper and Smith that 'the entries shouldn't have been made' (Pulliam and Solomon 2002). Indeed, he seems initially to have resisted making them, telling Sullivan 'the transfer couldn't be justified' (Pulliam 2003: M6).

It was the lack of support from Sullivan's fellow accountants that was fatal for him. When the audit committee reassembled on 24 June 2002, he continued to defend the disputed classification. However:

> KPMG told Sullivan that this theory for capitalizing operating line costs did not hold water. Representatives of Andersen, participating by telephone, said the accounting was not in accordance with GAAP [Generally Accepted Accounting Principles, the overall framework of financial reporting in the USA] and that Andersen was withdrawing its audit opinions for 2001 and its review of the first quarter of 2002. After the meeting, Salsbury [WorldCom General Counsel Michael Salsbury] asked Sullivan for his resignation. Myers, who was not present, was separately contacted and asked to resign. Myers later resigned. Sullivan did not, and was fired.
>
> (Beresford, Katzenbach, and Rogers 2003: 128–9)

Of course, context matters. Two weeks before the audit committee meeting, the huge auditing firm Arthur Andersen had been convicted of destroying evidence in connection with its client, Enron, and it was already clear that the firm had effectively collapsed: the 'big five' in auditing had become the 'big four'. So all those present at the audit committee meeting will have known that both criminal prosecution and corporate demise could follow from accounting decisions that others judged indefensible. In other circumstances, Sullivan's justification of the contested accounting classification might have been seen as allowable, as his earlier contentious reversal of the bad-debt provision seems initially to have been, but by June 2002 the risks of accepting it must have been viewed by those involved as too high.

Constraining Accounting

A crucial virtue of finitism as a theoretical perspective on financial reporting is that by suggesting that accounting cannot entirely be constrained by rules or by 'reality' it sharpens empirical curiosity as to the nature of the other sources of constraint. Unfortunately, existing research is insufficient fully to satisfy that empirical curiosity. Certainly, I do not pretend that the material presented in this chapter or in a small case study presented elsewhere (MacKenzie 2008) has done so. For reasons to be touched on below, the most promising approach to investigating the constraints on accounting is likely to be ethnographic, but research of that kind on financial reporting has so far been rare. The sociologically oriented literature in accounting, which is rich on topics such as professionalization, management accounting, and the regulation of accounting, is sparser in regard to the practices underpinning financial reporting: 'One of the disappointing characteristics of field studies in organizations is how few have examined how accounting and audit decisions are made' (Cooper and Robson 2006: 435). So my discussion of likely sources of constraint is speculative.

Although not intended as a comment on accounting, the passage from David Bloor already quoted in Chapter 2 is worth revisiting here as a way of orienting the discussion:

We *could* take our concepts or rules anywhere, in any direction ... We are not prevented by 'logic' or by 'meanings' from doing this ... The real sources of constraint [are] our instincts, our biological nature, our sense experience, our interactions with other people, our immediate purposes, our training, our anticipation of and response to sanctions, and so on through the gamut of causes, starting with the psychological and ending with the sociological.   (Bloor 1997: 19–20, emphasis in original)

Let me begin with a factor prominent in the unravelling of WorldCom and in any finitist analysis: 'interactions with other people'. Financial reporting is not an activity conducted by individuals in isolation. Often, others need to be persuaded that a classification or a measurement is appropriate, and this can be an important source of constraint. The most obvious such others are a corporation's auditors, and this, fortunately, is an area in which existing research is relatively strong. A particularly striking study is Beattie, Fearnley, and Brandt (2001), in which the authors took six UK companies and interviewed both the firms' finance director and the most senior external auditor. They showed that auditors are indeed a source of constraint, but a flexible one. When auditors disagree with a classification or a measurement, what ensues is often negotiation, rather than auditors dictating what must be done for them to 'sign off' the company's accounts.

In one case, for example, both the firm's finance director and its auditor suspected that its inventory was overvalued. To begin with, the auditors were unable to determine by how much. However, installation of a new computer system in the firm enabled 'slow-moving' and obsolescent stock to be identified. As the lead auditor put it: 'We just had the information from a stock obsolescence printout. But they [the firm] couldn't deny it because they … generated that information themselves and that came up with a big number' (Beattie, Fearnley, and Brandt 2001: 85). Instead, however, of insisting that the value of the stock should be written down immediately by the 'big number', the auditors agreed with company management that it should be written down only gradually over three years. Many accountants might have felt that this was wrong: in his foreword to Beattie, Fearnley, and Brandt's book, the leading accounting regulator Sir David Tweedie comments that 'the case-studies are anonymous—which is as well for the auditor who allowed over-valued stock to be written down over three years—for goodness sake!' (Beattie, Fearnley, and Brandt 2001: xxi). The senior auditor, however, had felt the need to reach a compromise: 'I'm afraid I take a pragmatic approach to auditing and you can't eat an elephant … so I had to dissect the thing and … get so much in one year and so much the next' (quoted in Beattie, Fearnley, and Brandt 2001: 86).

Interactions within a company are also likely to be important as a source of constraint on the construction of accounts, but have been much less studied from this viewpoint than interactions with auditors. Senior managers are likely to be a crucial audience for the work of accountants, and the literature on earnings management points strongly to their desire for favourable portrayals of financial performance often being an important factor shaping financial reporting. A less obvious set of others, however, are staff lower in corporate hierarchies than accountants, notably book-keepers. Like senior managers, they too will have what Bloor calls their 'immediate purposes', but these are likely to be 'getting the job done',[17] rather than portraying the economic condition of their company in one way rather than another. Their remuneration, unlike that of senior managers, is unlikely to be affected at all directly by that portrayal, and they are likely to be classifying a myriad of often small transactions, few or none of which will on their own be consequential to the portrayal.

The issue of the relationship between the situations and work of book-keepers and of more senior staff highlights a constraining factor that is not explicit in Bloor's list: technology. The technical systems of accounting—which for small entities can be standalone systems, but for the larger firms will now normally be aspects of continuously evolving Enterprise Resource Planning (ERP) systems such as Oracle or SAP (see, for example, Quattrone and Hopper 2006)—are neither merely neutral media nor simply means of increasing the efficiency of what unaided human beings might do. Technical systems link the work of the multiple people needed to do the accounts of any large entity in *structured* ways. In part to reduce opportunities for fraud, accounting systems are designed to constrain the ways in which any given person can alter the results of the work of another (and to prevent anyone other than a specific, limited set of individuals making such alterations), and to leave an ineliminable trace when an alteration is made.

Such deliberate 'technical' barriers then become 'social' constraints. The vast bulk of accounting classifications are, as already noted, made by staff low in corporate hierarchies such as book-keepers. Technical systems then 'solidify' those classifications by restricting what more senior staff can subsequently do to alter them. Is a senior manager going to attempt to influence in advance thousands or millions of 'primary' classifications made by dozens or hundreds of book-keepers, or subsequently to attempt to alter those classifications (especially if he or she does not have the access permissions to do so and if the alterations leave a visible audit trail)? The record of cases such as Enron or WorldCom suggests that these are not the most attractive paths. When Gene Morse was told by Cooper to 'go dig' into WorldCom's financial reporting, he did not discover efforts by Sullivan or others to alter these primary records. Instead, earnings management was being accomplished by leaving the primary classifications intact, and performing higher-level reclassifications. The latter, for example, is what the WorldCom accountant with which I began this chapter did on the Friday afternoon in 2001.

The material form taken by this technical constraint is password-controlled access to a firm's ERP system, together with a matrix specifying the 'read' and 'write' permissions of each user.[18] While senior accountants and perhaps some other top managers will have extensive or complete 'read' access to accounting data, the matrix normally restricts tightly their 'write' access: indeed, those at the top of corporate hierarchies may have no 'write' access at all. Processing sales orders and invoices, for example, is not part of their jobs—it is 'book-keepers' work'—and while they would usually be able to view the resultant records they would not normally have the 'write' permission needed to create such a record or to alter it.

Of course, technical constraint is not absolute. Any system's controls can be subverted if the technical staff in charge of a system's access-control matrix can be persuaded to alter it, if those who have the relevant permissions can be persuaded to disclose their passwords to those who do not, or if other ways (such as that used by Gene Morse) can be found to circumvent the controls. The creation of an audit trail is a deterrent only if an auditor is likely to scrutinize it and to contest the reclassifications it reveals, which returns us to the sphere of human constraints: of Bloor's 'interactions with other people' and 'anticipation of and response to sanctions'. Indeed, one can't entirely rule out the possibility that the apparent rarity of earnings management performed by the en masse alteration of primary records reflects success in doing so uncontested.

Nevertheless, such considerations do suggest that ethnographies of financial reporting will need to pay close attention to its technological bases. They also point to the importance of studying the work of book-keepers as well as of professional accountants. If my conjectures are correct, it is book-keepers—not accountants—who produce much of accounting's equivalent of science's observational base. Book-keepers' classifications are just as open to finitist analysis as those of accountants (and there is no 'theory-independent observation language' in accounting or in science), but their classificatory work has almost never been examined in ethnographic detail.[19]

Another issue worth attention *is* present explicitly on Bloor's list: training. Finitism suggests that classification and concept application are based on relations of similarity and difference that, ultimately, are learned ostensively—that is, by exposure to authoritative examples of 'correct' classification and 'appropriate' concept application. For instance, a scientific paradigm is at root a set of concrete, exemplary solutions to scientific problems. Scientific training consists in good part of learning of how to perform these exemplary solutions and how to extend them to similar cases (Kuhn 1970; Barnes 1982). Socialization into the 'paradigm' in the broader sense of an overarching disciplinary framework is not achieved solely by the framework being learned explicitly (if finitism is right, it could not be learned in its entirety in this way), but by repeated, authoritative ostension.

Accounting and book-keeping, I conjecture, are also learned in good part ostensively. The literature on the education of accountants—such as Power

(1991) and Anderson-Gough, Grey, and Robson (1998)—unfortunately does not offer a clear-cut answer to the question of the extent of ostensive learning, but it seems clear that while accountants and book-keepers do learn many explicit rules, they also have to learn how to apply these rules to particulars. Some of this training takes place in formal educational settings; much of it takes place 'on the job'. If training in accounting or book-keeping is like scientific training, we would expect it to consist largely in repeated experience of solving problems for which there are authoritative 'right' and 'wrong' answers. If the analogy with science holds, the result of such training will go beyond technical competence in any narrow sense. It will be found to be socialization into a way of viewing the world that is not wholly explicit, but is not for that reason any less powerful. That it is unlikely to be entirely explicit is one reason why ethnographic (rather than, for example, interview-based) research is needed. Those who practise the technical cultures of book-keeping and accounting may simply be unable to give a full verbal account of what they do and why they do it.

In particular, prolonged ostensively based socialization can 'achieve realism'. To neophytes, I conjecture, classifying items (in accounting, science, or elsewhere) will frequently 'feel' like classification: here is an item; here are possible classifications (X_1, X_2, X_3, ..., X_n); which shall I choose? (That, for example, is what I often feel when 'coding' research grant expenses.) The experienced practitioner, in contrast, will often feel 'This item *is* an X_3,' just as the experienced bird-watcher glances at a bird and thinks 'That is an oystercatcher,' not 'I am classifying that bird as an oystercatcher.' The classification can still be analysed as a choice (or so finitism insists), but to those involved it no longer feels like a choice, or indeed even a classification. From a finitist viewpoint, what happens in such cases is that training and habit have formed a strong sense of analogy: this bird resembles previous oystercatchers sufficiently strongly that it must be an oystercatcher. The reaction to Sullivan's contested classification of the costs of unused portions of line leases can also be read in this way. Sullivan may well have been correct that, as a matter of logic, this did not contradict the official definition of 'asset', but to the other accountants involved, such as Cooper, it did not resemble an asset, but seemed much more like an expense. What Sullivan was contending with, in other words, was precisely this deeply internalized sense of analogy. (Lay people will have lacked that internalized sense, which may have been why he had greater success persuading them.)

'When I obey a rule', wrote Wittgenstein (1967: 85e), 'I do not choose. I obey the rule *blindly*' (emphasis in original). Ostensively based socialization offers one possible reason why the rules and principles of accounting do in practice have force. (Participants certainly treat them as having force: the fierce debates occasioned by standards such as IAS 39 would have little point if rules had no force.) What a rule or principle implies for any concrete situation is undetermined logically (one can't, for example, calculate the value of an inventory simply by logical deduction from the relevant standard, IAS 2), but to those socialized into a particular culture of accounting, there may well be many cases in which the classification or other action that is demanded seems clear.

The extent to which accounting (or book-keeping) is in practice conducted in nominalist 'choice amongst classifications' mode or in 'realist' mode is an empirical question. My conjecture is that both modes will normally be present. Routine, familiar items, for example, may evoke 'realist' mode ('that *is* an X_3'); unfamiliar items provoke explicit choices ('is this an X_1 or an X_2?'). But, clearly, other factors will also be present. An accountant engaged in earnings management can be expected to operate in 'choice' mode, and will be a 'rule sceptic', viewing rules as open to interpretation and seeking favourable interpretations. He or she, however, will also need to take into account the classificatory impulses of those in 'realist' mode, such as Cooper's reaction to Sullivan's reversal of the bad-debt provision, which, as noted above, 'smelled funny' to her.

Conclusion

The set of factors discussed so far—interactions with other people, technological systems, training, and so on—is certainly not exhaustive. What I hope, however, is that this chapter begins to suggest the richness of the issues that a finitist perspective highlights. Financial reporting and the accounting practices underpinning it are complex sociotechnical matters that are, as noted, central to the economic governance of today's societies. In a profit-oriented economy, the measurement of profit is a central task, and one that is far from simple.

The finitist arguments that classifications are always in principle decisions and that rules in themselves do not determine their application to specific cases make finitism, I would argue, a useful perspective from which to analyse accounting and financial reporting. Even the most mundane of accounting classifications becomes of analytical interest from this perspective. Given that, if finitism is correct, any item could always in principle be classified differently, what determines the classification that is actually made? The answer, this chapter has suggested, is likely to be a combination of factors such as training and habit, the goals those involved are trying to achieve, the context within which they are making the classification, and the properties of the technological systems with which they have to interact.

This chapter has done little more than simply sketch questions such as this and speculate as to likely answers. Nevertheless, I am confident that research addressing these issues will be of great interest. The finitist accountant and finitist book-keeper are at the heart of economic life, and we badly need to know what determines their actions.

7

Constructing Emissions Markets

Universities contain rooms and buildings that academics never enter: boiler houses, for example. Amongst their contents are meters that measure the consumption of electricity, natural gas, and oil. Those readings determine the substantial sums that universities spend on energy: around £9 million per year for my university.

Some of the meters at the University of Edinburgh now have a second function too, indirectly measuring the carbon dioxide emitted by the boilers and combined heat and power units to which they are connected. Largely unnoticed, the meters have become part of what is in effect a measurement network stretching across Europe. Although not as extensive as the sociotechnical systems via which, as discussed in the previous chapter, profit is measured, this network is consequential. It is a crucial part of the material infrastructure of the European Union's Emissions Trading Scheme, a new market—it came into existence only in January 2005—which is the Union's main tool for combating global warming.

Amongst the activities to which the new trading scheme applies are '[c]ombustion installations with a rated thermal input exceeding 20 MW' (European Parliament, Council 2003: 42). One doesn't usually think of a university as a large combustion installation—aside from in inevitable jokes about the generation of hot air—but the capacity of two of my university's three highly efficient combined heat and power plants pushes them within the scope of emissions trading. It is perhaps not surprising that our science campus consumes a lot of energy, but even the plant in the area in which humanities and social sciences are taught totals 20.5 MW, and thus is over the threshold.

Like the other operators of Europe's large combustion installations, the University of Edinburgh has in consequence to hold permits to emit carbon dioxide. It receives an allocation of allowances, each permitting it to emit a tonne (1,000 kg) of CO_2. Its emissions are measured, and it has 'to surrender allowances equal to the total emissions of the installation in each calendar year' (European Parliament, Council 2003: 35). If it emits more CO_2 than it has allowances, it must buy further allowances on the market, or else it will be fined. If it emits less, it can sell its excess allowances.

Allowances are traded 'over the counter' (by direct institution-to-institution negotiation, or via brokers) and on organized exchanges such as the Nordic power exchange, Nord Pool. CO_2 futures are also traded, in their case on the European Climate Exchange, which uses the electronic trading platform of London's International Petroleum Exchange. A small over-the-counter market in CO_2 options already exists. The network of trading stretches beyond the European Union to encompass 'certified emission reductions' from projects in developing countries and 'emission reduction units' from projects in the former Soviet bloc. If a European operator such as Edinburgh University has a shortfall of allowances, it can meet its obligations by buying these reductions and units. Plans for emissions trading are gathering momentum in North America, in the north-east, midwest, and in California; political pressure is growing for a US national carbon market. Those involved in carbon trading indeed envisage the emergence of a global market, in which CO_2 will have a 'world price', just as gold has a world price.

This chapter begins by examining the intellectual roots of emissions trading within economics. It discusses the first large-scale experiment with emissions trading, one that has had a major influence on later debate: the sulphur-dioxide trading introduced by the US Clean Air Act Amendments of 1990. I next turn briefly to the 1997 Kyoto Protocol, in which carbon trading plays a central role, and to experiments in carbon trading in the post-Kyoto years by oil company BP and by the UK government. Drawing on a set of twenty-four interviews with carbon-market participants, I then discuss in more detail the European Union Emissions Trading Scheme, describing the process by which it came to be established, the factors that explain salient features of its design, the evolution of the scheme since its establishment in

2005, and the lessons to be learned from the experience. A major focus of the chapter is the processes of the allocation of emissions allowances. While the main initial proposal within economics for an emissions market assumed that allowances would be sold to emitters, political considerations have generally dictated that in practice they have been distributed free. This makes the mechanism of allocation and the total amounts allocated crucial technical and political matters, central to whether or not an emissions market is effective environmentally.

Economics and Emissions Markets

To a far greater extent than any of the other markets discussed in this book, markets in emissions permits are a creation of economics. They are a quintessential example of a strong form of the kind of process discussed in Chapter 2, in which economics has *done* something: its role has not been to analyse an already-existing market, but to help bring a new market into existence. While meteorologists and other natural scientists have been the experts on the extent to which human activities are increasing the 'greenhouse' warming of the planet, economists have played a leading role in discussing what should be done in response.

From an economic point of view, the effects of the production of carbon dioxide and other greenhouse gases by human activities are an instance of a familiar issue. They are an 'externality', a 'cost or benefit arising from any activity which does not accrue to the person or organization carrying on the activity' (Black 2002: 167). Research and development is an example of an activity that has positive externalities: its benefits typically accrue more widely than to the firm conducting it. Pollution, in contrast, is the textbook example of a negative externality:

The cost to society of having some of its labor and steel used up in a given factory is 'internalized' by the firm, because it has to pay for those inputs. But the firm does not have an economic incentive to minimize the 'external' costs of pollution.

(Jaffe, Newell, and Stavins 2005: 165)

The traditional response by economists to negative externalities such as pollution was to propose a tax set at a level that would 'internalize' the externality, in other words at a level corresponding to the wider social costs of the activity in question, thus forcing economic actors to take those wider costs into account. The argument, which goes back at least to Pigou (1920: 168, 193–4, and passim), is that 'when the market does not reflect the true social costs of some activity, be it switching on the air conditioning or driving into London at rush hour, the government can make society better off by imposing a tax that reflects that social cost' (Harford 2006). Governments could of course seek to control harmful activities directly, for example by banning them entirely, or by laying down how they should be conducted (for example, imposing fixed limits on the quantities or concentrations of pollutants). Economists have, however, generally held that environmental benefits can more efficiently be achieved by manipulating the price system via taxation than, for instance, by insisting on particular technological standards. That way, market processes—rather than centralized decision making—would determine the technological or other means by which reductions were achieved.

The idea that there was a third solution to the problem of negative externalities—beyond taxes and direct control measures—is generally traced to economist Ronald Coase. A 'mutually satisfactory bargain' (Coase 1960: 4) could be struck between those whose activities generate an externality and those affected by it, either by the former compensating the latter or the latter paying the former to reduce or cease the damaging activities; which would occur would depend upon whether there was legal liability for the damage caused. If rational agents could strike such bargains without incurring trans-action costs, the outcome would 'maximise . . . the value of production' (Coase 1960: 8). Taxes were unnecessary; bargaining between private agents could achieve the desired outcome.

While Coase's attack on Pigou and his sketch of an alternative to what he called 'the Pigovian tradition' (1960: 39) was influential, it did not directly inspire the idea of tradeable permits. Its most immediate progenitor was the University of Toronto economist and economic historian J. H. Dales, who was considering how to control pollution of the Great Lakes (Dales 1968a; 1968b).[1] In his analysis, Dales assumed it was possible to establish an 'equiva-lence . . . between different waste products', so that quantities of different prod-ucts could be translated into standardized 'equivalent tons'. He then supposed that it had been decided that 'no more than x equivalent tons of waste per year are to be dumped into the waters of region A, and that x represents a 10 per cent reduction from the amount of waste that is currently being discharged into the region's waters' (Dales 1968a: 800).

How, asked Dales, might a decision to reduce pollution to a fixed 'cap' be implemented at least total cost? For government simply to rule that each discharger must reduce its discharges by 10 per cent would not be optimal: some dischargers might be able cheaply to reduce their discharges by much more than a tenth, while others might face high costs in achieving the 10 per cent reduction. Nor could government plausibly minimize total costs by trying to work out an optimal allocation in which those who could cut waste cheaply would have to make bigger cuts than those for whom it was expensive. Mobilizing a standard argument against central planning (an argument associated above all with the economists Ludwig von Mises and Friedrich von Hayek),[2] Dales wrote:

To suppose that optimality in this sense is possible is to suppose that the administrative authority is able to solve a set of thousands of simultaneous equations, when the information required to write the equations in numerical form is not only not available, but also often unobtainable. (Dales 1968a: 800)

A better way to solve the problem of achieving a given overall reduction of pollution at minimum total cost, argued Dales, was a tax: an 'across-the-board' fee of 'so much per ton of waste discharged' (Dales 1968a: 800). With a tax or fee of this sort:

each polluter decides for himself by how much, if at all, he should reduce his wastes. The burden of pollution control is thus shared in exactly the right way, without the [Water Control Board] having to agonize over the question of how to find a just and reasonable sharing of the cost of the scheme. Since every polluter adjusts to the charges in whatever way minimizes *his* cost, the social cost of achieving the target amount of waste discharge—which is the sum of the costs borne by all polluters (and, of course, by the consumers of their products, in the case of industries)—will also be automatically minimized. (Dales 1968b: 92, emphasis in original)

Two quite demanding calculations nevertheless remained, Dales argued: finding the level of fee that would achieve the necessary overall reduction in discharges; and taking account of the 'new-comers (people or factories)' who would also discharge wastes. The former would require 'trial and error', and the latter was a 'guesstimate'. Those calculations could, however, be performed implicitly by setting up 'a "market" in "pollution rights" ':

Such markets would automatically set the correct level of the pollution charge (instead of its having to be set by some committee, after long and learned discussion) and would also automatically, and continuously, adjust the level of the charge to take account of economic growth. A simple market that can be operated by three or four people and a small staff of stenographers to register purchases and sales is very much cheaper, and just as efficient, as a large bureaucracy replete with computers to give answers to complicated pricing problems. If it is feasible to establish a market to implement a policy, no policy-maker can afford to do without one.

(Dales 1968b: 93, 100)

What Dales proposed was what has become known as a 'cap-and-trade' scheme. A Water Control Board or other government authority would decide on the cap, the total quantity of allowable discharges (for example, a 10 per cent reduction from current levels). It would then make the corresponding number of permits available for initial sale, and also set up a mechanism for a secondary market in which permits could be sold and bought at any point up to the date at which dischargers of waste have to surrender them to the authority to show they had the right to discharge the quantities they had. The fact that discharges were now costly would cause some firms and municipalities to reduce their emissions and the number of permits they thus needed to purchase, and 'when the price [of permits] has risen enough to reduce the demand' to the requisite level 'the market will be in equilibrium'. Those whose emissions were lower than they had anticipated 'would have rights to sell, and those in the contrary situation would be in the market as buyers'. 'All of these buyers and sellers, through their bids and offers, will establish the price of the Rights.' That price would, for example, be expected to rise if population or industrial activity grows, so increasing 'the incentive for waste dischargers to treat, or reduce, their wastes' (Dales 1968a: 801; 1968b: 93–4).

Dales's proposal was not put into practice in the Great Lakes. In the 1970s and 1980s, however, a small number of tradeable pollution permit schemes were introduced, mainly by the US Environmental Protection Agency. For example, as the use of lead additives in gasoline was phased out in the USA in the 1980s, refineries were allowed temporarily to trade 'lead credits', and did so to a reasonably large extent: 'Approximately 15 percent of the total lead rights used were traded' (Hahn 1989: 102).

Trading Sulphur Dioxide

More significant, however, than the limited and often clumsily implemented trading schemes of the 1970s and 1980s was the setting up in the USA in the 1990s of the market discussed briefly in Chapter 2: the market in permits to emit sulphur dioxide (SO_2) from electric power stations.[3] There had been considerable concern since the 1970s about the damaging effects of 'acid rain' and other acid depositions. Sulphur dioxide emissions, especially from coal-fired power stations, had been identified as the main cause. Numerous bills to address the problem were proposed in the 1980s, but all failed in the face of opposition from both the Reagan administration and Democrats from states that might suffer economically, such as those in Appalachia and the midwest that produced high-sulphur coal. Finally, however, the Clean Air Act Amendments of 1990 set the goal of reducing annual sulphur dioxide emissions in the USA dramatically—by 'ten million tons from 1980 emission levels'—a cut largely to be achieved by approximately halving SO_2 emissions from coal-fired power stations.[4]

Rather than lay down how power stations were to cut sulphur dioxide (for example, by mandating the installation of 'scrubbers' to remove SO_2 from flue gases), Congress established a two-phase market in emissions permits. Phase I, from 1995 to 1999, covered 'the 263 dirtiest large generating units'; in phase II, from 2000 onwards, the scheme was extended to include 'virtually all fossil-fueled electric generating plants' in the continental USA (Ellerman et al. 2000: 6). Operators of these plants were allocated allowances, and the owners of coal-fired plants were thus in effect left free to choose between doing nothing to reduce emissions (and thus most likely having to buy additional allowances on the market), paying the substantial costs of installing and operating scrubbers, or shifting to lower-sulphur coal.

The ultimate inspiration of the sulphur-dioxide market was the work within economics on emissions markets touched on above. However, economists did not simply propose the market and then sit back and see it adopted: they were politically active advocates of it. Particularly important in this respect were Robert Stavins of Harvard University's John F. Kennedy School of Government; MIT economist Richard Schmalensee, who was a member of President George H. W. Bush's Council of Economic Advisors; and Robert Hahn, one of the Council's professional staff.[5] Stavins, for example, had been an economist at the Environmental Defense Fund, an advocacy group which hired 'economists, engineers and computer analysts to find ways to help the environment without harming the economy',[6] and which was successfully positioning itself 'as the most pro-business of the major environmental NGOs in the United States' (Victor and House 2006: 2102). From Environmental Defense, Stavins moved to Harvard, where he directed 'Project 88', an investigation of 'Harnessing Market Forces to Protect the Environment', jointly chaired by the Republican Senator John Heinz and Democrat Timothy Wirth. Project 88's report publicized an estimate by consultants to the Environmental Protection Agency that 'a market-based approach to acid rain reduction could save us $3 billion per year, compared with the cost of a dictated technological solution' (Stavins 1988: 5).

Project 88's bipartisan sponsorship gave it potential for influence whoever won the 1988 presidential election. The victor, George H. W. Bush, 'had promised to be "the Environmental President" and had advocated looking "to the marketplace for innovative solutions" to environmental problems' (Ellerman et al. 2000: 21–2), and some important members of his new administration were favourably inclined to turning those words into action. For example, Robert Grady, who had been the chief speechwriter for the Bush–Quayle campaign, was given the responsibility for natural resources and energy in the powerful Office of Management and Budget, where he was an enthusiast for the proposal for a market in sulphur dioxide emissions (Stavins 1998: 78).

Despite channels of political influence of this sort, economists on their own could not have created the market in sulphur dioxide. Others were needed: not just technologists, who were needed in order to create the system of measurement described in Chapter 2, but also lawyers. For example, an especially important role, both as lobbyist and as drafter of Title IV of the Clean Air Act Amendments (the section that covered sulphur dioxide trading), was played by Joe Goffman. Like Stavins, Goffman worked originally for (and in his case eventually returned to) the Environmental Defense Fund, but he also served as associate counsel for the Senate committee working on the Clean Air Act, and then oversaw the detailed development of the trading programme's rules as an acting section chief at the Environmental Protection Agency.[7]

An emissions allowance is a subtle legal entity, so it is not surprising that lawyers as well as economists have been heavily involved in the development of emissions trading schemes more generally. A crucial issue is whether an allowance is a property right. Were it to be such a right, the constitutional protection awarded to private property in the United States would have made subsequent changes to the SO_2 trading programme difficult. Section 403(f) of the Clean Air Act Amendments laid down that an allowance was 'a limited authorization to emit sulfur dioxide...Such allowance does not constitute a property right.'[8] A decade later there was to be a similar assertion about the legal status of the units to be traded under the Kyoto Protocol, when the 2001 Marrakesh Accords decreed that the protocol 'has not created or bestowed any right, title or entitlement to emissions'.[9] Instead, Kyoto units are 'unitized and divisible embodiments of promises accepted by sovereign states in the context of a multilateral agreement which for that reason can be revoked, revised and altered through further negotiation' (Yamin 2005: 16).[10]

As well as requiring the skills of lawyers and others, economists found it necessary to accommodate to the demands of the political process, sometimes setting aside what their disciplinary inclinations might have led them to prefer. As Stavins put it: 'Policy instruments that appear impeccable from the vantage point of Cambridge, Massachusetts'—the home of Harvard, MIT, and much of the elite of academic economics—'but consistently prove infeasible in Washington, D.C., can hardly be considered "optimal" ' (Stavins 1998: 83). Two forms of accommodation stand out. First, an impulse of many economists would have been to perform a cost–benefit analysis, working out the optimum level of cuts in sulphur dioxide emissions by quantifying the costs of cuts and the benefits in terms of reduced damage to the environment and human health. Assigning dollar values to such damage would, however, have been intensely controversial, and the economists involved in promoting sulphur dioxide trading avoided it, simply 'accepting—implicitly or otherwise' (Stavins 1998: 77) the round-number reduction of 10 million tons that quickly became dominant in political debate. That reduction was in no sense demonstrably optimal—it was essentially a compromise between environmentalist demands for a cut of 12 million tons and industry proposals for 8 million (Burtraw et al. 2005: 259)—but instead of 'debating the costs and benefits of [the ten million ton] goal, they [economists] simply focused on the cost-effective means of achieving it' (Stavins 1998: 77).

Second, in Dales's proposed market, permits would have been sold to waste dischargers. A well-designed auction would quickly have established their market price, without having to wait for subsequent trading to do this. Auctioning sulphur dioxide permits, however, would have had a huge political disadvantage: it would have required the utility companies that owned power stations to pay large sums in order to continue to emit. There would have been a substantial transfer of resources from those companies to the Federal government. As the main study of the trading programme puts it, 'this alternative was simply not on the table' (Ellerman et al. 2000: 24).

In consequence, nearly all the sulphur allowances were simply distributed free of charge to the companies that ran the generating units that the scheme was to cover. (A small proportion of allowances—around 3 per cent—is held back and auctioned annually on behalf of the Environmental Protection Agency by the Chicago Board of Trade, in an auction in which private sellers can also take part.[11]) At the prices predicted at the start of the programme, phase I allowances would have been worth about $6 billion, and ten years of phase II allowances would have been worth $45–63 billion (Ellerman et al. 2000: 36). Those sums were in a sense notional, in that a utility would need to surrender allowances corresponding to its emissions, but they do indicate that a desirable commodity was about to be distributed. A favourable distribution would be valuable, and an unfavourable one could be expensive.

'With that sort of rent on the table, one would certainly expect to see serious rent seeking, and Washington did not disappoint' (Ellerman et al. 2000: 36). The basic allocation rule was that generating units received allowances proportional to the calorific value of the fuel they burned in the baseline years 1985–7.[12] There was, however, enormously complex jostling over deviations from the baseline rule, with the staff of Senators and Representatives lobbying for provisions that would favour mining and/or utility interests in their states, and other states, such as Florida, receiving favourable allocations because they were expected to be finely balanced in upcoming elections (Ellerman et al. 2000: 13–76).

For some of the economists involved, it was an education in the political process. Thus MIT's Richard Schmalensee recalled laughing when a special provision concerning lignite, the 'brown coal' common in North Dakota, was proposed at a meeting of Congressional staff members. 'He was forcefully reminded that North Dakota was a relatively poor state with bleak prospects and, more important, that Chairman Burdick [Quentin Burdick (D-ND), 1908–1992, Chair of the Senate Committee on Environment and Public Works] was not to be trifled with.' The provision duly became law.[13]

The Ratchet

The need to assuage powerful political actors by having rules that would generate favourable allocations for their constituents made the sections of the Clean Air Act Amendments governing those allocations complex. The Environmental Protection Agency (EPA) had three internal teams plus an external Acid Rain Advisory Committee at work on translating those sections into detailed rules and actual allocations. 'In order to record and defend its interpretation, EPA documented the allowance-allocation methods in detail', and produced and made public what were 'essentially [two] large spreadsheets' containing the calculations that generated the allocations to each of the 3,842 units covered.[14]

Accommodating special interests by granting favourable allocations could easily have undermined the environmental goals of the sulphur dioxide market. Crucially, however, the spreadsheet by which allowances were allocated had to have, in effect, a fixed total from 2000 onwards. That was the result of a provision known as 'the ratchet', which was added to the Clean Air Act Amendments early in the political infighting. Section 403(a) of the Amendments set a maximum on the total annual allowances that could be issued from 2000 on of 8.9 million tons. If the consequence of detailed rule-making was a total entitlement in excess of that, the allocations of each unit would be reduced *pro rata* to bring the total back down to the requisite level.

The ratchet survived the in-fighting almost intact. Except in one case,[15] it turned out to be possible to assuage special interests while keeping the ratchet mechanism—'which was not controversial' (Ellerman et al. 2000: 37)—outside the conflict. The ratchet's effects seem to have been under-estimated by those involved: a scaling-back of allowances of no more than 5 per cent was expected, but in fact allocations were reduced across the board by nearly 10 per cent (Ellerman et al. 2000: 37). It is worth noting that attacking the ratchet was a collective-action problem (see Chapter 2): any benefit from doing so would have been shared by all the utilities involved, making the balance of cost and benefit in fighting against the ratchet quite different from fighting for a rule that would have specific advantages for one's own state or company.

The ratchet made the game of allocation zero-sum: the extra allowances won by special interests were clawed back from all participants. The claw-back took place over a year after the legislation had been passed by the Senate and House of Representatives, by which time Washington political circles had moved on to other things.[16] So the assuaging of special interests caused no more than fairly minor loosening of the overall cap on SO_2.[17]

From Sulphur to Carbon

The 'ratchet' thus kept the politics of allocation, which was certainly intense, largely separate from the overall effects of the new market, which seems in general to have worked well. Certainly, the measurement system, sketched in Chapter 2, which underpinned the market appears to have functioned impeccably, giving rise to no dispute of which I am aware about the quantities of sulphur dioxide actually emitted. Large cuts in emissions were achieved,[18] at a cost far lower than industry lobbyists had predicted: around $1 billion per year, rather than $10 billion or more (Kerr 1998). The price of one-ton phase I allowances, originally expected to be in the range $290–410, in fact averaged only around $150 (Ellerman et al. 2000: 172–3; Swift 2000). Amongst the causes of reduced costs were that the capital cost of scrubbers fell sharply, the cost of operating them turned out to be lower than anticipated, and the option to buy allowances when necessary avoided the need to install spare modules in scrubber systems to be used when other modules were out of action (Burtraw et al. 2005: 268). Crucially, too, rail-freight deregulation reduced the cost of transportation from Wyoming's Powder River Basin, the main source of low-sulphur coal in the United States.

Some of the above factors would have reduced compliance costs even if sulphur emissions had been controlled (as they were in Europe) by mechanisms other than emissions trading: indeed, emissions were in decline in the USA in the 1980s before the trading scheme began, for example because coal with low levels of sulphur was already becoming more readily available (Lohmann 2006: 101). The effects of trading per se—which was sometimes quite limited in scale, for example because state-level regulations constrained utilities' options (Burtraw et al. 2005: 265)—are difficult to disentangle from the economic advantages of simply being able to choose between achieving abatement by installing scrubbers or by switching to low-sulphur coal. Despite these complications, however, the two main studies of the issue (Ellerman et al. 2000, and Carlson, Burtraw, Cropper, and Palmer 2000) are in broad agreement in suggesting savings of about 50 per cent by comparison with a traditional regulatory approach.

Sulphur dioxide trading can thus be judged at least a qualified success, and it was certainly perceived as successful.[19] That success—particularly the fact that the market price of allowances was much lower than had been predicted—moved emissions trading firmly into the political mainstream in the USA. Thus the economist William Nordhaus 'happened to be sitting between Richard Sandor [the Chicago Board of Trade's former chief economist, mentioned in Chapter 4] and Vice President Gore at the White House Climate Conference in October 1997. They were both pointing to the sulfur program as an argument against the "dismal" economists who were projecting that the costs of the [December 1997] Kyoto Protocol would be very high. They were asserting that once the markets for CO_2 were opened, the costs would plummet' (Nordhaus 2000: 65–6).

The Clinton administration entered the Kyoto negotiations determined that 'the agreement should include an array of flexible, market-based approaches for reducing emissions', and the administration was convinced that those approaches would keep the net costs 'relatively modest'. Detailed economic modelling conducted for the administration suggested that unrestricted international trading could reduce the costs to the USA to a fifth of what they would be if the necessary reductions had to be achieved domestically alone. The resultant cost, the administration claimed, would be a mere $7 billion a year, 0.07 per cent of anticipated 2010 gross domestic product (Clinton Administration 1998: 21, 39, 53).

In pushing for the use of emissions trading in curbing global warming, the Clinton administration faced opposition both from the European Union (which preferred mandatory measures, and which had already sought a Europe-wide carbon tax) and from third-world countries, many of which saw the argument that greenhouse gas emissions could more cheaply be curbed there as 'carbon colonialism'. The US negotiators, however, possessed energy, professionalism, the clout of the world's sole superpower, and strong conviction of the correctness of what one observer of the negotiations called 'economic ideology . . . dominated by general equilibrium concepts that focus upon economic efficiency and imply that flexibility achieves the same environmental benefits at lower costs: hence, the more flexibility the better' (Grubb 1999: 99, 112).

The USA prevailed. A key moment came in November 1997, just before the Kyoto meeting. Brazil had proposed that the industrialized countries should face a fine if they breached the commitments they were about to enter into. The fine 'would be paid into a Clean Development Fund that would be used to support appropriate projects in developing countries'. Needless to say, '[t]he idea that industrialized countries would agree' to such a fine 'seemed far-fetched to any seasoned politician'. However, a senior Brazilian negotiator started to canvass the idea of setting the fine 'at a rate set to fund projects that would save emissions equivalent to the degree of non-compliance' (Grubb 1999: 101–2).

US negotiators suddenly realized that with a minor tweak—turning the payment from a fine into a contribution towards meeting one's obligations—the Brazilian proposal was a route to international emissions trading. A 'US team dashed down to Rio to explore the options' (Grubb 1999: 103), and Kyoto's 'Clean Development Mechanism' was born. The core of the Kyoto Protocol was the undertaking of its 'Annex I' signatories (the industrialized countries) that by the time of the protocol's 2008–12 'commitment period' they would have limited their greenhouse-gas emissions to agreed proportions of their 1990 levels (93 per cent for the USA, 92 per cent for the European Community overall, and so on). However, under the protocol those countries can fund emission-reduction projects in 'Parties not included in Annex I' (developing countries), and count the 'certified emission reductions' from such projects against their Kyoto commitments.[20]

The Kyoto Protocol also provides for a similar 'Joint Implementation' mechanism whereby one industrialized Annex I country can pay for and receive 'emission reduction units' from a project in another (for example, in the Russian Federation or Ukraine, both of which are Annex I parties). More sweepingly, the protocol allows the Annex I countries, which have undertaken to limit emissions to the 'assigned amounts' determined by their Kyoto commitments, to trade those amounts amongst themselves, increasing one party's allowed emissions while making the equivalent reduction in another's.

The Kyoto Protocol was the barest skeleton of a market—it postponed for later discussion 'the relevant principles, modalities, rules and guidelines, in particular for verification, reporting and accountability for emissions trading'[21]—yet the US negotiators had succeeded in forging an agreement that largely reflected their preferences. Kyoto's irony is thus—as the reader will doubtless have anticipated—that having got much of what it wanted, the United States then walked away. In March 2001, the new administration of George W. Bush announced the withdrawal of the USA from the Kyoto Protocol.

European Carbon Trading

Although it was no surprise, the Bush administration's decision was a huge setback for greenhouse gas emissions trading. However, the idea did not die with the withdrawal of the country that was its author; it had started to take root outside the USA. Amongst the mechanisms by which this happened were the efforts of the Environmental Defense Fund, the key non-governmental proponent of the sulphur dioxide market, which also pushed for carbon trading. It viewed 'emissions trading as a way to end the polarity between business and environmental groups over the climate change issue' (Fialka 2000), and worked hard to secure the inclusion in Kyoto of the protocol's market-based provisions. In particular, Environmental Defense forged a partnership with British Petroleum (BP), which in 1997, under its new chief executive John Browne, broke ranks with the other major oil companies, announcing that it accepted that global warming was a major threat and that action was needed. Environmental Defense's President, Fred Krupp, 'lobbied John Browne to adopt a cap and trade system' (Victor and House 2006: 2102).

BP set up an internal trading scheme that Environmental Defense described as 'a microcosm of the global emissions trading system envisioned at Kyoto' (Environmental Defense Fund 1998: 7). BP undertook that by 2010 it would cut its emissions by a tenth from their level in 1990 (a goal roughly comparable in size to salient Kyoto targets). After pilot trading in autumn 1998 and 1999, BP allocated emissions ceilings to all its business units for the year 2000 of roughly 99 per cent of their 1998 emissions. These ceilings took the form of allowances recorded in a 'central database, where they could be electronically moved from one [business unit] to another'. Business units had either to limit their emissions to their allocation of allowances or to 'buy' allowances from units that expected to emit less than their allocations. Purchases were made without money changing hands, but the scheme was given force by incorporating it into BP's internal accounting and performance-measurement systems. The 'income' and 'expenses' earned or incurred via carbon trading by each business unit entered into the calculation of a closely monitored internal financial metric: the business unit's 'return on capital employed' (Victor and House 2006: 2102).

BP rapidly found that its year 2000 goal of a 1 per cent reduction in emissions was very easily achieved; the goal's modesty had arisen from an overoptimistic view of the growth of BP's business and what turned out to be exaggerated estimates by business units of projected growth in their emissions. In effect, the company had over-allocated emissions allowances. The cap for 2001 was therefore made much tighter, in effect forcing almost all the remainder of the 10 per cent reduction to be made in a single year, and with business units' caps being further readjusted quarterly in order, in the words of one participant, 'continuously [to] pull the behavioral levers to re-incentivize' (John Mogford, head of BP's Climate Steering Group, quoted in Victor and House 2006: 2105).

These reductions took place against a background of measurement uncertainty: BP's estimate of the uncertainty of its estimate of its 1990 emissions was 30–40 per cent, and even its 1998 estimate had an error band of 5 per cent (anon. 2002). When the scheme closed in December 2001, the equivalent of 4.5 million tonnes of carbon dioxide (around a twentieth of BP's overall emissions) had been traded between its business units at an average 'price' of $39.63 per tonne, and BP was able to conclude that the goal of a 10 per cent reduction in emissions had already been achieved, nine years earlier than anticipated. Although the measurement baseline prior to the scheme was acknowledged to be somewhat uncertain, BP was confident that a large, genuine reduction had been made. Overall, the company calculated that the emissions cut had been at no net cost to the company; indeed, the reductions had a positive net present value of $650 million, mainly because of energy savings and because the company could sell natural gas that previously would have been vented or flared (Victor and House 2006: 2105).

BP's motives in introducing internal trading were mixed: 'the desire to head off a standards-based or a tax-based policy' (Victor and House 2006: 2101) was amongst them. As with SO_2, it is unclear how much the trading mechanism itself had contributed to the success of BP's experiment. All of the reductions 'made economic sense without the financial return from emissions trading'

(Victor and House 2006: 2105). The bulk of the reductions, especially initially, were in emissions of methane (the main component of natural gas), not CO_2. Methane is a more potent greenhouse gas than CO_2—more than twenty times so over a 100-year period (Intergovernmental Panel on Climate Change 2007: 33)—and accordingly a tonne of avoided emissions of methane was accounted for in the BP scheme as equivalent to twenty tonnes of CO_2 (Victor and House 2006: 2103). Because reducing natural gas venting and flaring was relatively straightforward, it was thus possible cheaply to generate large savings in 'CO_2 equivalents'. The very creation of a company-wide metrological network, systematically measuring emissions, focused management attention. 'What gets measured gets managed', as John Browne put it in the speech at Stanford University in which he first announced that BP was taking climate change seriously (Browne 1997).

BP's embrace of carbon trading was influential, particularly because of the involvement of the increasingly prominent John Browne (now Lord Browne), and its broadly successful outcome was widely noted. BP staff became proselytizers for emissions markets, 'relentless in promoting [the BP scheme] as a model for international trading' (Engels 2006: 342). As a working example of carbon trading in one of Europe's leading companies, the BP scheme was to become 'a key driver in the policy debates' in Europe (Christiansen and Wettestad 2003: 9).[22]

In 2001, Denmark launched a scheme intended to promote CO_2 trading amongst eight large electric power generators.[23] The UK followed suit with a broader—but voluntary—trading scheme launched in 2002.[24] The Blair government that had come to power in the UK in 1997 was a particular enthusiast for emissions trading: like many 'New Labour' policies, greenhouse gas markets seemed a way to create a new market mechanism to achieve a goal that unfettered markets could not achieve by themselves and that traditional government regulatory tools would achieve only at greater expense.

While the other schemes discussed in this chapter involved free distribution of allowances to incumbents, usually on the basis of a baseline emissions level, the allocation mechanism in the UK scheme was an auction. However, the UK carbon auction was again not the sale of permits envisaged by Dales. The thirty-four voluntary participants in the UK scheme submitted bids for the quantities of emissions they would undertake in return for different levels of government subsidy. The 'descending clock' auction began at a subsidy of £100 per tonne of carbon dioxide, and the price was reduced until the product of prices and quantities bid fell within the scheme's £215 million budget, which occurred at a clearing price of £53.37/tonne (National Audit Office 2004). That high price—and thus substantial subsidy—made the scheme an expensive way of securing abatement, and as with the initial experience of the BP scheme, participants in the UK scheme found that they could easily meet the targets they had set themselves via the auction. Allowances were accordingly in surplus. By 2004, 'the demand for allowances [had] essentially vanished' (Christiansen and Arvanitakis 2004: 7).

The European Union Emissions Trading Scheme

In the USA, the 'Chicago Climate Exchange' established by Richard Sandor (see Chapter 4) set up a voluntary—but legally binding—trading scheme, in its case non-governmental and non-subsidized. But the 'geography' of emissions markets had shifted towards Europe. By far the most important carbon-trading scheme—far more important than the early initiatives described above—has been the European Union scheme with which I began this chapter, and which is the centre of what is potentially a global carbon market. Although the Emissions Trading Scheme can be analysed in several ways,[25] from the viewpoint of this book it is most interesting to see it as an exercise in market construction and, as discussed below, as an *in vivo* economic experiment (in the sense of Muniesa and Callon 2007). At the heart of market construction was a small team of officials of the European Commission, led by economist Jos Delbeke of the Commission's Environment Directorate-General.

As Peter Zapfel and Matti Vainio of the Environment Directorate-General put it, at the time of the 1997 Kyoto Protocol 'the concept of emissions trading was known [in Europe] only in narrow scientific circles encompassing professors and students of European environmental economics and to a very limited audience of environmental policymakers and administrators in environmental agencies' (Zapfel and Vainio 2002: 1). That situation rapidly changed. Academics and non-governmental organizations from the USA (including Environmental Defense and the Center for Clean Air Policy) were drawn into European policy discussions, and interviewees reported that the European Commission team studied the SO_2 experience intensively. European

consultants and auditing and certification firms 'saw a potential market arising', and some industry associations and corporations became interested in
emissions markets as a potentially 'cheap' alternative to expensive regulatory
measures (Zapfel and Vainio 2002: 1 and 7).

Amongst factors that turned this growing interest in Europe into an actual
carbon market was one that was specific to the political structure of the
European Union. As noted, the preference of many European environment
policy makers would have been for harmonized carbon taxes rather than
emissions trading. However, plans in 1992–5 to levy such taxes across Europe
had met with fierce industry opposition, and there was a structural disadvantage to trying to revive them. In the European Union, tax measures require
unanimity: a single dissenting country can block them. The initial proposal
for a harmonized European carbon tax was, as one policy-maker interviewee
put it, 'killed basically by the UK', which was concerned to keep jurisdiction
over tax at the national level, although other member states were potential
opponents as well, and 'if one member state, even a very tiny member state,
said no' to a tax measure, 'it was no'. As another interviewee said, 'taxation is
always fraught with obstacles, and if it isn't one member state who is objecting
it's another. And it [the objection] might rotate around the member states
because they all have their electoral cycles.'

The unanimity requirement was too demanding for a Europe-wide carbon
tax at any significant level to be feasible politically: 'We learned our lesson' in
that respect, said an interviewee involved in the tax proposal. European Union
decision making on environmental matters, however, falls into the terrain not
of unanimity but of 'qualified majority voting'. No single country can stop
an environmental measure: doing so takes a coalition of countries sufficiently
populous (since voting weights roughly follow population) to form a 'blocking minority'. The European Commission sought legal advice on whether a
cap-and-trade market could be classified under European Union procedures as
an environmental issue, and, as an interviewee reported, 'got the confirmation'
that it could: a CO_2 cap was an environmental matter, and thus would not
require unanimity. While the political structure of the European Union meant
it was not feasible to give carbon a substantial, harmonized price via a tax,
it potentially could be given a price via a cap-and-trade scheme. Emissions
trading, which had previously seemed in Europe to be, in an interviewee's
words, 'an academic idea which...was seen as too far...away from reality',
could in fact be made real more easily than a tax could.

There was certainly opposition to the compulsory Europe-wide trading scheme that eventually emerged. Environmental campaigners were (and often still are) sceptical of emissions markets that allow polluters the capacity to pay to keep polluting: a standard analogy is buying indulgences for sins. The European Commission team, however, took care to engage with leading, mainstream environmental NGOs, and the latter generally came to support the new market, albeit critically. Industry opposition was generally muted, with some sectors welcoming trading (certainly preferring it to a tax), though much of German industry was opposed, feeling it had already taken on onerous commitments under voluntary agreements with the German government. The UK was again a potential obstacle: interviewees reported that it wanted the European market to be similar in its design to the UK scheme described above. But even if Germany and the UK had united in opposition, they would have fallen short of the votes required to form a blocking minority (Christiansen and Wettestad 2003: 13). By the autumn of 2001, there were '[i]ndications that a qualified majority' in the premier decision-making body, the Council of the European Union (the 'Council of Ministers', as it used to be called), would indeed back emissions trading, and support in the European Parliament, whose agreement was also needed, was strong (Christiansen and Wettestad 2003: 7).

The emergence of the Danish and UK trading schemes, and a parliamentary commission on emissions trading set up in Sweden in 1999, were also a spur to action. They posed the threat that a partial 'patchwork of incompatible national trading schemes' could emerge (Christiansen and Wettestad 2003: 7). Some smaller countries such as Austria, Finland, and Ireland were inclined to support emissions trading but felt their domestic markets to be too small to support a national scheme (Zapfel and Vainio 2002: 10). The European Commission, one of whose key goals is harmonized European markets, saw 'the development of a coordinated EU-wide scheme with common rules' as a way of avoiding 'market fragmentation' (Christiansen and Wettestad 2003: 7). An interviewee reported, for example, that representatives of Denmark and the UK had met to discuss linking their two schemes, and found that the differences between the design of the two made it infeasible.

It also gradually became clear that the United States was not going to play the leading role it earlier had. The Clinton administration seemed unable to turn its Kyoto commitments into concrete proposals that stood a chance of succeeding in Congress, and, as noted, the Bush administration then abandoned the process. The initial belief in Europe had been that a system of international emissions trading, based around the United Nations but led by the USA, was on its way. As it became clear that this was not so, it was replaced by a sense that 'we have to make it happen at home first' (Zapfel and Vainio 2002: 8). Indeed, the withdrawal of the USA seems to have reduced opposition in Europe to carbon trading, perhaps because that trading was no longer something the USA was trying to impose on reluctant partners.[26] America's new unilateralism—on climate, and on much else—provoked hostility. The tortuous diplomatic process of adding flesh to Kyoto's skeleton market may, paradoxically, have been facilitated by the withdrawal of the USA: 'In a single stroke, the United States managed to focus the entire planet on a ... convoluted piece of diplomatic literature' (Benedick 2001). Four years after the Kyoto Protocol was signed, the 2001 Marrakesh Accords finally set out the detailed rules governing the international schemes—the Clean Development Mechanism and Joint Implementation—with which a European market could be linked.

With a significant current of opinion amongst European policy makers galvanized, momentum built up behind the project of building a Europe-wide trading scheme. By late 2002, the design of the European scheme was completed. By October 2003, the directive establishing the scheme was agreed and published (European Parliament, Council 2003), and it was followed in October 2004 by the 'linking directive' (European Parliament, Council 2004) laying the foundation for the interconnection to the Kyoto markets. In January 2005, Europe's carbon-trading scheme began operation.

Market Design

The factors influencing the design of the new market were heterogeneous. Measurement, for example, is key to any emissions market, and the practicalities of metrology meant that the market's architects quickly concluded that it would have been over ambitious to include either gases other than CO_2 or land-use changes that affect the biosphere's capacity to absorb or emit greenhouse gases. In a context of actual or potential opposition to the new market, unreliable measurement and monitoring would have been fatal, said one of my interviewees:

From a very early stage, the communications [policy papers] of '98 or '99, we had identified a CO_2-only scheme as being the most feasible ... It was basically a monitoring issue ... we felt that if other gases couldn't be monitored robustly we weren't able to affirm [the scheme's integrity]. And the criticism we were getting was that this will all be smoke and mirrors and we couldn't refute that criticism unless we've got a proposed robust monitoring.

Rather than building a new system of metrology, as the designers of the sulphur market had, the European scheme as far as possible measures CO_2 emissions by re-employing the existing meters and other mechanisms by which suppliers charge for energy. The measurements of coal, gas, and oil inputs thus obtained are turned into amounts of carbon dioxide by multiplying quantities of fuel by emission and oxidation factors, sometimes specific, for example to a particular type of coal, but more usually standard factors for the fuel in question. The scope of the scheme was, similarly, kept deliberately limited. It covers only around half of Europe's CO_2 emissions (Delbeke 2006: 293), essentially those from large fixed sources of CO_2. Public power and heat (primarily electricity generation) is the largest sector, accounting for roughly 60 per cent of the Emissions Trading Scheme, with the other sectors involved being energy-intensive industries, notably metals production, oil and gas, and cement, lime, and glass. Ground transport, marine transport, and aviation were all omitted, as was the domestic sector other than via the effects of the scheme on prices, especially of electricity. (Aviation is to be brought into the scheme, probably in 2012.)

Despite the decision to keep the scheme modest in its coverage, a whole new apparatus of verification had to be created to audit CO_2 measurements, along with National Registries, which are databases in which the issuance and transfer of CO_2 allowances are recorded, as is their cancellation when emitters surrender allowances corresponding to their emissions over the previous year. A 'Community Independent Transaction Log', registering transfers of allowances across national boundaries, was designed and made operational impressively quickly. (The corresponding system for Kyoto Protocol transactions was, in contrast, much delayed.)

Of course, not all the work to prepare the new market was done by the European Commission and its contractors. Europe's accounting regulators, for example, had to consider how CO_2 allowances should be treated, which involved deciding what kind of accounting item an allowance is. There was no existing body of practice that was directly relevant: because accounting regulation in the USA is different, the way SO_2 allowances are accounted for could not simply be adopted for CO_2 in Europe. With an unfamiliar item to classify, the finitist issues discussed in Chapter 6 came to the fore. CO_2 allowances had analogies to accounting items with established treatments, but to multiple such items, not just one. As an accountant interviewee put it, the carbon market is:

an emerging market in a commodity that has aspects of different types of market places. . . . It has some characteristics of a government grant, has some characteristics of an intangible asset, has some characteristics of inventory, has some characteristics of a financial instrument . . . and it depends how it's applied across which sectors.

Indeed, no fully satisfactory accounting treatment was found: a proposed 'Interpretation' of existing accounting standards to encompass the new commodity was withdrawn in June 2005 in the face of criticism, and at the time of writing no replacement has yet been agreed (Casamento 2005; Cook forthcoming).

The Politics of Allocation

The trickiest issue of all, however, was the allocation of CO_2 allowances. The March 2000 European Commission 'Green Paper' that was the basis for the consultation exercise on the proposed market laid out the case for auctioning allowances rather than allocating them free of charge:

Periodic auctioning is technically preferable, as it would give an equal and fair chance to all companies to acquire the allowances they want in a transparent manner. Auctioning applies the 'polluter pays' principle. The revenues raised by governments could be re-cycled in a variety of ways, even keeping the overall revenue effect neutral, or by using the revenues to promote energy efficiency investments, research and development or public investment in other greenhouse gas abatement efforts. Auctioning avoids the need to take the difficult and politically delicate decisions about how much to give each company covered by the trading scheme. The complex issues . . . about state aid and competition would largely disappear. It would also guarantee fair terms for new entrants to join the system as they, like existing sources, would also have the same opportunity to buy the allowances that they needed.[27]

Unsurprisingly, however, the market's architects 'were ... lobbied very hard by industry to allocate free' (interviewee). They knew the constraints they were under:

Interviewee: ... our decisions ... were driven by what we thought we could achieve ...
MacKenzie: Achieve politically?
Interviewee: Indeed.

While there were some actors—members of the European Parliament and one particular member state, Sweden—in favour of auctioning, the balance of forces was firmly in favour of free allocation. The SDP in Germany, for example, was unenthusiastic about the new market, and could be persuaded by its coalition partner, the Greens, to support it only if allocation was free. 'Once they'd agreed that, it was the foundation of their government and neither side could go back on it. And to some extent we knew that, so we couldn't force the issue', reported an interviewee. All that was feasible was a provision—in practice not heavily used—that gave member states the option to auction up to 5 per cent of allowances in the first phase of the scheme (January 2005 to December 2007), and 10 per cent in the second phase (January 2008–December 2012).

In a European Union made up of independent nation states, with their distinctive interests, priorities, and approaches to environmental matters, it was similarly infeasible politically, when setting up the new market, to insist upon standard, centralized rules for free allocation. At the heart of the Emissions Trading Scheme is a deep compromise between its architects' desire for, in an interviewee's words, 'an absolutely open market with one single market price' and the rootedness of many decision makers, even in the environmental sphere, in their national settings. 'The most national of things ... was the National Allocation Plan', which lays down both a country's overall allocation of CO_2 allowances and the rules by which they are distributed to sectors and companies. Although the market's architects knew that this decentralization held the potential for trouble, they also knew it was an unavoidable compromise: 'the *quid pro quo* was we got our market and the member states got their National Allocation Plan.'

For the market to work at all, however, National Allocation Plans had to be regulated, because of the obvious temptation for member states to be too generous in allocations to their industries so that the latter could profit by selling allowances they did not need to emitters in other countries. The Directive establishing the Emissions Trading Scheme laid down that proposed plans had to be submitted to the European Commission, gave the latter the right to reject them, and set out the rules to be applied by the Commission in judging them. The total quantity of allowances to be issued under a member state's National Allocation Plan:

(a) must be compatible with meeting the state's commitments under the Kyoto Protocol and its target under the 1998 'Burden Sharing Agreement', which allocates to each of the then fifteen member states an agreed share of the European Union's 8 per cent cut in emissions; and

(b) 'shall not be more than is likely to be needed' (European Parliament, Council 2003: 43).

The latter criterion is particularly pertinent to those member states that are on track to meet or over-fulfil their Kyoto or 'Burden Sharing' commitments (as, for example, most of the former Soviet-bloc countries that have joined the European Union are, because of the collapse of many of their heavy industries). The criterion was intended to stop such countries issuing more allowances than their industry was likely to require, taking account of anticipated economic growth and technological and other improvements that could reduce carbon intensity (emissions per unit of gross national product).

Applying the rules for assessing National Allocation Plans was—as a finitist analysis of the kind sketched in Chapter 2 would suggest—far from straightforward. The implications of the two criteria—consistency with Kyoto and no excess over what was 'needed'—were contestable. When the National Allocation Plans submitted for the first (2005–7) phase of the scheme were being assessed, the Kyoto 'commitment period' (2008–12) still lay in the future, and countries' undertakings for it could be met by abatement in the 'non-traded' sectors not covered by the scheme as well as via the scheme's caps. The predictions of economic growth and technological improvement needed to estimate 'need' for allowances could likewise be disputed. Above all, though, existing patterns of emissions were not known with any great certainty. At the level of national emissions totals, an interviewee told me, 'you find ridiculous things like leakage from gas pipelines, or complete gas pipelines, not having been considered'. Typical levels of uncertainty in overall national greenhouse gas emissions inventories were estimated to range from ±4 per cent to

±21 per cent (Monni, Syri, and Savolainen 2004). While there is reckoned to be less uncertainty in estimates of CO_2 produced from fuel combustion (perhaps ±2 per cent: see Monni, Syri, and Savolainen 2004: 93), such estimates were typically produced from aggregate totals of fuel consumption. Key data needed to assess how many allowances were 'likely to be needed'—in particular, existing patterns of plant-level emissions—had in many cases simply never been collected systematically.

In the run-up to the launch of the trading scheme, the installations to be covered were encouraged to supply, to their national governments, data on their existing emissions, and most did so, 'perhaps because the allocations to installations depended on these data' (Ellerman and Buchner 2007: 70). Later investigation suggested that, despite the incentive to exaggerate existing emissions to get more allowances, most of this reporting was done in good faith, but it nevertheless formed a less-than-secure backdrop against which to assess National Allocation Plans.

The architects of the Emissions Trading Scheme knew perfectly well that the combination of having each member state draw up its own National Allocation Plan and incomplete data against which to assess those plans was likely to give rise to an overgenerous distribution of allowances. As an interviewee put it: 'We were fearful of a first phase that wasn't sufficiently stringent', and for that reason refused to allow 'banking' of unused allowances for use in the second (2008–12) phase. The 'firewall' thus created was designed so that overgenerosity did not 'contaminate a second phase'. The scheme's architects also knew 'we couldn't have a war on all fronts' by rejecting almost all National Allocation Plans. With the Emissions Trading Scheme not yet launched, it was all too easy, as this interviewee put it, to imagine disgruntled member states convening 'a special European summit to postpone it by six months, or a year, or three if the going had been too tough'. Accordingly, while the most clearly excessive National Allocation Plans were indeed cut back substantially, others that in retrospect should also have been cut were left intact.

The Price of Carbon

Despite these and other problems, a functioning market was created, and from the start trading in it meant that carbon finally had a European-wide price: because allowances could be used in any of the European Union's member states, the potential for arbitrage kept that price close to uniform across Europe. Furthermore, with allowances traded both on organized exchanges and via brokers the price was public, and at least to a degree a fact, in the sense of reflecting perceptions of the changing economic value of allowances. On 25 February 2005, for example, the *Financial Times* carried, for what (as far as I am aware) was the first time, an article discussing the price of carbon and a determinant of it in terms very similar to those it uses when talking about other commodities: 'Carbon prices soared yesterday, sparked by a snap of cold weather across Europe ... Carbon reached €9.08 (£6.23) a tonne at the end of trade ... Brokers yesterday reported more than 800,000 tonnes of carbon changing hands in volatile trade' (Harvey 2005).

The European carbon price continued to rise during the first half of 2005, reaching almost €30/tonne by July. Both market participants and econometric analysis identified two main determinants of the changing price, both related to the way in which, as one interviewee put it, the European carbon market 'sits on top of the electricity market', the dominant sector in the scheme. The first was the pattern of fuel prices: as natural gas prices rose relative to those of coal, there was an incentive for electricity generators to shift to the latter, increasing their need for allowances because of coal's much higher emissions. The second was weather. As on the February day reported by the *Financial Times*, cold winter weather increases the demand for electricity and hence the need for allowances. Dry weather, similarly, was seen as tending to increase the carbon price, by reducing the future amounts of electricity that can be produced by hydropower (Point Carbon 2006).

So the carbon price was seen as reflecting factors that were 'real'. As Point Carbon, the market's leading analysts, put it in February 2006: 'the market is to a large extent trading on changes in the fundamentals ... This is yet another signal of the market working effectively ... the market price is not arbitrary.' However, politics (not generally seen by market participants as amongst the 'fundamentals') remained prominent: a survey of Point Carbon's subscribers revealed that in their aggregate opinion 'political factors' were the second most important driver (next to fuel prices) of the carbon price in the short term, and its most important driver in the long term. 'It would clearly be a positive development if the importance of politics was reduced and replaced by a more predictable fundamental both as a risk and a price driver' (Point Carbon 2006: 19, 21).

That carbon nevertheless had what was seen as at least to some extent a non-arbitrary price in Europe had global effects, above all via the link between the European scheme and Kyoto's Clean Development Mechanism. The CDM was, as suggested above, the centrepiece of Kyoto's effort to link the interests of the developed 'north' and developing 'south'. As one interviewee who had been involved in negotiating the CDM put it: 'I know first-hand that was a genuine bargain, one of the few real north/south bargains where there was something in it for us and something in it for them and everyone knew it.' But, he went on, it was a bargain that would be kept 'only if it works, only if they actually see money flow to them and we see credits go back'.

The CDM is broader in scope than the European carbon market. Its remit is the entire developing world (including China and even South Korea), and potentially it encompasses all the greenhouse gases and all the means of controlling them, including for example reforestation. To the resultant daunting problems of metrology were added a slow, cumbersome approval mechanism and, crucially, the necessity to demonstrate 'additionality'. To qualify under the CDM, it must be shown that a project will, in the words of article 12 of the Kyoto Protocol, result in '[r]eductions in emissions that are additional to any that would occur in the absence of the certified project activity'—a requirement that gives rise to the potentially tricky methodological problem of demonstrating, with credibility, what would happen in the absence of the project being assessed (see, e.g., Lohmann 2005; 2006).

Unsurprisingly, therefore, the bulk of emissions reductions under the CDM have so far come from developing countries with reasonably sophisticated infrastructures. In particular, a number of 'niches' have been found in which the problems of metrology and the demonstration of additionality are tractable. Particularly noteworthy—because they have been the largest single sector of the CDM—have been large-scale projects in Korea, India, and China to prevent emissions of HFC 23 (trifluoromethane), an especially damaging greenhouse gas that is a by-product of the production of the refrigerant and chemical feedstock HCFC 22 (chlorodifluoromethane).[28] Also prominent have been projects to reduce emissions of nitrous oxide from plants producing adipic and nitric acids.

As one interviewee involved in the CDM put it, 'what we've discovered is that there are people out there who are fantastically expert at nitrous oxide and HFC 23 . . . and we put a little bit of money with them and go round the world and collect in emission reductions by applying catalytic technologies to industrial processes'. However, for that 'little bit of money' to be forthcoming from investors for projects of this sort—or, for example, for the smaller but more numerous renewable energy projects, such as the Mongolian wind farm of which the above interviewee was proud—the credits ('certified emissions reductions') from such projects have to have a monetary value. The link between European carbon trading and the CDM gives projects under the latter this monetary value because those credits can be used in Europe in place of Emissions Trading Scheme carbon allowances. Europe's emitters have therefore been funding projects under the Clean Development Mechanism in order to earn credits that they can use, and other firms fund projects in order to have credits to sell at a profit. These latter firms were in effect conducting 'carbon arbitrage' (see Chapter 5). In the autumn of 2005, for example, with allowances trading in Europe at €20–5/tonne, the rights to certified emission reductions from CDM projects could still be purchased at around €7–8/tonne.

It was only a potential arbitrage. If CDM credits were paid for only when they were certified and delivered, funding problems might cause the underlying projects not to be completed; if credits were paid for in advance, then there was the risk they would not be forthcoming, for example because of failure to achieve certification or because of the bankruptcy of the entity running the project. Nevertheless, the potential arbitrage cast its shadow ahead of it, infusing factual status into the price of certified emission reductions (CERs) from CDM projects. One climate-change newsletter commented in April 2005 that 'the operation of the EU ETS [Emissions Trading Scheme] seems to have made the value of CERs more "real" to investors' (Latham & Watkins LLP 2005: 3). As an interviewee put it: 'we're creating a value associated with reducing emissions. And it's monetizable.' There were other sources of monetizability— via voluntary carbon offset schemes, and because CDM credits can be bought by countries to meet their Kyoto commitments—but because of its size the European carbon market was the crucial source. As prices in that market rose, so too did the price of contracts that would produce CERs. By early 2006, CERs from firm contracts with near-term delivery and perceived low risk were commanding up to €14/tonne (Point Carbon 2006: 25). Abatement projects throughout the world had thus become tightly linked to the European Emissions Trading Scheme.

Emissions Markets as Economic Experiments

Emissions markets had moved from a proposal by economists to having global effects. The seventh of the precepts sketched in Chapter 2 is 'economics *does* things', and that is clearly the case here: emissions markets would not have come into being without economics and economists. As in the celebrated case of the use of economics in the design of the auctions of the frequency spectrum by the Federal Communications Commission and other agencies, not just economists' proposals but 'economists themselves had to circulate' (Muniesa and Callon 2007: 183). In that case, economists became directly involved in the design of the auctions and in advising firms on their bidding strategies. Here, especially in the case of the pivotal early market—in SO_2 emissions—a key role of economists was as policy entrepreneurs.

What policy-entrepreneur economists did was to help launch a set of what, following Muniesa and Callon (2007), can be described as 'economic experiments'. By the term, they include more than the increasingly prominent field of 'experimental economics', in which 'markets' are created in laboratory conditions and subjects' behaviour in them is studied. Economic experiments are:

> research activities in the sense that they aim at observing and representing economic objects, but also—and quite explicitly—in the sense that they seek to intervene on these economic objects: to seize them, to modify and then stabilize them, to produce them in some specific manner. To experiment is to attempt to solve a problem by organizing trials that lead to outcomes that are assessed and taken as starting points for further actions. Experimentation is action and reflection.
>
> (Muniesa and Callon 2007: 163)

Of the two main markets discussed in this chapter, the SO_2 market and European Union Emissions Trading Scheme, the latter is more explicitly an experiment in this sense. As noted, it is being implemented in phases: phase 1 2005–7; phase 2 2008–12; and phase 3 from 2013 onwards. Phase 1 was largely dominated by the practicalities (both technical and political) of ensuring that the scheme—Muniesa and Callon's 'economic object'—was indeed brought into being. The broad framework of rules for phase 2 was established in the 2003 Directive establishing the scheme, but important aspects of what is being done in that phase, especially in respect to allowance allocation, were influenced— as discussed below—by what was learned from phase 1 and, crucially, by the

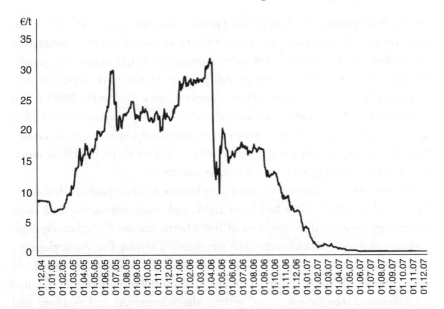

Figure 7.1. The price of allowances for phase 1 of the European Union Emissions Trading Scheme
Source: Courtesy Point Carbon.

way in which the very creation of the 'economic object' reshaped its technical and political context. The process, under way at the time of writing, of designing phase 3 (the plans for which were not laid down at the start of the scheme) is, likewise, being shaped in part by the accumulating effects of the evolving process of market construction.

That the first phase of the Emissions Trading Scheme should be seen as an economic experiment is important because many observers concluded on the basis of it that the scheme was a failure. After generally climbing in early 2005 and 2006—at one point reaching €31/tonne (see Figure 7.1)—the European carbon price fell by over 30 per cent in a single day, 26 April (Morrison 2006). By mid-May, allowances were trading as low as €9/tonne. Despite a slight recovery in summer 2006,[29] prices then continued to slide. By December 2007, one could buy a one-tonne carbon dioxide allowance for as little as 4 euro cents,[30] little more than a thousandth of the peak prices of the previous year.

The initial cause of the price collapse was the leaking-out of the information that a number of countries—the Czech Republic, the Netherlands, Estonia, the Walloon region of Belgium, and France—had reported to the European Commission 2005 emissions of CO_2 by their industries that were substantially lower than the number of allowances issued to those industries. It gradually then emerged that this was the overall pattern: by the start of June 2006, it was being calculated that the total of allowances issued exceeded 2005's actual emissions by 3.4 per cent, or around 60 million tonnes (Carbon Market Data 2006). Installations in several countries—notably Italy, Spain, and, especially, the UK—were left with sizeable net shortages of allowances, but those shortages were far outweighed by the surpluses elsewhere.

There were various possible reasons for Europe's net surplus of allowances. The weather late in 2005 had been mild, and some abatement had most likely been prompted by the start of the scheme and by the relatively high carbon price in 2005 and early 2006 (see below). By far the most plausible explanation, however, was that too many allowances had been issued. As noted above, although the most exaggerated claims of national 'needs' had been rejected, the exigencies of getting the scheme up and running and the paucity of detailed data against which to assess claims had led to more allowances having been created than were actually needed for 'business as usual'. It was a damaging outcome. The European carbon price, having earlier seemed a 'fact' reflecting fundamentals of the market such as weather, was revealed by the 2006 crisis to have been arbitrary after all, the result of political processes of allocation the effects of which had initially not been understood fully.

Also problematic for the reputation of the Emissions Trading Scheme was that analysis of electricity prices suggested that despite doing relatively little to reduce their emissions generators had earned significant income from the scheme, in effect passing on to electricity consumers the price of carbon allowances, when these had been allocated to the generators free of charge (see, e.g., Sijm, Neuhoff, and Chen 2006; Point Carbon 2007). Standard economics predicted that they would do that. Even with free allocation of allowances, companies will, other things being equal, increase prices to take into account the 'opportunity cost' of using those allowances to produce electricity (or other goods), rather than selling them: '[I]n principle and in line with economic theory, a company is expected to add the costs of CO_2 emission allowances to its other marginal (variable) costs when making (short-term) production or trading decisions' (Sijm, Neuhoff, and Chen 2006: 50).

For example, Sijm, Neuhoff, and Chen estimate that when the average allowance price was around €20/tonne the electricity sector of Netherlands was making the equivalent of around €300–600 million per year profit from the Emissions Trading Scheme (2006: 67). The UK's producers are reckoned to have profited in total by around £2 billion in 2005–7 (Crooks 2007). My interviewees in the electricity sector firmly defended the appropriateness of adding the opportunity cost of allowances to electricity prices, citing the above economic argument, but to others the resultant income was 'windfall profits'. In Germany, for example, the Bundeskartellamt (Federal Cartel Office) charged generator RWE with behaving illegally in passing on prices in this way (RWE AG 2007); the case was settled out of court.

So was the experiment a failure? Against these real problems of the Emissions Trading Scheme are three substantial achievements. First, there is tentative evidence that it did produce some abatement even in its first (2005–7) phase. Ellerman and Buchner (2007) report that total 2005 emissions from the sectors covered by the scheme were around 7 per cent lower than would have been predicted simply by extrapolating pre-2005 emissions in the light of economic growth and the trend in carbon intensity in European economies. Of course, that apparent abatement would be partially or entirely spurious if pre-2005 emissions had been exaggerated to gain additional allowances. As noted above, however, there seems to have been less 'gaming' of this sort than might have been expected, so some genuine abatement probably took place. In particular, my interviewees in the electricity sector told me that when the European carbon price was high it did provide an incentive to supply electricity where possible from gas-fired plants rather than the more carbon-intensive coal-fired plants.

Second, the coming into being of the European carbon market has been essential to the growth of the Clean Development Mechanism. There are unquestionably problems with the CDM, ranging from the protracted and demanding approval process to doubts about the genuine 'additionality' of significant numbers of projects, questions about local environmental and social impact, and concerns that CDM funding of the elimination of HFC 23 is generating windfall profits for the producers of HCFC 22 (and even providing a perverse incentive to increase production of HCFC 22).[31] Furthermore, the scale so far of the CDM has been small in relation to what would be needed significantly to restrain global emissions, especially from countries such as

China and India. However, an institutional structure has successfully been created that does allow for significant flows of capital from the developed to the developing world in order to achieve abatement. While the problems of ensuring that projects would not have taken place in any case and of monitoring and verifying abatement are unquestionably real, those problems have to be set in context by considering the likely analogous difficulties of the other main means of achieving significant capital transfers: direct government aid.

Third, as the first large-scale working carbon market, the European Union Emissions Trading Scheme serves as a vital example for those developing such markets in other places. In North America in particular, momentum is growing behind the construction of carbon markets. One significant regional carbon market is already well on the way: ten states in the north-eastern USA (Connecticut, Delaware, Massachusetts, Maine, New Hampshire, New Jersey, New York, Rhode Island, Vermont, and Maryland) have set up the Regional Greenhouse Gas Initiative, a cap-and-trade market for their electricity generators. In August 2006, the state of California approved a bill intended to return the state's carbon emissions to their 1990 levels by 2020—a significant task, given California's rates of population and economic growth—and laid the foundation for an emissions trading scheme to help achieve that goal. The Californian scheme may expand into a wider regional market (including Canadian provinces as well as states in the USA), and indeed there have been a slew of proposals in the form of Congressional bills aimed at constructing a USA-wide market. The European experience has become a vital part of the debate in the USA:

One of the key areas that Hill staffers and the western state counterparts will home-in on is how RGGI [the Regional Greenhouse Gas Initiative] handles the allocation of allowances. Everyone is hoping to prevent what happened in the first phase of Europe's Emission Trading Scheme, when the spot price of a tonne of CO_2 dropped from more than €30 ($43) in the spring of last year to below €0.10 today [December 2007]. . . . Additionally, the free allocation of permits in Europe led to accusations of windfall profits for generators . . .   (Volcovici 2007: 28)

While such problems could have been predicted on other grounds (as noted above, the 'windfall profits' are the result of a mechanism that economists would anticipate), their appearance in an *in vivo* economic experiment makes them far more compelling as an input into the policy debate in the United States.

The Experiment Changes its Context

It would, of course, be quite mistaken to regard the European Union Emissions Trading Scheme as analogous to a classic laboratory experiment, in which considerable effort is devoted to tight control of experimental conditions. The 'economic object' that has been constructed is not a static one, nor is there a single 'experimenter' who is changing the experimental conditions. As already noted, the scheme's architects have had to work under tight political constraints, but the very existence of the experiment has begun to shift those constraints.

The way the experiment changed its context can be seen most clearly in the contrast between the process of assessing National Allocation Plans for phase 1 of the scheme (2005–7) and phase 2 (2008–12). As noted above, the need to get the scheme up and running and the weakness of the data that could be drawn upon to assess proposed plans led in phase 1 to over-allocation of allowances and to a price crash. In phase 2, in contrast, only four of the twenty-seven member-state plans submitted to the Commission were approved (Denmark, France, Slovenia, and the UK). For example, the National Allocation Plan of Europe's largest emitter, Germany, was cut from 482 million tonnes to 453.1, and swingeing cuts were imposed on some other member states' proposals. Latvia, for example, had its desired cap of 7.7 million tonnes reduced to 3.43 million, and Lithuania's proposed 16.6 million was cut to 8.8 million (anon. 2007: 3).

Key to the cuts was the application of what participants came to call the European Commission's 'NAP formula' (see, e.g., Wyns 2007; NAPs are National Allocation Plans). Setting complexities aside, the core of this is the following expression for calculating a country's 'needed' annual average allocation of allowances for 2008–12:

$$(2005\ emissions) \times (GDP\ growth\ factor) \times (carbon\ intensity\ improvement)$$

The GDP growth factor reflects the anticipated increase in economic activity between 2005 and 2010 (the mid-year of the second phase of the scheme). In the case of Latvia, for example, whose GDP was expected to grow by 50 per cent between 2005 and 2010, the GDP growth factor used by the European Commission was thus 1.5 (Commission of the European Communities 2006). The carbon intensity improvement factor similarly takes into account anticipated changes in emissions per unit of GDP.

The NAP formula is a way of making concrete the rule that countries should not allocate more allowances than are needed. Again, though, it should not surprise us that all the three factors in the formula are contestable and contested. (At the time of writing, nine member states were suing the European Commission over its rulings cutting their emissions caps.) For example, should 2005 emissions be used as the baseline, or should an average over several years be employed? Member states arguing for averaging typically suggested that their 2005 emissions were anomalously low, for example because of weather conditions. From the Commission's viewpoint, however, the great virtue of the use of 2005 emissions was that these had been verified under the Emissions Trading Scheme, which meant they were unlikely to be exaggerations: companies' immediate economic interests would have been served by underestimating rather than overestimating emissions, because of the need to surrender allowances corresponding to those emissions. The 2005 emissions were therefore 'harder' facts than estimates of emissions in earlier years. In the case of Latvia, for example, the Commission noted that 'it cannot be excluded that emissions figures reported by Latvia in respect of earlier years overstate actual emissions' (Commission of the European Communities 2006: 4).

GDP growth factors and carbon intensity improvements were, likewise, challengeable. Again, though, the Commission was able to avoid simply relying on the estimates of these that member states submitted in the spreadsheet accompanying their draft National Allocation Plan (the spreadsheet can be found in Commission of the European Communities 2005). The Commission's crucial resource in this respect was an economic model, PRIMES, 'a modelling system that simulates a market equilibrium solution for energy supply and demand in the European Union (EU) member states. The model determines the equilibrium by finding the prices of each energy form such that the quantity producers find best to supply match the quantity consumers wish to use' (National Technical University of Athens n.d.: 3). In its decision in respect to Latvia, for example, the Commission spelled out the advantages of PRIMES as a way of determining GDP growth factor and carbon intensity improvement:

Of all the data at its disposal, including those in the public domain, the Commission considers the data indicated in the PRIMES model as the most accurate and reliable estimations of both GDP growth and carbon intensity improvement rates. The PRIMES model has been used for analysis of energy and climate policy for a long time and the baseline assumptions are updated on a regular basis to reflect the most likely future trend. Furthermore, baseline assumptions are validated with the involvement of experts from Member States. ... There is no other data source at the disposal of the Commission which offers a comparable degree of consistency and uniform accuracy across all Member States, thus ensuring equal treatment of Member States.

(Commission of the European Communities 2006: 5–6)

The use of the 'NAP formula', the 2005 data, and PRIMES meant a process of the assessment of National Allocation Plans that in the eyes of carbon-market participants came to be seen as having the virtue of predictability. After the January 2007 decisions on the Belgian and Dutch National Allocation Plans, Kjersti Ulset of the consultancy Point Carbon asked, 'Should anyone be surprised by the NAP decisions?' and answered no: 'anyone should now be able to predict how the Commission will rule on the remaining countries, or at least come very close. The EC's methodology for NAP assessments is crystal clear' (Ulset 2007: 1).

The very existence of the European Union Emissions Trading Scheme, even in its experimental first phase, had changed the forms of assessment that were feasible. First, as noted above, the 2005 emissions measurements under the scheme provided a credible baseline. Second, the implicit threat in the background to phase 1 assessments—that disgruntled member states might succeed in having the scheme's launch postponed or conceivably even cancelled—was no longer present when phase 2 plans were being assessed in 2006–7. The assessment of phase 2 allocations thus took place in what one interviewee called 'a completely different context': 'Feasibility, data availability. ... Facts are in place. One is that the emissions trading [scheme] is there, and the idea of it ever not being there is not on the agenda and would shock the political process.'

Even in phase 2 of the Emissions Trading Scheme, the abatement required of participants is modest. The total Europe-wide annual cap, 2.10 billion tonnes, is only slightly lower than the equivalent 2005 emissions (around 2.23 billion tonnes), and given that credits from the Clean Development Mechanism can be used (up to set proportions) in place of European allowances, even phase 2 is compatible with a growth in emissions in Europe. Nevertheless, reasonably substantial phase-2 allowance prices, nearly €30/tonne at the start of July 2008, indicated perhaps that the goal of giving carbon a meaningful price was gradually being achieved. The terms of policy debate were also changing.

The European Union's 2007 decision to commit itself to have cut its emissions by 2020 by 20 per cent of their 1990 levels, whatever other countries did (and by 30 per cent if others joined in international action), made it possible to canvass far more stringent phase-3 caps, and large-scale auctioning—politically infeasible in the earlier phases of the scheme—was likewise being proposed influentially.

The verdict of one carbon broker I interviewed—that 'now you've got a dial that you can turn', in other words that it was now possible to reduce emissions by tightening the European caps—understated the extent to which 'turning the dial' downwards was still politically contentious, but there was some justice in his verdict that 'we do seem to have set up a working system'. Of course, the problem of combating climate change is much too far-reaching and complex to be solved by a single class of instruments such as emissions markets: direct regulation, large-scale public investment in research and development and in infrastructure, international aid, and (in contexts in which they are politically feasible) carbon taxes are all likely to be part of the necessary armoury, as is the removal of the many subsidies that exist globally for the extraction and use of fossil fuels (see, for example, Lohmann 2006, and Prins and Rayner 2007). Nevertheless, the experiment of European carbon trading had demonstrated that constructing a working greenhouse gas emissions market, though enormously demanding, might indeed be feasible.

Conclusion

The construction of emissions markets has many aspects. For example, a feature of economic experiments in laboratory conditions is that participants often have to be 'taught' to behave as economically rational agents (see, for example, Muniesa and Callon 2007). So it is with European carbon trading: the construction of economic agents is in a sense still incomplete. For example, even a company in the Emissions Trading Scheme that has been allocated, free, as many allowances as it 'needs' for business as usual should nevertheless be motivated to achieve abatement, if that abatement costs less than the market price of emissions allowances, because it can then earn profit by selling unneeded allowances. Interviewees, however, reported little clear evidence of this happening. Instead of treating a carbon market as a profit opportunity, most energy-intensive industry (the electricity sector aside) was treating the new and unfamiliar scheme primarily as a compliance matter, a business of ensuring that it had enough allowances to cover its emissions. In phase 1, even allowances that a typical industrial emitter was clearly unlikely to need were often held back until its emissions in the year in question were known with certainty, which may explain why allowances were able temporarily to command high prices even though they were in aggregate surplus. Even after the extent of over-allocation became clear in spring 2006, prices only very gradually dropped to close to zero (see Figure 7.1), with many companies not selling unneeded allowances even when they could still earn substantial income by doing so.

Such issues must, however, be left for future discussion. Instead, let me end by returning to the central theme running through this chapter's discussion of the construction of emissions markets: the tendency to over-allocation. In each of the cap-and-trade markets discussed—the sulphur dioxide market, the BP scheme, and the first phase of the European Union Emissions Trading Scheme—there were strong forces pushing in the direction of over-allocation, and even the UK scheme, though differently structured, manifested an equivalent phenomenon. It seems likely that the tendency to over-allocation will manifest itself whenever a new emissions market is created. Free allocation will typically be more attractive politically than auctioning, measurements of existing levels of emissions are often far more uncertain than one might imagine, the potential straightforwardly and cheaply to achieve abatement is often grossly underestimated, and—crucially—the political exigencies of getting markets established may make stringency in allocation infeasible.

A tendency to over-allocation is, therefore, a predictable feature of what might be called the 'technopolitics' of constructing emissions markets, and an over-allocated market is pointless.[32] Yet this chapter has also emphasized the possibility of finding technopolitical means of combating this tendency. The 'ratchet' in the sulphur dioxide market was a crucial such means, and the European Commission's mobilization of the NAP formula, the 2005 emissions data, and the PRIMES model to move in phase 2 of the Emissions Trading Scheme to what one interviewee called 'more mechanistic' allocation may also prove to have been effective in ending over-allocation, although at the time of writing it is still too early in phase 2 to be certain.

I use the expression 'technopolitics' because the politics of emissions markets runs far deeper than the questions on which much of the existing literature tends to focus, such as the reasons for the choice of a market rather than a tax. Take the phase-2 allocations, for example. Apparently 'technical' matters such as the use of 2005 emissions as the baseline (rather than an average over a longer period) or the employment of the PRIMES model are not matters of 'mere detail' but central to whether over-allocation can be avoided, and thus to whether an emissions market achieves its environmental goals. Such matters often escape notice: for example, I have been able to discover only one brief discussion of sulphur's 'ratchet' in the existing literature, despite its crucial role in the success of the much-discussed SO_2 market (Ellerman et al. 2000: 37, 38, and 49). Yet such specifics—the technopolitical 'nuts and bolts' of the design of markets and of allocation mechanisms—cannot be ignored.

Hence, I would argue, the appropriateness to understanding emissions markets of an approach of the kind proposed in this book. Scales aren't stable: 'micro' phenomena (details, technicalities) are crucial to the success or failure of emissions markets. Emissions markets are politically attractive, making possible coalitions of 'left-wing' environmentalism and 'right-wing' pro-market sentiment. Yet to make them successful we need a politics of market design, one that focuses not just on the overall virtues and demerits of market solutions but on technopolitical specifics such as the ratchet and NAP formula. The need for such a politics is large. As noted, carbon-market construction is gathering momentum in North America, and it is likely that if a successor to the Kyoto Protocol can be negotiated a global carbon market is likely to be at its heart. In this evolving context, restraining the tendency to over-allocation, and in other ways making emissions markets effective, are daunting, difficult problems that are simultaneously technical and political. They are, however, problems that must be faced: the issues at stake are far too important for them to be evaded.

8

Conclusion: Opening the Black Boxes of Finance

Friday, 14 September 2007: Britain's high streets. It was a scene from a different time or a different place: from Depression-era America, perhaps, or modern Argentina. The United Kingdom's first large-scale bank run since Victorian times had begun, after the previous night's leak to the BBC that Northern Rock had had to turn to the lender of last resort, the Bank of England, for emergency funding. As one depositor queuing outside the stricken bank's branch in Kingston-upon-Thames told a journalist from the *Financial Times*: 'I'm here to take the lot out, because they're going under, aren't they?' (Braithwaite and Tighe 2007).

For a few days, confidence in the UK's banking system wavered, as depositors' concerns about other banks grew, and as international financial institutions, alarmed by the dramatic TV pictures, grew wary of lending to British banks. Panic was eased only by a government guarantee to Northern Rock's depositors—and to those of any other UK bank in similar difficulties—and by the Bank of England reversing its earlier policy and making funds more readily available to cash-strapped banks.

The run on Northern Rock and the temporary loss of confidence in UK banking were part of a global financial crisis that began in the summer of 2007. A serious but apparently limited problem—rising default rates on 'sub-prime' mortgages in the United States—had spread through the financial system. Amongst the vectors of the credit crisis was a collapse of confidence in the markets' fact-generation systems. As losses and downgrades hit even the most highly rated, AAA, mortgage-backed securities, the ratings system itself was called into question. As one manager of a money-market fund—previously a substantial investor in the apparently safe 'commercial paper' issued by the credit world's special purpose vehicles—put it to *Bloomberg Markets* in early autumn: 'In today's market, you really can't trust any ratings' (Evans 2007: 46).

The buyers of commercial paper are the 'photoplankton' of the markets, one interviewee told me. The metaphor mixed scorn for those who based their investment decisions solely on ratings with acknowledgement of their crucial importance to funding the system. As they stopped buying, the special purpose vehicles they had previously supported turned, where they could, to their parent banks. Those banks themselves were in many cases already carrying losses that were both large and alarmingly indeterminate. Modern accounting regulation forces much of banks' portfolios to be 'marked to market'—revalued as market prices change—but securities of many kinds (bonds backed by Northern Rock's mortgages, for example) either could not be sold at all, or sold only at distressed prices.

Banks' preparedness to lend money to each other—except perhaps for the shortest possible period, overnight—evaporated. As noted in Chapter 4 LIBOR, the most solid of financial facts, lost some of its authority, criticized for example as a measure of interest rates in what was in some cases a market in which one could no longer actually borrow. 'The Libor rates are a bit of a fiction', said one large bank's treasurer (Tett 2007).

The credit crisis—far from over at the time of writing—is, amongst other things, a crisis of the infrastructure of the financial world: not of its technological infrastructure, where only limited difficulties were manifest, but of its cognitive infrastructure, of its fact-generation mechanisms. It remains unclear just how wide the ramifications of the collapse of fact will be. Many Americans—some estimate as many as two million, others even larger numbers—will lose their homes, unable to repay loans arranged for them by intermediaries who knew they themselves carried no risk of default, because mortgages and the credit risk they involve could be sold on. Pensions and many forms of investment have already suffered. The overall squeeze on credit will dampen economic activity, but how much and for how long is, at the time of writing, unclear. Confidence in facts will no doubt return, but not in all facts.

From the viewpoint of this book, the credit crisis illustrates the importance of the kind of phenomena upon which the social studies of finance
focuses. Of course, the crisis reflects 'big' phenomena: the global imbalances
caused by a glut of savings in countries such as China and massive borrowing and balance-of-payments deficits in countries such as the USA and
UK; the deregulation of financial systems; the neoliberal ideas that promoted
deregulation; and so on. Yet equally crucial were apparently 'little' things.
At the heart of the expansion of credit, for example, was a particular set of
investment vehicles—the collateralized debt obligations (CDOs) mentioned
in Chapter 2—that are sufficiently complicated that their properties can be
grasped only with mathematical models, in particular the 'Gaussian copula'
models touched on in that chapter. Without the capacity to model CDOs, the
rating agencies would have been hard pressed to award ratings to products
based on them, and without ratings most investors would not have bought
them. In particular, CDOs were a crucial—perhaps the crucial—source of
demand for securities based upon sub-prime mortgages: central to the attractiveness of CDOs to investors was that a CDO could be used to package
high-risk debt into forms that could still achieve high ratings, while offering
greater rates of return than simpler products such as bonds with the same
ratings.

The crisis showed, in other words, that scales aren't stable. At the heart of an
epochal event—in the view of many, the most serious financial crisis since the
Second World War—were 'technical' matters such as mathematical models
and credit ratings. If this book has a single dominant theme to convey, it is
that technical matters of this kind are not 'mere details' that can safely be set
aside by social scientists looking for 'the big picture'. Yes, global imbalances
and the influence of the neoliberal ideas matter, but so too does the gamut of
phenomena of the kind discussed here, from bodily capacities such as broker's
ear to the algorithm that generates LIBOR.

As suggested in Chapter 1, the social studies of finance is a material sociology of markets, one that emphasizes their physicality, their corporeality, and
their technicality. I am, of course, painfully aware of the book's limitations
in these respects. Access difficulties mean that the data upon which I draw
are predominantly interview based rather than directly observational: getting
permission to conduct ethnographic observation in financial markets can be
extraordinarily hard. This in turn means that the preceding chapters have

given less emphasis to physicality and corporeality than I would have liked: those aspects of markets are more easily documented by witnessing objects, technological systems, and human bodies in interaction than by listening to people talk about them. Even on the particular topics discussed here, there is in consequence much more to be discovered in these respects, and many other aspects of markets remain *terra incognita* from the viewpoint of material sociology.

It is also appropriate to be modest about the academic ambitions of the social studies of finance. It is all too easy for the proponents of a new approach to overemphasize its novelty, or to claim that it supplants all previous approaches. Neither is the case here. Take, for example, the relationship between social studies of finance and mainstream economic sociology. There is much work in the latter field that is fully compatible with a social studies of finance approach, for example the insightful analysis by Carruthers and Stinchcombe, already touched upon in Chapter 2, of how 'liquidity presumes assets that are knowable by a large group of potential buyers and sellers' and involves creating 'generalized impersonal knowledge out of idiosyncratic personal knowledge' (1999: 356). The collapse of liquidity following the loss of confidence in financial facts in the credit crisis is a perfect illustration of their argument.

Similarly, the social studies of finance complements, rather than displaces, what is perhaps the central tradition of recent economic sociology, which focuses on the consequences for economic action of the embedding of actors in networks of interpersonal connections, and is a line of research inspired above all by the work of Mark Granovetter (see, for example, Granovetter 1973; 1985; 1992). It is not that human beings are embedded in systems of technologies, cognitive frameworks, simplifying concepts, and calculative mechanisms rather than in networks of personal connections, but that they are embedded, simultaneously and inextricably, in both.

Take traders, for example. The research reported here and the earlier work described in MacKenzie (2006) has involved some fifty interviews with traders. Even those involved in the most 'technical' forms of trading, such as options or credit derivatives, reported the need to pay attention not just to calculative tools such as models but also to who was doing what and why, which is information typically acquired through networks of personal connections. Furthermore, models matter in part simply because others use them. Traders in credit derivatives, for example, reported that it was sometimes productive to request price quotations for sets of derivatives from several different investment bank trading desks, work out from patterns of quoted prices the characteristics of the models that trading desks must be using, and arbitrage the differences between the models used by different banks, in effect buying credit protection cheaply from one bank and selling it expensively to another.

The example of how traders use models illustrates a general point: the 'technical' and the 'social' are not two separate spheres, but two sides of the same coin, as a long tradition in the social studies of science and technology has emphasized.[1] Any market—indeed any society (see, for example, Latour 2005)—is a sociotechnical construction. A central role of the social studies of finance and similar 'material sociology' approaches to markets is thus to add to the well-honed set of tools for analysing the more directly 'social' aspects of markets—such as the work pioneered by Granovetter, the different form of network analysis developed by Harrison White (1981; 2001), the 'political-cultural' approach of Fligstein (2001), and so on—a set of tools for making sense of their more 'technical' aspects. Because the 'social' and 'technical' are inextricably linked in market construction, the two sets of tools will ultimately need to be integrated fully: a challenging but important academic task.

The ambitions of the social studies of finance, however, should not be academic alone. There has been in recent years within sociology a greatly enhanced attention to the topic of 'public sociology' (forms of sociology that go beyond academia, and engage with multiple publics in multiple ways), attention sparked above all by Michael Burawoy's Presidential Address to the American Sociological Association (Burawoy 2005). While the specifics of what Burawoy calls for are contentious—amongst many critiques is Holmwood (2007), and I offer a critical comment of my own below—his impulse is surely correct. When dealing with topics, such as markets, that have enormous implications for people's lives, researchers should surely aim not just at high-quality academic research, but also should seek to reach out beyond academia to wider publics. This is an issue for all social scientists, not just sociologists: at stake is not just public sociology, but public social science more generally.

What sort of public social science might the social studies of finance foster? There are many possibilities, but one particularly attractive one is a potential broadening of the forms of political engagement with markets. All too frequently, existing political debate treats 'the market' as a singular entity with inherent characteristics, which should either be promoted (as the political right normally suggests) or opposed (as the left often prefers). For example, for all the strengths of his advocacy of public sociology, Burawoy's writing tends to remain lodged within this dichotomy, treating 'the market' as something with a fixed essence against which 'society' needs protection (see, especially, Burawoy 2007).

At the heart of the social studies of finance is the conviction that treating 'the market' as a singular entity is mistaken: the best-known book by Michel Callon, one that has been deeply influential in the field, is titled *The Laws of the Markets* (Callon 1998). If this conviction is correct, and multiple forms of markets with diverse characteristics and substantially different consequences are possible, then politics divided between 'pro-market' and 'anti-market' (both in the singular) is wholly impoverished, and even a 'third way' that seeks simply to position itself between the two is insufficient. Of the many markets that are possible, *which* markets we have matters, and that is a question not simply of their overall characteristics but of the details of their design, the technological infrastructures that support them, and the way economic agents in them are constructed: the systematic forms of knowledge those agents deploy; the phenomena to which they pay attention and to which they do not; the ways in which complexities are made simple enough for economic agents to grasp; and so on.

The need for a form of political engagement with markets that tackles such phenomena is perhaps clearest in emissions markets. As Chapter 7 emphasizes, such markets certainly do not have fixed characteristics. A well-designed, well-functioning emissions market can be an effective and economical tool of abatement, as the US SO_2 market largely was. On the other hand, a poorly designed emissions market can be useless or worse. Which outcome happens depends not just on the overall advantages and disadvantages of markets as policy tools, but on the details of market design, for example of the allocation mechanisms discussed in Chapter 7.

A detailed politics of market design is already being practised by leading environmental NGOs, which have gone beyond the 'pro-market'/'anti-market' dichotomy to seek to influence the key, detailed matters that make emissions markets effective or otherwise. But that is unusual. There are, for example, only limited examples of similar engagement with the design of financial markets. Such markets are just as 'political' as emissions markets—they operate within frameworks still largely set by governments and regulatory bodies, and channel huge amounts of resources with major consequences for patterns of economic growth, employment, wealth, and poverty—but the crucial specifics that shape financial markets seldom become matters for public debate.

Much of what goes on in the processes shaping markets is what Beck (1996) calls 'subpolitics', involving consequential decision making taking place outside the formal political system and concerning phenomena not traditionally thought of as political. Provision for old age, for example, is a traditional, recognizably political topic. The accounting rules that govern the financial reporting of pension provision, in contrast, are treated as a technical matter to be decided by specialists. Yet those rules deeply affect what kind of pension provision prevails.

A financial innovation that has a strong case for being the twentieth century's finest is not any sophisticated derivative but the 'final salary', defined-benefit, pension scheme, in which it is predominantly employers who bear the financial risks of provision for old age. (In the other main type of scheme, defined contribution, it is the employee who bears the risk of market fluctuations.) In recent years, defined-benefit schemes have declined sharply in the private sector in the UK, and amongst the causes, argues Avrahampour (2007), was the introduction of UK Financial Reporting Standard 17 (and now International Accounting Standard 19), governing employees' pension benefits. These standards make a firm's pension provision far more central to its financial reporting than previously, causing the financial risks in such provision to become far more salient to investors. In this context, defined-contribution schemes tend to be far more attractive to firms than defined-benefit schemes, precisely because the former shift the risk away from the firm and its investors. Even apparently very detailed technicalities can be deeply consequential. For example, an employer's pension liabilities largely lie in the future, so a discount rate must be chosen to work out their present value for reporting purposes. Whether one uses the yield of an AA-rated corporate bond as the discount rate (as is current practice) or (as some are now advocating) uses the lower yield on a government bond has a major effect; the latter option makes liabilities seem much larger.

Another example of financial reporting mattering in terms of wider outcomes concerns whether multinational companies in sectors such as oil and mining can simply produce accounts for their aggregate global activities or have to report on their operations country by country. In 2006 a group of eighty NGOs prompted the International Accounting Standards Board to begin considering requiring country-by-country reporting; the coalition's aim was to force corporations to provide figures on matters such as their payments to each specific government (Jopson 2006). Of course, the 'finitist' issues outlined in Chapter 6 would bear upon the effectiveness with which such reporting could be turned into a tool to increase transparency and deter corruption, but the initiative is an excellent example of the 'nuts and bolts' politics of markets that this book advocates.

Consider, too, the regulation of banking. The British government's rescue of Northern Rock made clear that it has become close to inconceivable for a developed-country government to allow a major bank to collapse in such a way that large-scale losses were caused to substantial numbers of the voting public. In consequence, there is an asymmetry (long-standing, but currently especially prominent) in the construction of a bank as an economic agent: the rewards of taking risks in banking are captured privately, while the most extreme potential losses are implicitly borne by taxpayers. This first asymmetry is further reinforced by a second: the prevailing system of rewarding banks' employees, especially traders. Their salaries and bonuses increase, often dramatically, if they generate profits, but losses are not penalized by negative salaries or by negative bonuses. Because of the first asymmetry—the second, though also consequential, has until very recently featured much less often in policy debate—it is almost universally acknowledged that banking requires close regulation. Yet the specifics of such regulation—the models employed to calculate banks' 'value at risk'; whether such models and the marking to market of portfolios are 'pro-cyclical' (that is, encourage too much risk taking in booms and feed downward spirals in bad times: see Goodhart and Persaud 2008); the role of credit ratings in determining the capital reserves banks must hold; ways to reduce incentives to adopt strategies that promise enhanced returns (and thus bonuses) most of the time, but run the risk of occasional catastrophic losses; and so on—are 'subpolitical' rather than 'political' matters, seldom, for example, the topic of debate by legislators.

Of course, matters such as accounting standards and banking regulations *are* technical: that is the main barrier to making them objects of wider debate. An important form of public social science that the social studies of finance could practise is therefore to highlight the importance of such matters and to explain them in ways that wider audiences can grasp. *How* academics in the field write is thus affected, but also *where* they write. Publishing in academic journals with limited circulation is not enough, and even academic books have their limitations. An article for a more generalist magazine (see, for example, MacKenzie 2007b) can reach a readership at least ten times as large; a newspaper article can boost the potential audience a hundredfold. Furthermore, the necessary public sociology, as Burawoy (2005) emphasizes, goes beyond simply writing for print or Internet outlets with wide readership. We academics have at least as much to learn from those who are seeking to alter the characteristics of markets as they from us. Especially in spheres such as emissions markets where the specifics of design are already the subject of wider discussion and political action, 'public sociology brings sociology into a conversation with publics, understood as people who are themselves involved in conversation' (Burawoy 2005: 7).

The material sociology of markets exemplified in the social studies of finance has thus the potential not just to broaden the academic study of markets but to help widen—and in turn to be enriched by—public discussion and action in relation to them. Markets are of course central to modern life, and are here to stay: a comprehensive move away from market forms of economic provision is close to inconceivable. Yet most people's direct experience of markets is limited. The credit crisis, for example, suddenly threw into the spotlight entities such as SIVs (structured investment vehicles), structured products such as CDOs (collateralized debt obligations), and firms such as monolines (insurers of bonds), which few outsiders had previously even heard of. Financial markets are littered with what the social studies of science and technology tends to call 'black boxes' of this kind. As noted in Chapter 2, 'black boxes' are devices, practices, regulations, organizations, models, and so on, the internal structure of which can be disregarded or which are opaque to outsiders, often because their contents are regarded as 'technical' (see MacKenzie 2005).

Research that opens the black boxes of finance can thus contribute to public as well as to academic life. This book has sought, in modest and preliminary ways, to open some black boxes: hedge funds (often regarded as particularly opaque organizations), derivatives markets (often deeply technical in their operations), arbitrage (a crucial market operation but seldom examined in its sociotechnical specifics), accounting (seldom studied by non-accountants), and emissions markets (which in their complication can be deeply daunting when first encountered). I hope that in so doing it has shown that black boxes can be opened, and that gaining a better understanding of their contents is both interesting intellectually and, at least in some cases, potentially consequential for real-world action. If the book has succeeded even partially in doing this, then its author's hopes for it will have been fulfilled.

GLOSSARY

The financial market terms in this glossary often have a range of meanings, and I have given only the meaning relevant to this book. For wider meanings, see Moles and Terry (1999), which has been my main source.[1]

arbitrage   In financial market parlance, arbitrage is trading that seeks to make low-risk profits from price discrepancies, for example between the prices of similar assets. In finance theory, arbitrage is trading that generates riskless profit with no net capital outlay.

bond   A tradeable form of debt. Bonds normally commit the issuer (most commonly, a government or corporation) to repay a fixed sum (the principal) on a given date and to make periodic interest payments (coupons) of fixed amounts until that date. The owner of a bond can sell it to another investor.

collateralized debt obligation (CDO)   An investment vehicle that acquires pools of debt instruments such as *bonds*, loans, securities backed by mortgages, etc., and sells on to investors, repackaged in structured form, the cash flow from these instruments but also the risk that their issuers will default.

coupon   See *bond*.

derivative   A contract or security (such as a *forward*, *future*, *option*, or *swap*), the value of which depends upon the price of another 'underlying' asset, on the level of an index, exchange rate, or interest rate, or on other parameters such as the probability of a *bond* issuer defaulting.

discount   To calculate the amount by which future costs, payments, or other benefits must be reduced to give their present value.

forward   A contract in which one party undertakes to buy, and the other party to sell, a set quantity of an asset of a particular type at a set price at a given future time. If the contract is standardized and traded on an organized exchange, it is referred to as a *future*.

future   A standardized contract traded on an organized exchange in which one party undertakes to buy, and the other to sell, a set quantity of an asset of a particular type at a set price at a given point in time in the future. The term is also used for contracts that are economically close to equivalent to such future purchases/sales but which are settled by cash payments.

hedge fund   A special category of investment vehicle, often registered offshore and/or falling within the 'private funds' exemption from the US Investment Company Act of 1940, which typically permits only very large investments and/or a strictly limited number of investors and is banned from advertising, but is exempt from many regulatory requirements and is free to adopt strategies (such as *short selling* and using borrowed funds to enhance returns) that many other categories of investor are prohibited from using.

implied volatility   The *volatility* of a stock or index consistent with the price of *options* on the stock or index.

LIBOR   London Interbank Offered Rate, the average rate of interest at which a panel of major banks report other banks as being prepared to lend them funds in a particular currency for a particular period. See Chapter 4 for how the average is calculated.

long position   A portfolio of an asset and/or *derivative* of that asset that will rise in value if the price of the asset rises. Cf. *short position*.

open outcry   Trading by voice and/or hand signals that takes place within a fixed arena and is audible/visible to those in the arena.

option   A contract, the purchaser of which gains the right, but is not obliged, to buy ('call') or to sell ('put') an asset at a given price (the strike price or exercise price) on, or up to, a given future date (the expiration). The seller (or 'writer') of the option is obliged to fulfil his or her part of the contract if so demanded.

pit   The physical location (often stepped around the sides) of *open outcry* trading.

share   See *stock*.

short position   A portfolio of an asset and/or *derivative* of that asset that will rise in value if the price of the asset falls. A short position can, for example, be constructed by *short selling* an asset. Cf. *long position*.

short selling   A process in which a trader sells a security he or she does not yet own, or owns only temporarily. Short selling is often accomplished by finding an owner of the security who is prepared, for a fee, to 'lend' it to the trader: in other words, to transfer ownership of it to the trader, who in turn undertakes to replace it. The trader who short sells may, for example, expect that the price of the security will have fallen by the time he or she has to replace it, so he or she can keep the difference in price (minus the fee).

stock (US) or **share** (UK)   A security that confers part-ownership of a corporation.

swap   A contract to exchange two income streams, for example fixed-rate and floating-rate interest on the same notional principal sum.

volatility   The extent of the fluctuations of the price of an asset, conventionally measured by the annualized standard deviation of continuously compounded returns on the asset.

yield   The yield of a *bond* is the rate of return it offers over its lifetime at its current market price, normally measured by finding the rate of interest at which a bond's coupons and principal have to be *discounted* so that their total present value is the bond's current price.

Chapter 1

1. Unfortunately, precision is impossible because the relevant data source, the Bank for International Settlements (<http://www.bis.org>, accessed 13 June 2007), does not specify the interest rate underlying interest-rate derivatives. My rough estimate of $170 trillion is based upon the total notional amounts of interest-rate swaps outstanding ($169,106 billion) at the end of December 2005. (In an interest-rate swap, the notional amount is the sum on which one party agrees to pay a fixed rate of interest while receiving a variable rate. The latter is most usually, but not always, a specified LIBOR.) My estimate thus assumes that interest-rate swaps based upon rates other than LIBOR are at least equalled by other kinds of interest-rate derivatives (such as 'forward rate agreements', and futures and options on interest rates) that are based upon LIBOR. (The notional amounts of interest-rate derivatives other than swaps totalled $95 trillion.) That assumption is plausible, but I have made my estimate conservative by ignoring the rise in the total notional amounts of interest-rate swaps between end December and the time of my observations in February 2006 (by the end of June, the total had risen to $207 trillion).

2. See, for example, the classic work of Max Weber, recently translated as Weber (2000a; 2000b), also Rose (1951; 1966), Smith (1981), Adler and Adler (1984), and Baker (1984a; 1984b).

3. For a collection of articles covering social studies of finance in both the broad and the narrower sense discussed in the text, see Knorr Cetina and Preda (2005); another useful collection is Kalthoff, Rottenburg, and Wagener (2000). Aside from the chapters in those volumes, other noteworthy recent contributions to the social studies of finance include Abolafia (1996; 1998), Arnoldi (2004), Beunza and Stark (2003; 2004; 2005), Caliskan (2005), Clark (2000), Godechot (2000; 2001; 2004), de Goede (2005), Hassoun (2000), Hertz (1998), Holzer and Millo (2005), Izquierdo (1998; 2001), Knorr Cetina and Bruegger (2000; 2002a; 2002b), Lépinay (2004; 2007), Levin (2001), LiPuma and Lee (2004; 2005), McDowell (1997), Maurer (2001; 2002; 2005), Millo (2003), Millo, Muniesa, Panourgias, and Scott (2005), Miyazaki (2003; 2005), Muniesa (2003; 2005), Podolny (1993; 2001); Preda (2001a; 2001b; 2004a; 2004b; 2006), Pryke and Allen (2000), Riles (2004), Thrift (1994),

Tickell (1998; 2000), Uzzi (1999), Widick (2003), Zaloom (2003; 2004; 2006), Zorn (2004), and Zuckerman (1999; 2004).

4. Amongst the field's leading scholarly bodies are the Society for Social Studies of Science (<http://www.4sonline.org/>) and the European Association for the Study of Science and Technology (<http://www.easst.net/>). Amongst its most prominent journals are *Social Studies of Science* and *Science, Technology, and Human Values*.

5. On materiality more generally, see e.g. Miller (2005).

6. Baker did not name the exchange he studied, but when I began to research options trading (MacKenzie and Millo 2003; MacKenzie 2006), it quickly became clear that his fieldwork site must be the Chicago Board Options Exchange.

7. For another set of precepts for social studies of finance, with a different emphasis, see Preda (2001c).

Chapter 2

1. *Shorter Oxford English Dictionary*, 5th edition.

2. On the historically specific nature of the modern 'experimental life', see Shapin and Schaffer (1985).

3. According to Knorr Cetina (2005: 45), there were over 300,000 Reuters terminals and 150,000 Bloomberg terminals worldwide in 2001, and the numbers (especially of Bloomberg terminals) will have risen considerably since then.

4. Chicago Mercantile Exchange traders pointed to the close regulation of the market by the Commodity Futures Trading Commission, and suggested that 'complaints are arising now largely because milk prices are relatively low' (Grant 2006).

5. See MacKenzie (2006), and, for a contrary view, Moore and Juh (2006) and Mixon (2006).

6. A market that is of particular interest from the viewpoint of chartism is foreign exchange, where very large numbers of traders are chartists, and econometric analysis suggests that chartist techniques do indeed successfully predict short-term rate movements (see the literature cited by Osler 2003: 1791). Thus two prominent chartist beliefs are that 'trends tend to reverse course at predictable support and resistance levels' and that 'trends tend to be unusually rapid after rates cross such levels' (Osler 2003: 1791). Osler suggests that the clustering of 'take-profit' orders at round-number rates, and of 'stop-loss' orders immediately beyond those rates, may explain the apparent empirical validity of these two beliefs. Donaldson and Kim (1993) similarly demonstrate anomalous behaviour of the Dow Jones Industrial Average in the vicinity of round-number index levels.

7. 'Base correlation' is well explained by its developers in McGinty, Beinstein, Ahluwalia, and Watts (2004).

8. The work of Hutchins belongs primarily within cognitive science rather than science and technology studies, but its relation to the work of Bruno Latour (especially Latour 1986) is clear and made explicit by Hutchins (1995a: 132).

9. The so-called 'large pool' approximation does lead to analytical solutions, but the approximation seems to be regarded as too radical, and the models that are used in practice are at best 'semi-analytical' (that is, they involve techniques such as numerical integration and fast Fourier transforms).

10. <http://www.epa.gov/airmarkets/monitoring/factsheet.html>, accessed 4 September 2006.

11. On metrology, see, for example, Latour (1987: 247–57), Schaffer (1992), and Alder (1997). The significance of metrology for markets is noted, for instance, by Callon (1998: 23) and Levin and Espeland (2002).

12. The concentration of nitrogen oxides is also measured, as is 'diluent gas' (oxygen or carbon dioxide) and opacity ('the percentage of light that can be seen through the flue gas'): <http://www.epa.gov/airmarkets/monitoring/factsheet.html>, accessed 4 September 2006.

13. See <http://www.epa.gov/airmarket/emissions/raw/index.html>, accessed 4 September 2006.

14. See, for example, EPA (1997).

15. See, for example, Greimas (1987).

16. The few social-science studies of the content of what book-keepers do that I have been able to trace come exclusively from ethnomethodological and similar ethnographic research on work and on its automation: see, especially, Anderson, Hughes, and Sharrock (1989: 123–37), and also, for example, Suchman (1983) and Button and Harper (1993).

17. For examples, see Abolafia (1996).

18. See, for example, Ledyard (1995: 121), Baker (1984a; 1984b), Pirrong (1996), and MacKenzie and Millo (2003).

19. See Levy (1993). Unfortunately, the extent to which behaviour was actually changed by 'tote-board' diplomacy is unclear, since the relevant protocols may 'merely [have] codified what most of the parties were planning to do anyway' (Barrett 2003: 10).

20. There's a sense in which the failure was indeed only apparent. The United Kingdom refused to adopt the 1985 Helsinki Protocol, which required a cut of 30% in sulphur emissions, but then UK emissions actually fell by the requisite amount (Barrett 2003: 9). This was largely a by-product of the shift in electricity generation towards natural gas, but Levy (1993: 124) suggests that political pressure may have been involved too.

21. Ethnomethodology as developed by Garfinkel (especially in Garfinkel 1967) is another major source of finitism, and Latour (2005: 54) describes actor-network theory as 'half Garfinkel and half Greimas'. I think he has got the proportions wrong, at least as far as Garfinkel's finitism is concerned: it does not seem a strong influence on actor-network theory.

22. A lease can be in effect a way of borrowing money to buy an asset, and regulators have been concerned that such leases—'finance leases'—should appear on a corporation's balance sheet and so enter into calculations of the extent of a corporation's borrowing and the level of return on its assets. See IAS [International Accounting Standard] 17, 'Leases' (IASB 2005: 887–914).

23. On microworlds, see, for example, Collins (1990).

24. In the summer of 2005 the pawn-promotion rule was changed with the apparent aim of blocking the interpretation discussed in the text. The word 'new' was added, so it now reads 'exchanged ... for a *new* queen, rook ...' (FIDE 2005b: rule 3.7.e, emphasis added). However, the solution to the puzzle might still under some circumstances be argued to be allowable. Imagine the game is being played with an old wooden set, but that some pieces have been lost and the white rook currently on the board is a modern plastic replacement. Is that not 'a new ... rook'?

25. See MacKenzie (2006) and MacKenzie, Muniesa, and Siu (2007).

26. Thus Mirowski and Nik-Khah (2007) use Nik-Khah's rich case study of the role of economists in the Federal Communication Commission's spectrum auctions in the USA as a refutation of the idea of the performativity of economics, while I see it as (strong) evidence against linear views of performativity.

27. For dissent from Edgerton's claim that the linear model is simply a 'straw man', see Hounshell (2004). Paul Forman has fiercely attacked critics of a linear view, especially within the history of technology, for example suggesting that they (including this author) are guilty of 'animosity toward science' (2007: 62). He does not, however, put forward evidence that a linear view is correct, and indeed does not appear to believe that it is.

28. For other possible innocent explanations, see Ingebretsen (2002: 136–7).

29. The issue was the 'inside spread'—the difference between highest broker-dealer bid and lowest broker-dealer offer in the entire market—not the spread quoted by any individual dealer (Department of Justice 1996: 9–10).

Chapter 3

1. Indeed, this chapter and the article (Hardie and MacKenzie 2007) on which it builds contain what is, to our knowledge, the first study of a hedge fund that includes direct observation (albeit brief observation) of its operations (for a

previous sociological—but retrospective—study of a hedge fund, see MacKenzie 2003). There have, however, been a number of sociological or anthropological observational studies of other kinds of actor and action in financial markets that are particularly pertinent to our analysis: in particular, Knorr Cetina and Bruegger (2002a) and Beunza and Stark (2004); the latter is drawn on in Chapter 5. See also, for example, Heath, Jirotka, Luff, and Hindmarsh (1993), Abolafia (1996), and Zaloom (2003; 2006).

2. Investment Company Act, section 3 (especially paragraph c.1) and section 12, paragraph a. The text of the act is available at <http://www.law.uc.edu/CCL/InvCoAct>, accessed 11 May 2005.

3. Data from International Financial Services London, <http://www.ifsl.org.uk>, accessed 23 May 2005.

4. Data (for end 2003) from <http://www.ifsl.org.uk>, accessed 23 May 2005.

5. In certain markets—notably that for small-capitalization stocks—behaviour in December and January has unusual aspects to do with matters such as the end of the US tax year (Reinganum 1983), but as far as we could tell there was no such effect on what we were observing, though it is possible that a period of observation right at the start of the calendar year and after the markets were closed for a holiday may have been busier than normal.

6. For discussions on the relative influence of endogenous and exogenous factors on emerging market bond spreads, see for example Manzocchi (2001) and Eichengreen and Mody (2000).

7. On the controversy, see for example Collins and Yearley (1992).

8. We owe this way of framing the point to Fabian Muniesa.

Chapter 4

1. See, for example, Tufano (2003) and Black (1986).

2. See, especially, Tickell (1998; 2000), Pryke and Allen (2000), Maurer (2001; 2002), LiPuma and Lee (2004; 2005), and Arnoldi (2004).

3. Most computer systems employ both fast 'main memory' (the contents of which programs can access and modify), which in the early years of computing was expensive and limited in its capacity, and 'secondary storage', which is slower, not directly accessible, but larger capacity. In the late 1950s and early 1960s, computer scientists learned how to design operating systems that automatically transfer data between the two in such a way as to free programs from the limited physical capacity of main memory by giving them access to an 'address space' ('virtual memory') that is much larger.

4. The recent growth of property derivatives is the subject of ongoing research by Susan Smith of Durham University.
5. See, e.g., Sandor and Sosin (1983: 260–7).
6. US Court of Appeals, Federal Circuit, 149 F.3d 1368.
7. See <http://fedcir.gov/about.html>, accessed 4 December 2006.
8. It is also worth noting that the extent to which Chicago's competitive ethos translated into the actuality of fierce competition was in fact variable, as beautifully demonstrated by Baker (1984a; 1984b).
9. On weather derivatives, see Pryke (forthcoming). The potential demand for longevity derivatives—still largely in the planning stage—arises from the desire of pension funds to hedge the risk that their members may live longer than anticipated.
10. Leo Melamed, electronic mail message to author, 13 January 2006.
11. See, e.g., <http://www.igindex.co.uk/>.

Chapter 5

1. A purist should replace the word 'arbitrage' in what follows with 'relative-value trading'.
2. Three of the fifty-one are repeat interviews of traders interviewed in MacKenzie's original study.
3. I owe this point to Juan Pablo Pardo-Guerra.

Chapter 6

1. On the history of interchangeable parts, see Alder (1997).
2. I owe the idea of this list, and many items on it, to a comment by Mike Power on an earlier version of this chapter.
3. An analogous issue arises in the measurement of liabilities, which for reasons of space I ignore.
4. See, for example, Hines (1988: 253).
5. On the history of ratio analysis, see Miller and Power (1995).
6. Again, see Hines (1988).
7. The latter is of course Merton's famous example of self-fulfilling prophecy: see Merton (1948).
8. IAS 39 can be found in International Accounting Standards Board (2005: 1657–946).
9. '[A] man's income [is] the maximum value which he can consume during a week, and still expect to be as well off at the end of the week as he was at

the beginning' (Hicks 1946: 172). The difficulty of this definition lies in making precise what is meant by 'as well off'. As Hicks pointed out, that leads into issues such as future interest rates, future prices, and depreciation. On the episode, see Hopwood and Bromwich (1984).

10. <http://www.fasb.org>, accessed 5 July 2008. For example, Standard 133 ('Accounting for Derivative Instruments and Hedging Activities') stretches over 165 pages.

11. In the original, this sentence is in bold, which is how the International Accounting Standards Board signals a precept's status as a principle.

12. OC [Optical Carrier] 192 is a standard data rate (9,953,280 kbit/s) for high-speed, high-capacity synchronized data transmission via optical fibre.

13. SEC Staff Accounting Bulletin, No. 101: 'Revenue Recognition in Financial Statements', available at <http://www.sec.gov/interps/account/sab101.htm>, accessed 19 February 2008.

14. Financial Accounting Standards Board, Statement No. 91: 'Accounting for Non-refundable Fees and Costs Associated with Originating or Acquiring Loans and Initial Direct Costs of Leases', available at <http://www.fasb.org/pdf/fas91.pdf>, accessed 19 February 2008.

15. Tsalavoutas's sample suggests that the costs of acquiring customer relationships via mergers and acquisitions are increasingly being recognized as a distinct asset, rather than simply part of 'goodwill'.

16. I owe this point to David Leung.

17. See Suchman (1983), which is one of only a limited number of empirical studies of the content of book-keeping work, and also, e.g., Button and Harper (1993).

18. This paragraph draws upon a conversation with Christine Grimm, an experienced SAP implementer.

19. The ethnomethodologically influenced corpus of workplace ethnographies offers the closest approach to the study of book-keepers' classifications. Again see, for example, Suchman (1983) and Button and Harper (1993).

Chapter 7

1. Also relevant, though less detailed than Dales's proposal, was the emissions trading proposal put forward by Thomas D. Crocker, then of the University of Wisconsin at Milwaukee (Crocker 1966). Montgomery (1972) is an early formal analysis.

2. For von Hayek, see Caldwell (2004).

3. Markets were also set up in the USA in emissions of nitrogen oxides, starting with the Los Angeles Regional Clean Air Incentives Market (RECLAIM) in 1994. Their history is chequered (see Burtraw et al. 2005), and they were much less

influential than the sulphur dioxide market as exemplars drawn on in shaping policy for carbon dioxide.

4. Title IV of the 1990 Clean Air Act Amendments is available at <http://www.epa.gov/air/caa/title4.html>, accessed 2 September 2006. The 'tons' in question are US or 'short' tons (2,000 lb; around 907 kg).

5. See Stavins (1998: 78) and Sorrell (1994: 76).

6. <http://www.environmentaldefense.org/aboutus.cfm?tagID=362&linkID=9>, accessed 2 September 2006.

7. Sorrell (1994: 76); see also <http://www.rff.org/rff/Events/Choosing-Environmental-Policy-Bios.cfm>, accessed 11 September 2006.

8. On the issue of the legal status of SO_2 allowances, see Dennis (1993).

9. Marrakesh Accords, Decision 15/CP.7. The text of the Marrakesh Accords is available at <http://unfccc.int/documentation/documents/advanced_search/items/3594.php?rec=j&priref=600001728,>, accessed 19 September 2006.

10. For an eloquent argument that despite these assertions emission allowances are nevertheless property rights, see Lohmann (2006: 73–87).

11. Ellerman et al. (2000: 38). In view of the salience of auction design in the debate over the performativity of economics (see, especially, Mirowski and Nik-Khah 2007), it is worth noting that the form of auction that the Environmental Protection Agency believes is mandated by section 416 of the Clean Air Act Amendments is not what many economists would have recommended. Instead of the auction being used to identify a single market-clearing price which all buyers pay and all sellers receive, bids and asks are matched in such a way that the seller with the lowest asking price receives the highest price that is bid, and so on. This form of auction was sharply criticized by experimental economists Timothy Cason and Charles Plott, who concluded on the basis of laboratory studies that it 'may provide poor price signals' and in particular 'biases market-clearing prices downward' (Cason and Plott 1996: 133–4). In practice, however, the role of the auction in the emissions market has been too small for the mechanism to matter much. It also seems that the form of behaviour predicted by Cason and Plott's experiments did not occur in practice: 'in fact private sellers have tended to set their reservation prices too high to produce sales' (Ellerman et al. 2000: 299).

12. The rate was 2.5 lb (1.13 kg) of sulphur dioxide for each million British thermal units input (Ellerman et al. 2000: 7).

13. Ellerman et al. (2000: 46). The lignite provision is section 405(b)(3) of the Clean Air Act Amendments of 1990.

14. Ellerman et al. (2000: 38). The current version of the main spreadsheet, the National Allowance Data Base, is available at <http://www.epa.gov.airmarket/allocations/index.html>, accessed 18 September 2006.

15. The exception, contained in section 404(a)(3) of the Amendments, was an additional allocation to Illinois, Indiana, and Ohio (with the exception of 'units at Kyger Creek, Clifty Creek, and Joppa Stream'). All three states had well-placed Representatives in the House. The three excluded plants mainly sold electricity to Department of Energy facilities that processed uranium, which involved 'cost plus' contracts in which operators could claim back the costs of allowances (Ellerman et al. 2000: 40).

16. The complexity of the calculations involved meant that the actual size of the ratchet did not become known until early in 1992 (Ellerman et al. 2000: 37).

17. The concession, over and above the ratchet, to Illinois, Indiana, and Ohio seems to have had the effect of increasing the cap on emissions by 0.24 million tons per year (calculated from the figures in Ellerman et al. 2000: 37 n. 10).

18. See, e.g., Kinner and Birnbaum (2004).

19. A particular worry had been that even if emissions were reduced overall, the trading of allowances might have led to 'hot spots': localized increases in SO_2 emissions to levels that were damaging to human health or the environment. One study reported that of 617 facilities that were in operation in 1990, 282 had actually increased emissions by 2000–2 (Kinner and Birnbaum 2004). The total of such increases (1.2 million tons) was, however, much less than the total reductions (6.3 million tons) by the remainder. Though concerns remain, 'geographic effects' such as hot spots seem 'small compared to the aggregate benefits' (Burtraw et al. 2005: 262).

20. The text of the Kyoto Protocol to the United Nations Framework Convention on Climate Change is available at <http://unfccc.int/resource/docs/convkp/kpeng.html>, accessed 24 March 2006.

21. The quotation is from article 17 of the Protocol: see previous note.

22. Royal Dutch/Shell and the US chemicals giant DuPont also set up internal trading schemes similar to BP's (Fialka 2000).

23. In fact, little or no trading seems to have taken place.

24. Two other UK schemes involving an element of trading are the Renewables Obligation, under which electricity suppliers must buy increasing proportions of their electricity from certified renewable sources, and the Energy Efficiency Commitment, under which gas and electricity suppliers have obligations to deliver energy savings, with a particular focus on low-income customers. For the schemes, see Sorrell (2003).

25. See, e.g., Christiansen and Wettestad (2003), Damro and Méndez (2003), Wettestad (2005), Cass (2005), and Engels (2006).

26. Although I know of no direct evidence on the point, another factor in reducing opposition may have been that the withdrawal of the USA, potentially a huge

purchaser of credits such as Clean Development Mechanism-certified emission reductions, reduced the costs to others of meeting Kyoto commitments.

27. The Green Paper is reproduced in Delbeke (2006: 279–313, quote on p. 299).

28. HCFC 22 is an ozone depleter, albeit not amongst the most damaging such agents. Its production will be phased out under the Montreal Protocol, but will cease only in 2030. HCFC 22's main feedstock use is in the production of polytetrafluoroethylene (PTFE, or Teflon®), the uses of which range from aerospace to non-stick frying pans.

29. A factor in the partial recovery was that the German federal government inserted into its plan a provision for 'ex-post adjustments', giving itself the right to claw back allowances if there was 'malpractice' or 'undesirable over-allocations' (Freshfields Bruckhaus Deringer 2005: 3). Although the legality of Germany's proposed ex-post adjustments was challenged by the European Commission, on 15 May 2006 Germany announced that it would employ the provision to claw back allowances equivalent to around ten million tonnes of carbon dioxide. Since Germany had made what appeared to be in absolute terms the largest single over-allocation, the announcement was significant not just because it would reduce the overall surplus of allowances: it was read as 'news that Germany had acknowledged being too generous in its 2005 allocation' (Milner and Gow 2006). Although the European carbon price did not return to its pre-crisis level, it rose by 80% on the day of the announcement.

30. Spot offer price, as reported on <http://www.pointcarbon.com>, accessed 3 December 2007.

31. See, e.g., Lohmann (2006) and Wara (2007).

32. On technopolitics, see e.g. Mitchell (2002).

Chapter 8

1. Particularly central here has been the actor-network theory of Latour (e.g. 1987) and Callon (e.g. 1986), discussed in Chapter 2.

Glossary

1. Most of the definitions in this glossary are taken from D. MacKenzie, *An Engine, not a Camera: How Financial Models Shape Markets* (Cambridge, Mass.: MIT Press, 2006). I am grateful to MIT Press for permission to reuse them here.

REFERENCES

ABOLAFIA, MITCHEL Y. 1996. *Making Markets: Opportunism and Restraint on Wall Street.* Cambridge, Mass.: Harvard University Press.

—— 1998. 'Markets as Cultures: An Ethnographic Approach'. Pp. 69–85 in *The Laws of the Markets*, edited by Michel Callon. Oxford: Blackwell.

ABREU, DILIP, and BRUNNERMEIER, MARKUS D. 2002. 'Synchronization Risk and Delayed Arbitrage', *Journal of Financial Economics*, 66: 341–60.

ADLER, PATRICIA A., and ADLER, PETER (eds.). 1984. *The Social Dynamics of Financial Markets.* Greenwich, Conn.: JAI Press.

ALDER, KEN. 1997. *Engineering the Revolution: Arms and Enlightenment in France, 1763–1815.* Princeton: Princeton University Press.

ALLEN, FRANKLIN, and GALE, DOUGLAS. 1994. *Financial Innovation and Risk Sharing.* Cambridge, Mass.: MIT Press.

ANDERSON, R. J., HUGHES, J. A., and SHARROCK, W. W. 1989. *Working for Profit: The Social Organisation of Calculation in an Entrepreneurial Firm.* Aldershot: Avebury.

ANDERSON-GOUGH, FIONA, GREY, CHRISTOPHER, and ROBSON, KEITH. 1998. *Making Up Accountants: The Organizational and Professional Socialization of Trainee Chartered Accountants.* Aldershot: Ashgate.

ANON. 2002. 'BP's Credibility Gap over Carbon Emissions'. *ENDS Report* no. 326: 3–4.

—— 2005a. 'The Vision Thing [Lex Column]', *Financial Times*, 20 April: 18.

—— 2005b. 'Case for a Closer Look at Hedge Funds', *Financial Times*, 12 May: 18.

—— 2007. 'EU ETS 2008–2012 Allocation Overview', *Carbon Market Europe*, 6/43 (2 November): 3.

ARNOLDI, JAKOB. 2004. 'Derivatives: Virtual Values and Real Risks', *Theory, Culture and Society*, 21/6: 23–4.

ARTHUR, W. BRIAN. 1984. 'Competing Technologies and Economic Prediction', *Options*, April: 10–13.

ATTARI, MUKARRAM, MELLO, ANTONIO S., and RUCKES, MARTIN E. 2005. 'Arbitraging Arbitrageurs', *Journal of Finance*, 60: 2471–511.

AUSTIN, J. L. 1962. *How To Do Things With Words.* Oxford: Clarendon.

AVRAHAMPOUR, YALLY. 2007. 'Agency, Networks and Professional Rivalry: The Valuation and Investment of UK Pension Funds (1948–2006)'. Ph.D. thesis: University of Essex.

BAKER, WAYNE E. 1981. 'Markets as Networks: A Multimethod Study of Trading Networks in a Securities Market'. Ph.D. thesis: Northwestern University.

—— 1984a. 'The Social Structure of a National Securities Market', *American Journal of Sociology*, 89: 775–811.

—— 1984b. 'Floor Trading and Crowd Dynamics'. Pp. 107–28 in *The Social Dynamics of Financial Markets*, edited by Patricia A. Adler and Peter Adler. Greenwich, Conn.: JAI Press.

BARNES, BARRY. 1982. *T. S. Kuhn and Social Science*. London: Macmillan.

—— 1983. 'Social Life as Bootstrapped Induction', *Sociology*, 17: 524–45.

—— 1988. *The Nature of Power*. Cambridge: Polity.

—— 1995. *The Elements of Social Theory*. London: UCL Press.

—— BLOOR, DAVID, and HENRY, JOHN. 1996. *Scientific Knowledge: A Sociological Analysis*. London: Athlone.

—— and EDGE, DAVID (eds.). 1982. *Science in Context: Readings in the Sociology of Science*. Milton Keynes: Open University Press.

BARRETT, SCOTT. 2003. *Environment and Statecraft: The Strategy of Environmental Treaty-Making*. Oxford: Oxford University Press.

BAY, WOLF, and BRUNS, HANS-GEORG. 2003. 'Multinational Companies and International Capital Markets'. Pp. 385–404 in *International Accounting*, edited by Peter Walton, Axel Haller, and Bernard Raffournier. London: Thomson.

BEALES, RICHARD, and TETT, GILLIAN. 2007. 'Hedge Funds Rival Banks for Share of US Treasury Market', *Financial Times*, 9 March: 1.

BEAR, KEITH, HOD, ZOHAR, ENNESS, PHIL, and GRAHAM, ANDREW. 2006. 'Tackling Latency: The Algorithmic Arms Race'. London: IBM UK.

BEATTIE, VIVIEN, FEARNLEY, STELLA, and BRANDT, RICHARD. 2001. *Behind Closed Doors: What Company Audit is Really About*. Basingstoke: Palgrave.

BECK, ULRICH. 1996. 'World Risk Society as Cosmopolitan Society? Ecological Questions in a Framework of Manufactured Uncertainties', *Theory, Culture and Society*, 13/4: 1–32.

BENEDICK, RICHARD E. 1991. *Ozone Diplomacy: New Directions in Safeguarding the Planet*. Cambridge, Mass.: Harvard University Press.

—— 2001. 'Striking a New Deal on Climate Change'. Available at <http://www.issues.org/18.1/benedick.html>, accessed 26 May 2006.

BERESFORD, DENNIS R., KATZENBACH, NICHOLAS DE B., and ROGERS, C. B., JR. 2003. 'Report of Investigation by the Special Investigative Committee of the Board of Directors of WorldCom, Inc'. Available at <http://news.findlaw.com/legalnews/lit/worldcom#documents>, accessed 17 March 2006.

BEUNZA, DANIEL, and GARUD, RAGHU. 2004. 'Security Analysts as Frame-Makers'. Paper presented to workshop 'The Performativities of Economics', Paris, 29–30 August.

—— HARDIE, IAIN, and MACKENZIE, DONALD. 2006. 'A Price is a Social Thing: Towards a Material Sociology of Arbitrage', *Organization Studies*, 27: 721–45.

BEUNZA, and MUNIESA, FABIAN. 2005. 'Listening to the Spread Plot'. Pp. 628–33 in *Making Things Public: Atmospheres of Democracy*, edited by Bruno Latour and Peter Weibel. Cambridge, Mass.: MIT Press.

——and STARK, DAVID. 2003. 'The Organization of Responsiveness: Innovation and Recovery in the Trading Rooms of Lower Manhattan', *Socio-Economic Review*, 1: 135–64.

————2004. 'Tools of the Trade: The Socio-Technology of Arbitrage in a Wall Street Trading Room', *Industrial and Corporate Change*, 13: 369–400.

————2005. 'Resolving Identities: Successive Crises in a Trading Room after 9/11'. Pp. 293–320 in *Wounded City: The Social Impact of 9/11*, edited by Nancy Foner. New York: Russell Sage Foundation Press.

BIGGS, BARTON. 2006. *Hedge Hogging*. Hoboken, NJ: Wiley.

BLACK, DEBORAH G. 1986. 'Success and Failure of Futures Contracts: Theory and Empirical Evidence'. New York University: Salomon Brothers Center for the Study of Financial Institutions, Monograph 1986–1.

BLACK, FISCHER, and SCHOLES, MYRON. 1973. 'The Pricing of Options and Corporate Liabilities', *Journal of Political Economy*, 81: 637–54.

BLACK, JOHN. 2002. *A Dictionary of Economics*. Oxford: Oxford University Press.

BLOOR, DAVID. 1997. *Wittgenstein, Rules and Institutions*. London: Routledge.

BRADY, CHRIS, and RAMYAR, RICHARD. 2006. 'White Paper on Spread Betting'. London: Cass Business School.

BRAITHWAITE, TOM, and TIGHE, CHRIS. 2007. 'I'm here to take the lot out; they're going under, aren't they?' *Financial Times*, 15–16 September: 1.

BRAV, ALON, and HEATON, J. B. 2002. 'Competing Theories of Financial Anomalies', *Review of Financial Studies*, 15: 575–606.

BROWNE, JOHN. 1997. 'Addressing Climate Change'. Speech at Stanford University. Available at <http://www.bp.com/genericarticle.do?categoryId=98&contentId=2000427>, accessed 19 September 2006.

BURAWOY, MICHAEL. 2005. 'For Public Sociology', *American Sociological Review*, 70: 4–28.

——2007. 'Public Sociology vs. the Market', *Socio-Economic Review*, 5: 356–67.

BURGSTAHLER, DAVID, and DICHEV, ILIA. 1997. 'Earnings Management to Avoid Earnings Decreases and Losses', *Journal of Accounting and Economics*, 24: 99–126.

BURT, RONALD S. 2005. *Brokerage and Closure: An Introduction to Social Capital*. Oxford: Oxford University Press.

BURTRAW, DALLAS, EVANS, DAVID A., KRUPNICK, ALAN, PALMER, KAREN, and TOTH, RUSSELL. 2005. 'Economics of Pollution Trading for SO_2 and NO_x', *Annual Review of Environmental Resources*, 30: 253–89.

BUTTON, GRAHAM, and HARPER, R. H. R. 1993. 'Taking the Organisation into Accounts'. Pp. 98–107 in *Technology in Working Order: Studies of Work, Interaction and Technology*, edited by Graham Button. London: Routledge.

CALDWELL, BRUCE. 2004. *Hayek's Challenge: An Intellectual Biography of F. A. Hayek*. Chicago: University of Chicago Press.

CALISKAN, KORAY. 2005. 'Making a Global Commodity: The Production of Markets and Cotton in Egypt, Turkey, and the United States'. Ph.D. thesis: New York University.

CALLON, MICHEL. 1986. 'Some Elements of a Sociology of Translation: Domestication of the Scallops and the Fishermen of St Brieuc Bay'. Pp. 196–233 in *Power, Action and Belief: A New Sociology of Knowledge?*, edited by John Law. London: Routledge and Kegan Paul.

—— (ed.) 1998. *The Laws of the Markets*. Oxford: Blackwell.

—— 2005. 'Why Virtualism Paves the Way to Political Impotence: A Reply to Daniel Miller's Critique of *The Laws of the Markets*', *Economic Sociology: European Electronic Newsletter*, 6/2 (February): 3–20.

—— 2007. 'What does it mean to say that Economics is Performative?' Pp. 311–57 in *Do Economists Make Markets? On the Performativity of Economics*, edited by Donald MacKenzie, Fabian Muniesa, and Lucia Siu. Princeton: Princeton University Press.

—— and CALISKAN, KORAY. 2005. 'New and Old Directions in the Anthropology of Markets'. Paper presented to Wenner-Gren Foundation for Anthropological Research, New York, 9 April.

—— and LATOUR, BRUNO. 1981. 'Unscrewing the Big Leviathan: How Actors Macro-Structure Reality and How Sociologists Help Them To Do So'. Pp. 277–303 in *Advances in Social Theory and Methodology: Toward an Integration of Micro- and Macro-Sociologies*, edited by Karin Knorr Cetina and A. V. Cicourel. Boston: Routledge and Kegan Paul.

—— and LAW, JOHN. 2005. 'On Qualculation, Agency and Otherness', *Environment and Planning D: Society and Space*, 23: 717–33.

CALVO, GUILLERMO A., and MENDOZA, E. G. 2000. 'Capital-Markets Crises and Economic Collapse in Emerging Markets: An Informational-Frictions Approach', *American Economic Review*, 90: 59–64.

CARBON MARKET DATA. 2006. 'Carbon Market Data Publishes Key Figures on the European Emissions Trading Scheme'. Available at <http://www.carbonmarketdata.com/pages/news.php>, accessed 26 June 2006.

CARLSON, CURTIS, BURTRAW, DALLAS, CROPPER, MAUREEN, and PALMER, KAREN. 2000. 'SO_2 Control by Electric Utilities: What Are the Gains from Trade?' *Journal of Political Economy*, 108: 1292–326.

CARRUTHERS, BRUCE G., and STINCHCOMBE, ARTHUR L. 1999. 'The Social Structure of Liquidity: Flexibility, Markets, and States', *Theory and Society*, 28: 353–82.

CASAMENTO, ROBERT. 2005. 'Accounting for and Taxation of Emission Allowances and Credits'. Pp. 55–70 in *Legal Aspects of Implementing the Kyoto Protocol Mechanisms: Making Kyoto Work*, edited by David Freestone and Charlotte Streck. Oxford: Oxford University Press.

CASON, TIMOTHY N., and PLOTT, CHARLES R. 1996. 'EPA's New Emissions Trading Mechanism: A Laboratory Evaluation', *Journal of Environmental Economics and Management*, 30: 133–60.

CASS, LOREN. 2005. 'Norm Entrapment and Preference Change: The Evolution of the European Union Position on International Emissions Trading', *Global Environmental Politics*, 5/2: 38–60.

CHRISTIANSEN, ATLE CHRISTER, and ARVANITAKIS, ANDREAS. 2004. 'What Determines the Price of Carbon in the European Union?' N.p.: Point Carbon and Chicago Climate Exchange.

——— and WETTESTAD, JØRGEN. 2003. 'The EU as a Frontrunner on Greenhouse Gas Emissions Trading: How Did It Happen and Will the EU Succeed?' *Climate Policy*, 3: 3–18.

CHRISTIE, WILLIAM G., and SCHULTZ, PAUL H. 1994. 'Why Do NASDAQ Market Makers Avoid Odd-Eighth Quotes?' *Journal of Finance*, 49: 1813–40.

CLARK, G. 2000. *Pension Fund Capitalism*. Oxford: Oxford University Press.

CLINTON ADMINISTRATION. 1998. 'The Kyoto Protocol and the President's Policies to Address Climate Change: Administration Economic Analysis'. Available at <http://yosemite.epa.gov/OAR/globalwarming.nsf/content/ResourceCenterPublications-PositionPapersWhyKyoto.html #execsum>, accessed 24 April 2006.

COASE, R. H. 1960. 'The Problem of Social Cost', *Journal of Law and Economics*, 3: 1–44.

COLLIN, PETER, KNOX, HELEN, LEDÉSERT, MARGARET, and LEDÉSERT, RENÉ (eds.). 1982. *Harrap's Shorter French–English Dictionary*. London: Harrap.

COLLINS, HARRY M. 1974. 'The TEA Set: Tacit Knowledge and Scientific Networks', *Science Studies*, 4: 165–86.

——— 1990. *Artificial Experts: Social Knowledge and Intelligent Machines*. Cambridge, Mass.: MIT Press.

——— and YEARLEY, STEVEN. 1992. 'Epistemological Chicken'. Pp. 301–26 in *Science as Practice and Culture*, edited by Andrew Pickering. Chicago: Chicago University Press.

COMMISSION OF THE EUROPEAN COMMUNITIES. 2005. 'Further Guidance on Allocation Plans for the 2008 to 2012 Trading Period of the EU Emission Trading Scheme'. Brussels: Commission of the European Communities. Available at <http://ec.europa.eu/environment/climat/emission.htm>, accessed 16 March 2007.

——— 2006. 'Commission Decision of 29 November 2006 Concerning the National Allocation Plan for the Allocation of Greenhouse Gas Emission Allowances Notified by Latvia in Accordance with Directive 2003/87/EC of the European Parliament and of the Council'. Brussels: Commission of the European Communities. Available at <http://ec.europa.eu/environment/climat/pdf/nap2006/20061128_lv_nap_en.pdf>, accessed 6 January 2008.

COOK, ALLAN. Forthcoming. 'Emission Rights: From Costless Activity to Market Operations', *Accounting, Organizations and Society*.

COOPER, DAVID J., and ROBSON, KEITH. 2006. 'Accounting, Professions and Regulation: Locating the Sites of Professionalization', *Accounting, Organizations and Society*, 31: 415–44.

CRAMER, JAMES J. 2002. *Confessions of a Street Addict*. New York: Simon and Schuster.

CROCKER, THOMAS D. 1966. 'The Structuring of Atmospheric Pollution Control Systems'. Pp. 61–86 in *The Economics of Air Pollution*, edited by Harold Wolozin. New York: Norton.

CRONON, WILLIAM. 1991. *Nature's Metropolis: Chicago and the Great West*. New York: Norton.

CROOKS, ED. 2007. 'Electricity Generators Gain from Emissions Trading', *Financial Times*, 18 June: 4.

DALES, J. H. 1968a. 'Land, Water, and Ownership', *Canadian Journal of Economics*, 1: 791–804.

—— 1968b. *Pollution, Property and Prices: An Essay in Policy-Making and Economics*. Toronto: University of Toronto Press.

DAMASIO, ANTONIO R. 1995. *Descartes's Error: Emotion, Reason and the Human Brain*. London: Picador.

DAMRO, CHAD, and MÉNDEZ, PILAR LUACES. 2003. 'Emissions Trading at Kyoto: From EU Resistance to Union Innovation', *Environmental Politics*, 12/2: 71–94.

DAVID, PAUL A. 1992. 'Heroes, Herds and Hysteresis in Technological History: Thomas Edison and "The Battle of the Systems" Reconsidered', *Industrial and Corporate Change*, 1: 129–80.

DECHOW, PATRICIA M., RICHARDSON, SCOTT A., and TUNA, IREM. 2003. 'Why Are Earnings Kinky? An Examination of the Earnings Management Explanation', *Review of Accounting Studies*, 8: 355–84.

DELBEKE, JOS (ed.). 2006. *EU Environmental Law: The EU Greenhouse Gas Emissions Trading Scheme*. Leuven: Claeys & Castells.

DELEUZE, GILLES, and GUATTARI, FÉLIX. 2004. *A Thousand Plateaus: Capitalism and Schizophrenia*. London: Continuum.

DENNIS, JEANNE M. 1993. 'Smoke for Sale: Paradoxes and Problems of the Emissions Trading Program of the Clean Air Act Amendments of 1990', *UCLA Law Review*, 40/4: 1101–25.

DEPARTMENT OF JUSTICE. 1996. 'United States of America, Plaintiff v. Alex. Brown & Sons Inc. [and others]: Competitive Impact Statement'. Available at <http://www.usdoj.gov/atr/cases/f0700/0739.htm>, accessed 25 September 2006.

DONALDSON, R. GLEN, and KIM, HAROLD Y. 1993. 'Price Barriers in the Dow Jones Industrial Average', *Journal of Financial and Quantitative Analysis*, 28: 313–30.

EDGERTON, DAVID. 2004. ' "The Linear Model" Did Not Exist: Reflections on the History and Historiography of Science and Research in Industry in the Twentieth Century'.

Pp. 31–57 in *The Science-Industry Nexus: History, Policy, Implications,* edited by Karl Grandin, Nina Wormbs, and Sven Widmalm. Sagamore Beach, Mass.: Science History Publications.

EICHENGREEN, BARRY, and MODY, ASHOKA. 2000. 'What Explains Spreads on Emerging-Market Debt: Fundamentals or Market Sentiment?' National Bureau of Economic Research Working Paper 6408.

ELLERMAN, A. DENNY, and BUCHNER, BARBARA K. 2007. 'The European Union Emissions Trading Scheme: Origins, Allocation, and Early Results', *Review of Environmental Economics and Policy,* 1: 66–87.

—— SCHMALENSEE, RICHARD, BAILEY, ELIZABETH M., JOSKOW, PAUL L., and MONTERO, JUAN-PABLO. 2000. *Markets for Clean Air: The U.S. Acid Rain Program.* Cambridge: Cambridge University Press.

ENGELS, ANITA. 2006. 'Market Creation and Transnational Rule-Making: The Case of CO_2 Emissions Trading'. Pp. 329–48 in *Transnational Governance: International Dynamics of Regulation,* edited by Marie-Laure Djelic and Kerstin Sahlin-Andersson. Cambridge: Cambridge University Press.

ENVIRONMENTAL DEFENSE FUND. 1998. '1998 Annual Report'. New York: Environmental Defense Fund, available at <http://www.environmentaldefense.org/documents/218_AR98.pdf>, accessed 2 September 2006.

EPA (ENVIRONMENTAL PROTECTION AGENCY). 1997. 'EPA Traceability Protocol for Assay and Certification of Gaseous Calibration Standards'. Research Triangle Park, NC: EPA National Exposure Research Laboratory, EPA-600/R-97/121. Available at <http://www.epa.gov/ttn/emc/news/sec1.pdf>, accessed 7 September 2006.

EUROPEAN PARLIAMENT, COUNCIL. 2003. 'Directive 2003/87/EC of the European Parliament and of the Council', *Official Journal of the European Union,* 275 (25 October): 32–46.

—— 2004. 'Directive 2004/101/EC of the European Parliament and of the Council', *Official Journal of the European Union,* 338 (13 November): 18–23.

EVANS, DAVID. 2007. 'Unsafe Havens', *Bloomberg Markets,* October: 36–54.

FALLOON, WILLIAM D. 1998. *Market Maker: A Sesquicentennial Look at the Chicago Board of Trade.* Chicago: Chicago Board of Trade.

FASB (FINANCIAL ACCOUNTING STANDARDS BOARD). 1985. 'Statement of Financial Accounting Concepts No. 6: Elements of Financial Statements'. Norwalk, Conn.: FASB.

FENTON-O'CREEVY, MARK, NICHOLSON, NIGEL, SOANE, EMMA, and WILLMAN, PAUL. 2005. *Traders: Risks, Decisions, and Management in Financial Markets.* Oxford: Oxford University Press.

FIALKA, JOHN J. 2000. 'Green Leader Lobbies Hard to Gain Corporate Support', *Wall Street Journal Europe,* 22 November: 2.

FIDE (FÉDÉRATION INTERNATIONALE DES ÉCHECS). 2005a. 'FIDE Laws of Chess'. Available at <http://www.fide.com>, accessed 16 May 2005.

—— 2005b. 'FIDE Laws of Chess'. Available at <http://www.fide.com>, accessed 11 October 2005.

FINANCIAL SERVICES AUTHORITY. 2005. 'Final Notice to Citigroup Global Markets Limited, June 28'. Available at <http://www.fsa.gov.uk/pubs/final/cgml>, accessed 30 June 2005.

FLECK, JAMES. 1994. 'Learning by Trying: The Implementation of Configurational Technology', *Research Policy*, 23: 637–52.

FLIGSTEIN, NEIL. 2001. *The Architecture of Markets*. Princeton: Princeton University Press.

FORMAN, PAUL. 2007. 'The Primacy of Science in Modernity, or Technology in Postmodernity, and of Ideology in the History of Technology', *History and Technology*, 23: 1–160.

FRESHFIELDS BRUCKHAUS DERINGER. 2005. 'EU ETS Trading Commences'. Available at <http://www.freshfields.com/practice/environment/publications/pdfs/10573.pdf>, accessed 26 September 2006.

GANGAHAR, ANUJ. 2007. 'Chicago Trio Shake Up Markets', *Financial Times*, 20 March: 39.

GARFINKEL, HAROLD. 1967. *Studies in Ethnomethodology*. Englewood Cliffs, NJ: Prentice-Hall.

GEMMILL, GORDON, and DICKINS, PAUL. 1986. 'An Examination of the Efficiency of the London Traded Options Market', *Applied Economics*, 18: 995–1010.

GODECHOT, OLIVIER. 2000. 'Le Bazar de la rationalité: Vers une sociologie des formes concrètes de raisonnement', *Politix*, 13/52: 17–56.

—— 2001. *Les Traders: Essai de sociologie des marchés financiers*. Paris: La Découverte.

—— 2004. 'L'Appropriation du profit: Politiques des bonus dans l'industrie financière'. Ph.D. thesis: Conservatoire National des Arts et Métiers.

—— 2007. *Working rich: Salaires, bonus et appropriation du profit dans l'industrie financière*. Paris: La Découverte.

GOEDE, MARIEKE DE. 2005. *Virtue, Fortune, and Faith: A Genealogy of Finance*. Minneapolis: University of Minnesota Press.

GOODHART, CHARLES, and PERSAUD, AVINASH. 2008. 'A Proposal for How to Avoid the Next Crash', *Financial Times*, 31 January: 13.

GRANOVETTER, MARK. 1973. 'The Strength of Weak Ties', *American Journal of Sociology*, 78: 1360–80.

—— 1985. 'Economic Action and Social Structure: The Problem of Embeddedness', *American Journal of Sociology*, 91: 485–510.

—— 1992. 'Economic Institutions as Social Constructions: A Framework for Analysis', *Acta Sociologica*, 35: 3–11.

GRANT, JEREMY. 2006. 'CME in Cheese Price-Fix Investigation', *Financial Times*, 18 August: 19.

GREIMAS, ALGIRDAS J. 1987. *On Meaning: Selected Writings in Semiotic Theory*. London: Pinter.

—— and COURTÉS, JOSEPH. 1982. *Semiotics and Language: An Analytical Dictionary*. Bloomington, Ind.: Indiana University Press.

GRUBB, MICHAEL. 1999. *The Kyoto Protocol: A Guide and Assessment*. London: Royal Institute of International Affairs.

HACKING, IAN. 1983. *Representing and Intervening: Introductory Topics in the Philosophy of Natural Science*. Cambridge: Cambridge University Press.

HAHN, ROBERT W. 1989. 'Economic Prescriptions for Environmental Problems: How the Patient Followed the Doctor's Orders', *Journal of Economic Perspectives*, 3/2: 95–114.

HALL, PETER A., and SOSKICE, DAVID (eds.). 2001. *Varieties of Capitalism: The Institutional Foundations of Comparative Advantage*. New York: Oxford University Press.

HARDIE, IAIN. 2004. ' "The Sociology of Arbitrage": A Comment on MacKenzie', *Economy and Society*, 33: 239–54.

—— 2007. 'Trading the Risk: Financialisation, Loyalty and Emerging Market Government Policy Autonomy'. Ph.D. thesis: University of Edinburgh.

—— and MACKENZIE, DONALD. 2007. 'Assembling an Economic Actor: The *Agencement* of a Hedge Fund', *Sociological Review*, 55: 57–80.

HARFORD, TIM. 2006. 'Green Taxes and Posturing Politicians', *Financial Times*, 21 July: 13.

HARRIS, L. 1991. 'Stock Price Clustering and Discreteness', *Review of Financial Studies*, 4: 389–415.

HARVEY, FIONA. 2005. 'Cold Snap Pushes Up Carbon Price', *Financial Times*, 25 February: 3.

HASSOUN, JEAN-PIERRE. 2000. 'Trois interactions hétérodoxes sur les marchés à la criée du MATIF', *Politix*, 13/52: 99–119.

HATHERLY, DAVID, LEUNG, DAVID, and MACKENZIE, DONALD. Forthcoming. 'The Finitist Accountant: Classifications, Rules and the Construction of Profits'. In *Living in a Material World: On the Mutual Constitution of Technology, Economy, and Society*, edited by Trevor Pinch and Richard Swedberg. Cambridge, Mass.: MIT Press, in press.

HAWAWINI, GABRIEL, and VORA, ASHOK. 2007. 'A Brief History of Yield Approximations'. Pp. 19–30 in *Pioneers of Financial Economics, ii: Twentieth-Century Contributions*, edited by Geoffrey Poitras and Franck Jovanovic. Cheltenham: Elgar.

HEALY, PAUL M., and WAHLEN, JAMES M. 1999. 'A Review of the Earnings Management Literature and its Implications for Standard Setting', *Accounting Horizons*, 13: 365–83.

HEATH, CHRISTIAN, JIROTKA, MARINA, LUFF, PAUL, and HINDMARSH, JON. 1993. 'Unpacking Collaboration: The Interactional Organisation of Trading in a City Dealing Room'. Proceedings of the Third European Conference on Computer-Supported Collaborative Work, 13–17 September, Milan.

HENKER, THOMAS, and MARTENS, MARTIN. 2005. 'Index Futures Arbitrage before and after the Introduction of Sixteenths on the NYSE', *Journal of Empirical Finance*, 12: 353–73.

HENRY, DAVID. 2004. 'Fuzzy Numbers', *Business Week*, 4 October: 50–4.

HERTZ, ELLEN. 1998. *The Trading Crowd: An Ethnography of the Shanghai Stock Market*. Cambridge: Cambridge University Press.

HESSE, MARY. 1974. *The Structure of Scientific Inference*. London: Macmillan.

HICKS, JOHN R. 1946. *Value and Capital: An Inquiry into Some Fundamental Principles of Economic Theory*. Oxford: Clarendon.

HINES, RUTH D. 1988. 'Financial Accounting: In Communicating Reality, We Construct Reality', *Accounting, Organizations and Society*, 13: 251–61.

HOLMWOOD, JOHN. 2007. 'Sociology as Public Discourse and Professional Practice: A Critique of Michael Burawoy', *Sociological Theory*, 25/1: 46–66.

HOLZER, BORIS, and MILLO, YUVAL. 2005. 'From Risks to Second-Order Dangers in Financial Markets: Unintended Consequences of Risk Management Systems', *New Political Economy*, 10: 223–45.

HOPWOOD, ANTHONY G., and BROMWICH, MICHAEL. 1984. 'Accounting Research in the United Kingdom'. Pp. 133–61 in *European Contributions to Accounting Research: The Achievements of the Last Decade*, edited by Anthony G. Hopwood and Hein Schreuder. Amsterdam: Free University Press.

HOUNSHELL, DAVID A. 2004. 'Industrial Research: Commentary'. Pp. 59–65 in *The Science-Industry Nexus: History, Policy, Implications*, edited by Karl Grandin, Nina Wormbs, and Sven Widmalm. Sagamore Beach, Mass.: Science History Publications.

HUTCHINS, EDWIN. 1995a. *Cognition in the Wild*. Cambridge, Mass.: MIT Press.

—— 1995b. 'How a Cockpit Remembers its Speeds', *Cognitive Science*, 19: 265–88.

IASB (INTERNATIONAL ACCOUNTING STANDARDS BOARD). 2005. *International Financial Reporting Standards (IFRSs) 2005*. London: IASB.

INGEBRETSEN, MARK. 2002. *NASDAQ: A History of the Market that Changed the World*. Roseville, Calif.: Forum.

INTERGOVERNMENTAL PANEL ON CLIMATE CHANGE. 2007. *Climate Change 2007: The Physical Science Basis*. Cambridge: Cambridge University Press.

IZQUIERDO MARTIN, A. JAVIER. 1998. 'El declive de los grandes números: Benoit Mandelbrot y la estadística social', *Empiria: Revista de metodología de ciencias sociales*, 1: 51–84.

—— 2001. 'Reliability at Risk: The Supervision of Financial Models as a Case Study for Reflexive Economic Sociology', *European Societies*, 3: 69–90.

JAFFE, ADAM B., NEWELL, RICHARD G., and STAVINS, ROBERT N. 2005. 'A Tale of Two Market Failures: Technology and Environmental Policy', *Ecological Economics*, 54: 154–74.

JENKINS, PATRICK, and MILNE, RICHARD. 2005. 'Hedge Funds Hold a Quarter of Germany's Blue-Chips', *Financial Times*, 2 September: 17.

JETER, LYNNE W. 2003. *Disconnected: Deceit and Betrayal at WorldCom*. Hoboken, NJ: Wiley.

JOHNSON, STEVE, and SIMENSEN, IVAR. 2006. 'Iceland's Collapse Has Global Impact', *Financial Times*, 23 February: 42.

JONES, JENNIFER J. 1991. 'Earnings Management during Import Relief Investigations', *Journal of Accounting Research*, 29: 193–228.

Jopson, Barney. 2006. 'Activists Trigger Accounting Review', *Financial Times*, 22 November: 6.

Kahneman, Daniel, and Tversky, Amos. 1979. 'Prospect Theory: An Analysis of Decision under Risk', *Econometrica*, 47: 263–91.

Kalthoff, Herbert, Rottenburg, Richard, and Wagener, Hans-Jürgen. 2000. *Ökonomie und Gesellschaft, Jahrbuch 16. Facts and Figures: Economic Representations and Practices*. Marburg: Metropolis.

Kay, John. 2004. 'Ignore the Wisdom of Accounting at Your Own Risk', *Financial Times*, 7 September: 21.

Kerr, Richard A. 1998. 'Acid Rain Control: Success on the Cheap', *Science*, 282/5391 (6 November): 1024–6.

Kinner, Amy, and Birnbaum, Rona. 2004. 'The Acid Rain Experience: Should We Be Concerned about SO_2 Emissions Hotspots?'. Available at <http://www.epa.gov/airmarkets/articles/arpexperience.ppt>, accessed 2 September 2006.

Kirkham, Linda M., and Loft, Anne. 1993. 'Gender and the Construction of the Professional Accountant', *Accounting, Organizations and Society*, 18: 507–58.

Knorr Cetina, Karin. 2005. 'How Are Global Markets Global? The Architecture of a Flow World'. Pp. 38–61 in *The Sociology of Financial Markets*, edited by Karin Knorr Cetina and Alex Preda. Oxford: Oxford University Press.

—— and Bruegger, Urs. 2000. 'The Market as an Object of Attachment: Exploring Postsocial Relations in Financial Markets', *Canadian Journal of Sociology*, 25: 141–68.

—— —— 2002a. 'Global Microstructures: The Virtual Societies of Financial Markets', *American Journal of Sociology*, 107: 905–51.

—— —— 2002b. 'Inhabiting Technology: The Global Lifeform of Financial Markets', *Current Sociology*, 50: 389–405.

—— and Preda, Alex (eds.). 2005. *The Sociology of Financial Markets*. Oxford: Oxford University Press.

Kuhn, Thomas S. 1970. *The Structure of Scientific Revolutions*. Chicago: Chicago University Press, 2nd edition.

Kynaston, David. 1997. *LIFFE: A Market and its Makers*. Cambridge: Granta.

Lakatos, Imre. 1976. *Proofs and Refutations: The Logic of Mathematical Discovery*. Cambridge: Cambridge University Press.

Latham & Watkins LLP. 2005. 'Global Climate Change News: April'. Available at <http://www.lw.com/resource/Publications/_pdf/pub1385_1.2.pdf>, accessed 26 September 2006.

Latour, Bruno. 1986. 'Visualization and Cognition: Thinking with Eyes and Hands'. Pp. 1–40 in *Knowledge and Society: Studies in the Sociology of Culture Past and Present*, vol. vi, edited by Henrika Kuklick and Elizabeth Long. London: JAI.

—— 1987. *Science in Action*. Cambridge, Mass.: Harvard University Press.

—— 2005. *Reassembling the Social: An Introduction to Actor-Network Theory*. Oxford: Oxford University Press.

—— and WOOLGAR, STEVE. 1986. *Laboratory Life: The Construction of Scientific Facts*. Princeton: Princeton University Press.

LAW, JOHN. 1999. 'After ANT: Complexity, Naming and Topology'. Pp. 1–14 in *Actor Network Theory and After*, edited by John Law and John Hassard. Oxford: Blackwell.

LEDYARD, JOHN O. 1995. 'Public Goods: A Survey of Experimental Research'. Pp. 111–94 in *The Handbook of Experimental Economics*, edited by John H. Kagel and Alvin E. Roth. Princeton: Princeton University Press.

LÉPINAY, VINCENT-ANTONIN. 2004. 'The Concrete Abstraction of Capital: Hilferding Meets Callon in a Trading Room'. Paper presented to workshop 'The Performativities of Economics', Paris, 29–30 August.

—— 2007. 'Decoding Finance: Articulation and Liquidity around a Trading Room'. Pp. 87–127 in *Do Economists Make Markets? On the Performativity of Economics*, edited by Donald MacKenzie, Fabian Muniesa, and Lucia Siu. Princeton: Princeton University Press.

LERNER, JOSH. 2002. 'Where Does *State Street* Lead? A First Look at Financial Patents, 1971 to 2000', *Journal of Finance*, 57: 901–30.

LESLIE, JAMES, and WYATT, GEOFFREY. 1992. 'Futures and Options'. Pp. 85–110 in *Markets and Dealers: The Economics of the London Financial Markets*, edited by David Cobham. Harlow: Longman.

LEVIN, PETER. 2001. 'Gendering the Market: Temporality, Work, and Gender on a National Futures Exchange', *Work and Occupations*, 28: 112–30.

—— and ESPELAND, WENDY NELSON. 2002. 'Pollution Futures: Commensuration, Commodification, and the Market for Air'. Pp. 119–47 in *Organizations, Policy, and the Natural Environment: Institutional and Strategic Perspectives*, edited by Andrew J. Hoffman and Marc J. Ventresca. Stanford, Calif.: Stanford University Press.

LEVITT, ARTHUR. 1998. 'The "Numbers Game"'. Available at <http://www.sec.gov/news/speech/speecharchive/1998/spch220.txt>, accessed 7 April 2004.

LEVY, MARC A. 1993. 'European Acid Rain: The Power of Tote-Board Diplomacy'. Pp. 75–132 in *Institutions for the Earth: Sources of Effective Environment Protection*, edited by Peter M. Haas, Robert O. Keohane, and Marc A. Levy. Cambridge, Mass.: MIT Press.

LIPUMA, EDWARD, and LEE, BENJAMIN. 2004. *Financial Derivatives and the Globalization of Risk*. Durham, NC: Duke University Press.

—— —— 2005. 'Financial Derivatives and the Rise of Circulation', *Economy and Society*, 34. 404–27.

LOHMANN, LARRY. 2005. 'Marketing and Making Carbon Dumps: Commodification, Calculation and Counterfactuals in Climate Change Mitigation', *Science as Culture*, 14: 203–35.

LOHMANN, LARRY. 2006. 'Carbon Trading: A Critical Conversation on Climate Change, Privatisation and Power', *Development Dialogue*, 48 (September): 4–359.

LOOMIS, CAROL J. 1966. 'The Jones Nobody Keeps Up With', *Fortune*, April: 237–47.

LYNN, CARI. 2004. *Leg the Spread: A Woman's Adventures inside the Trillion-Dollar Boys' Club of Commodities Trading*. New York: Broadway.

McDOWELL, LINDA. 1997. *Capital Culture: Gender at Work in the City*. Oxford: Blackwell.

McGINTY, LEE, BEINSTEIN, ERIC, AHLUWALIA, RISHAD, and WATTS, MARTIN. 2004. 'Credit Correlation: A Guide'. London: JP Morgan. Available at <http://www.math.nyu.edu/~cousot/Teaching/IRCM/Lecture10/Base%20correlationJPM.pdf>, accessed 24 June 2006.

MACKENZIE, DONALD. 1990. *Inventing Accuracy: A Historical Sociology of Nuclear Missile Guidance*. Cambridge, Mass.: MIT Press.

—— 2003. 'Long-Term Capital Management and the Sociology of Arbitrage', *Economy and Society*, 32: 349–80.

—— 2004. 'The Big, Bad Wolf and the Rational Market: Portfolio Insurance, the 1987 Crash and the Performativity of Economics', *Economy and Society*, 33: 303–34.

—— 2005. 'Opening the Black Boxes of Global Finance', *Review of International Political Economy*, 12: 555–76.

—— 2006. *An Engine, not a Camera: How Financial Models Shape Markets*. Cambridge, Mass.: MIT Press.

—— 2007a. 'The Material Production of Virtuality: Innovation, Cultural Geography and Facticity in Derivatives Markets', *Economy and Society*, 36: 355–76.

—— 2007b. 'The Political Economy of Carbon Trading', *London Review of Books*, 29/7 (5 April): 29–31.

—— 2008. 'Producing Accounts: Finitism, Technology and Rule Following'. Pp. 99–117 in *Knowledge as Social Order: Rethinking the Sociology of Barry Barnes*, edited by Massimo Mazzotti. Aldershot: Ashgate.

—— and MILLO, YUVAL. 2003. 'Constructing a Market, Performing Theory: The Historical Sociology of a Financial Derivatives Exchange', *American Journal of Sociology*, 109: 107–45.

—— MUNIESA, FABIAN, and SIU, LUCIA (eds.). 2007. *Do Economists Make Markets? On the Performativity of Economics*. Princeton: Princeton University Press.

—— and WAJCMAN JUDY (eds.). 1999. *The Social Shaping of Technology*. Buckingham: Open University Press.

MACKINTOSH, JAMES. 2006. 'Hedge Funds Ahead of Estimates', *Financial Times*, 29 November: 30.

McNICHOLS, MAUREEN F. 2000. 'Research Design Issues in Earnings Management Studies', *Journal of Accounting and Public Policy*, 19: 313–45.

MANZOCCHI, STEFANO. 2001. 'Capital Flows to Developing Economies throughout the Twentieth Century'. Pp. 51–73 in *Financial Globalization and Democracy in Emerging Markets*, edited by Leslie Elliott Armijo. Basingstoke: Palgrave.

MASON, WILLIAM. 1999. 'Rate Setting in London'. British Bankers' Association, typescript.

MAURER, BILL. 2001. 'Engineering an Islamic Future: Speculations on Islamic Financial Alternatives', *Anthropology Today*, 17/1: 8–11.

——2002. 'Repressed Futures: Financial Derivatives' Theological Unconscious', *Economy and Society*, 31: 15–36.

——2005. *Mutual Life, Limited: Islamic Banking, Alternative Currencies, Lateral Reason*. Princeton: Princeton University Press.

MELAMED, LEO, and TAMARKIN, BOB. 1996. *Leo Melamed: Escape to the Futures*. New York: Wiley.

MERGES, ROBERT P. 2000. 'One Hundred Years of Solicitude: Intellectual Property Law 1900–2000', *California Law Review*, 88: 2187–240.

MERTON, ROBERT C. 1973. 'Theory of Rational Option Pricing', *Bell Journal of Economics and Management Science*, 4: 141–83.

——and BODIE, ZVI. 2005. 'Design of Financial Systems: Towards a Synthesis of Function and Structure', *Journal of Investment Management*, 3: 1–23.

MERTON, ROBERT K. 1948. 'The Self-Fulfilling Prophecy', *Antioch Review*, 8: 193–210.

MILLER, DANIEL (ed.). 2005. *Materiality*. Durham, NC: Duke University Press.

MILLER, PETER, and POWER, MICHAEL. 1995. 'Calculating Corporate Failure'. Pp. 51–76 in *Professional Competition and Professional Power: Lawyers, Accountants and the Social Construction of Markets*, edited by Yves Dezalay and David Sugarman. London: Routledge.

MILLO, YUVAL. 2003. 'Where Do Financial Markets Come From? Historical Sociology of Financial Derivatives Markets'. Ph.D. thesis: University of Edinburgh.

——MUNIESA, FABIAN, PANOURGIAS, NIKIFOROS S., and SCOTT, SUSAN V. 2005. 'Organized Detachment: Clearinghouse Mechanisms in Financial Markets', *Information and Organization*, 15: 229–46.

MILNER, MARK, and GOW, DAVID. 2006. 'In Theory, Only the Virtuous Are Rewarded', *The Guardian*, 16 May: 4.

MIROWSKI, PHILIP. 2002. *Machine Dreams: Economics Becomes a Cyborg Science*. Cambridge: Cambridge University Press.

——and NIK-KHAH, EDWARD. 2007. 'Markets Made Flesh: Performativity, and a Problem in Science Studies, Augmented with Consideration of the FCC Auctions'. Pp. 190–224 in *Do Economists Make Markets? On the Performativity of Economics*, edited by Donald MacKenzie, Fabian Muniesa, and Lucia Siu. Princeton: Princeton University Press.

MITCHELL, TIMOTHY. 2002. *Rule of Experts: Egypt, Techno-Politics, Modernity*. Berkeley and Los Angeles: University of California Press.

MIXON, SCOTT. 2006. 'Option Markets and Implied Volatility: Past versus Present'. Typescript.

MIYAZAKI, HIROKAZU. 2003. 'The Temporalities of the Market', *American Anthropologist*, 105/2: 255–65.

——2005. 'The Materiality of Finance Theory'. Pp. 165–81 in *Materiality*, edited by Daniel Miller. Durham, NC: Duke University Press.

MOLES, PETER, and TERRY, NICHOLAS. 1999. *The Handbook of International Financial Terms*. Oxford: Oxford University Press.

MONNI, SUVI, SYRI, SANNA, and SAVOLAINEN, ILKKA. 2004. 'Uncertainties in the Finnish Greenhouse Gas Emission Inventory', *Environmental Science and Policy*, 7: 87–98.

MONTGOMERY, W. DAVID. 1972. 'Markets in Licenses and Efficient Pollution Control Programs', *Journal of Economic Theory*, 5: 395–418.

MOORE, LYNDON, and JUH, STEVE. 2006. 'Warrant Pricing 60 Years before Black Scholes: Evidence from the Johannesburg Stock Exchange', *Journal of Finance*, 62: 3069–98.

MORRISON, KEVIN. 2006. 'Lower Pollution in EU Sees CO_2 Permits Fall 30%', *Financial Times*, 27 April: 19.

MOSLEY, LAYNA. 2003. *Global Capital and National Governments*. Cambridge: Cambridge University Press.

MUNIESA, FABIAN. 2003. 'Des marchés comme algorithmes: Sociologie de la cotation électronique à la Bourse de Paris'. Ph.D. thesis: École Nationale Supérieure des Mines.

——2005. 'Contenir le marché: La transition de la criée à la cotation électronique à la Bourse de Paris', *Sociologie du travail*, 47: 485–501.

——and CALLON, MICHEL. 2007. 'Economic Experiments and the Construction of Markets'. Pp. 163–89 in *Do Economists Make Markets? On the Performativity of Economics*, edited by Donald MacKenzie, Fabian Muniesa, and Lucia Siu. Princeton: Princeton University Press.

NATIONAL AUDIT OFFICE. 2004. *The UK Emissions Trading Scheme: A New Way to Combat Climate Change*. London: Stationery Office.

NATIONAL TECHNICAL UNIVERSITY OF ATHENS. n.d. 'The Primes Energy System Model: Summary Description'. Athens: National Technical University, available at <http://www.e3mlab.ntua.gr/manuals/PRIMsd.pdf>, accessed 6 January 2008.

NORDHAUS, WILLIAM D. 2000. 'From Porcopolis to Carbopolis: The Evolution from Pork Bellies to Emissions Trading'. Pp. 61–73 in *Emissions Trading: Environmental Policy's New Approach*, edited by Richard F. Kosobud. New York: Wiley.

O'BRIEN, RICHARD. 1992. *Global Financial Integration: The End of Geography*. London: Pinter.

O'MALLEY, PAT. 2003. 'Moral Uncertainties: Contract Law and Distinctions between Speculation, Gambling, and Insurance'. Pp. 231–57 in *Risk and Morality*, edited by Richard V. Ericson and Aaron Doyle. Toronto: University of Toronto Press.

OSLER, CAROL L. 2003. 'Currency Orders and Exchange Rate Dynamics: An Explanation for the Predictive Success of Technical Analysis', *Journal of Finance*, 58: 1791–819.

OUDSHOORN, NELLY, and PINCH, TREVOR (eds.). 2003. *How Users Matter: The Co-Construction of Users and Technology*. Cambridge, Mass.: MIT Press.

PATEL, KANAK. 1994. 'Lessons from the FOX Residential Property Futures and Mortgage Interest Rate Futures Market', *Housing Policy Debate*, 5: 343–60.

PERKS, ROBERT. 2004. *Financial Accounting for Non-Specialists*. Maidenhead: McGraw-Hill.

PIGOU, ARTHUR CECIL. 1920. *The Economics of Welfare*. London: Macmillan.

PIRRONG, CRAIG. 1996. 'Market Liquidity and Depth on Computerized and Open Outcry Trading Systems: A Comparison of DTB and LIFFE Bund Contracts', *Journal of Futures Markets*, 16: 519–43.

PODOLNY, JOEL M. 1993. 'A Status-Based Model of Market Competition', *American Journal of Sociology*, 98: 829–72.

—— 2001. 'Networks as the Pipes and Prisms of the Market', *American Journal of Sociology*, 107: 33–60.

POINT CARBON. 2006. 'Carbon 2006: Towards a Truly Global Market'. Oslo: Point Carbon.

—— 2007. 'Carbon 2007: A New Climate for Carbon Trading'. Oslo: Point Carbon.

PORTER, THEODORE M. 1995. *Trust in Numbers: The Pursuit of Objectivity in Science and Public Life*. Princeton: Princeton University Press.

POWER, MICHAEL K. 1991. 'Educating Accountants: Towards a Critical Ethnography', *Accounting, Organizations and Society*, 16: 333–53.

—— 1992. 'The Politics of Brand Accounting in the United Kingdom', *European Accounting Review*, 1: 39–68.

PREDA, ALEX. 2001a. 'The Rise of the Popular Investor: Financial Knowledge and Investing in England and France, 1840–1880', *Sociological Quarterly*, 42: 205–32.

—— 2001b. 'In the Enchanted Grove: Financial Conversations and the Marketplace in England and France in the 18th Century', *Journal of Historical Sociology*, 14: 276–307.

—— 2001c. 'Sense and Sensibility: Or, How Should Social Studies of Finance Behave: A Manifesto', *Economic Sociology: European Electronic Newsletter*, 2/2: 15–18.

—— 2004a. 'Informative Prices, Rational Investors: The Emergence of the Random Walk Hypothesis and the Nineteenth-Century "Science of Financial Investments"', *History of Political Economy*, 36: 351–86.

—— 2004b. 'Epistemic Performativity: The Case of Financial Chartism'. Paper presented to workshop, 'The Performativities of Economics', Paris, 29–30 August.

PREDA, ALEX. 2006. 'Socio-Technical Agency in Financial Markets: The Case of the Stock Ticker', *Social Studies of Science*, 36: 753–82.

PRINS, GWYN, and RAYNER, STEVE. 2007. 'Time to Ditch Kyoto', *Nature*, 449 (25 October): 973–5.

PRYKE, MICHAEL D. Forthcoming. 'Geomoney: An Option on Frost, Going Long on Clouds', *Geoforum*.

—— and ALLEN, JOHN. 2000. 'Monetized Time-Space: Derivatives—Money's "New Imaginary" '? *Economy and Society*, 29: 264–84.

PULLIAM, SUSAN. 2003. 'Accountant Balked, then Caved', *Wall Street Journal Europe*, 24 June: M6–M7.

—— and SOLOMON, DEBORAH. 2002. 'How 3 Unlikely Sleuths Uncooked WorldCom's Books', *Wall Street Journal Europe*, 31 October: A8.

QUATTRONE, PAOLO, and HOPPER, TREVOR. 2006. 'What is IT? SAP, Accounting, and Visibility in a Multinational Organisation', *Information and Organization*, 16: 212–50.

REINGANUM, MARC R. 1983. 'The Anomalous Stock Market Behavior of Small Firms in January: Empirical Tests for Tax-Loss Selling Effects', *Journal of Financial Economics*, 12: 89–104.

RILES, ANNELISE. 2004. 'Real Time: Unwinding Technocratic and Anthropological Knowledge' *American Ethnologist*, 31: 392–405.

RIPLEY, AMANDA. 2002. 'The Night Detective'. Available at <http://www.time.com/time/subscriber/personoftheyear/2002/>, accessed 2 February 2007.

ROBOTTI, PAOLA. n.d. 'Arbitrage/Short Selling: A Political Economy Approach'. Typescript.

ROSE, ARNOLD M. 1951. 'Rumor in the Stock Market', *Public Opinion Quarterly*, 15: 461–86.

—— 1966. 'A Social Psychological Approach to the Study of the Stock Market', *Kyklos*, 19: 267–87.

RUBIN, ROBERT E., and WEISBERG, JACOB. 2003. *In an Uncertain World: Tough Choices from Wall Street to Washington*. New York: Random House.

RWE AG. 2007. 'RWE erzielt Einigung mit Bundeskartellamt in CO_2-Verfahren'. Essen: RWE AG, 27 September. Available at <http://www.rwe.com>, accessed 28 September 2007.

SANDLER, LINDA. 1998. 'U.S. Universities Get Burned by Rash of Risky Strategies', *Wall Street Journal Europe*, 13 October: 5B.

SANDOR, RICHARD L., and SOSIN, HOWARD B. 1983. 'Inventive Activity in Futures Markets: A Case Study of the Development of the First Interest Rate Futures Market'. Pp. 255–72 in *Futures Markets: Modelling, Managing and Monitoring Futures Trading*, edited by Manfred E. Streit. Oxford: Blackwell.

SANFEY, ALAN G., RILLING, JAMES K., ARONSON, JESSICA A., NYSTROM, LEIGH E., and COHEN, JONATHAN D. 2003. 'The Neural Basis of Economic Decision-Making in the Ultimatum Game', *Science*, 300 (13 June): 1755–8.

SCHAFFER, SIMON. 1992. 'Late Victorian Metrology and its Instrumentation: A Manufactory of Ohms'. Pp. 23–56 in *Invisible Connections: Instruments, Institutions, and Science*, edited by Robert Bud and Susan Cozzens. Bellingham, Wash.: SPIE Optical Engineering Press.

SCHIPPER, KATHERINE. 1989. 'Commentary on Earnings Management', *Accounting Horizons*, 3: 91–102.

SHALEN, CATHERINE. n.d. 'The Nitty-Gritty of CBOT^R DJIA^{SM} Futures Index Arbitrage'. Available at <http://www.cbot.com/cbot/docs/29685.pdf>, accessed 30 July 2005.

SHAPIN, STEVEN. 1994. *A Social History of Truth: Civility and Science in Seventeenth-Century England.* Chicago: University of Chicago Press.

——— and SCHAFFER, SIMON. 1985. *Leviathan and the Air-Pump: Hobbes, Boyle, and the Experimental Life.* Princeton: Princeton University Press.

SHLEIFER, ANDREI, and VISHNY, ROBERT W. 1997. 'The Limits of Arbitrage', *Journal of Finance*, 52: 35–55.

SIJM, JOS, NEUHOFF, KARSTEN, and CHEN, YIHSU, 2006. 'CO_2 Cost Pass-Through and Windfall Profits in the Power Sector', *Climate Policy*, 6: 49–72.

SILBER, WILLIAM L. 1981. 'Innovations, Competition, and New Contract Design in Futures Markets', *Journal of Futures Markets*, 1: 123–55.

SIMON, HERBERT. 1955. 'A Behavioral Model of Rational Choice', *Quarterly Journal of Economics*, 69: 99–118.

SKORECKI, ALEX, and MUNTER, PÄIVI. 2005. 'Dealers Get the Squeeze', *Financial Times*, 2 February: 41.

SLIMMINGS, SIR WILLIAM. 1981. 'The Scottish Contribution'. Pp. 12–26 in *British Accounting Standards: The First 10 Years*, edited by Sir Ronald Leach and Edward Stamp. Cambridge: Woodhead-Faulkner.

SMITH, CHARLES W. 1981. *The Mind of the Market: A Study of Stock Market Philosophies, Their Uses, and Implications.* Totowa, NJ: Rowman & Littlefield.

SØRENSEN, KNUT H., and WILLIAMS, ROBIN (eds.). 2002. *Shaping Technology, Guiding Policy: Concepts, Spaces and Tools.* Cheltenham: Elgar.

SORRELL, STEVE. 1994. 'Pollution on the Market: The US Experience with Emissions Trading for the Control of Air Pollution'. Brighton: University of Sussex, Science Policy Research Unit.

——— 2003. 'Who Owns the Carbon? Interactions between the EU Emissions Trading Scheme and the UK Renewables Obligations and Energy Efficiency Commitment', *Energy and Environment*, 14: 677–703.

STAVINS, ROBERT N. 1988. 'Project 88: Harnessing Market Forces to Protect the Environment'. Available at <http://ksghome.harvard.edu/~rstavins/Monographs_&_Reports/Project_88–1.pdf>, accessed 11 September 2006.

——— 1998. 'What Can We Learn from the Grand Policy Experiment? Lessons from SO_2 Allowance Trading', *Journal of Economic Perspectives*, 12/3: 69–88.

STEEN, DAVID. 1982. 'How Traded Options Started', *Money Observer*, 27 April.

STERN, NICHOLAS. 2007. *The Economics of Climate Change: The Stern Review*. Cambridge: Cambridge University Press.

SUCHMAN, LUCY A. 1983. 'Office Procedure as Practical Action: Models of Work and System Design', *ACM Transactions on Office Information Systems*, 1: 320–8.

SULLIVAN, SCOTT. 2002. ' "White Paper" Submitted to Board of WorldCom, Inc'. Available at <http://news.corporate.findlaw.com/legalnews/documents/archive_w. html>, accessed 8 September 2006.

SWAN, EDWARD J. 2000. *Building the Global Market: A 4000 Year History of Derivatives*. London: Kluwer.

SWIFT, BYRON. 2000. 'Allowance Trading and Potential Hot Spots: Good News from the Acid Rain Program', *Environment Reporter*, 31 (12 May): 954–9.

TAMARKIN, BOB. 1993. *The Merc: The Emergence of a Global Financial Powerhouse*. New York: HarperCollins.

TEOH, SIEW HONG, WONG, T. J., and RAO, GITA R. 1998. 'Are Accruals during Initial Public Offerings Opportunistic?' *Review of Accounting Studies*, 3: 175–208.

TETT, GILLIAN. 2007. 'Libor's Value is Called into Question', *Financial Times*, 26 September: 43.

THOMAS, DANIEL. 2007. 'Hedge Fund Assets Soar to almost $2,500 bn', *Financial Times*, 10 October: 23.

THOMPSON, PAUL. 1997. 'The Pyrrhic Victory of Gentlemanly Capitalism: The Financial Elite of the City of London, 1945–90', *Journal of Contemporary History*, 32: 283–304 and 427–40.

THRIFT, NIGEL. 1994. 'On the Social and Cultural Determinants of Financial Centres: The Case of the City of London'. Pp. 327–55 in *Money, Power, and Space*, edited by Stuart Corbridge and Ron Martin. Oxford: Blackwell.

—— 2000. 'Pandora's Box? Cultural Geographies of Economies'. Pp. 689–704 in *Oxford Handbook of Economic Geography*, edited by Gordon L. Clark, Meric S. Gertler, and Maryann P. Feldman. Oxford: Oxford University Press.

TICKELL, ADAM. 1998. 'Unstable Futures: Controlling and Creating Risks in International Money', *Socialist Register*: 248–77.

—— 2000. 'Dangerous Derivatives: Controlling and Creating Risks in International Money', *Geoforum*, 31: 87–99.

TRICKS, HENRY, and BUCK, TOBIAS. 2004. 'ASB Tells UK Companies to Ignore EU Ruling on Accounting Standards', *Financial Times*, 12 October: 1.

—— and HARGREAVES, DEBORAH. 2004. 'Accounting Watchdog Sees Trouble', *Financial Times*, 10 November: 19.

TUFANO, PETER. 1989. 'Financial Innovation and First-Mover Advantages', *Journal of Financial Economics*, 25: 213–40.

—— 2003. 'Financial Innovation'. Pp. 307–35 in *Handbook of the Economics of Finance, ia: Corporate Finance*, edited by George M. Constantinides, Milton Harris, and René M. Stulz. Amsterdam: Elsevier.

ULSET, KJERSTI. 2007. 'Should Anyone Be Surprised by the NAP Decisions?' *Carbon Market Europe*, 6/13 (19 January): 1.

UZZI, BRIAN. 1999. 'Embeddedness in the Making of Financial Capital: How Social Relations and Networks Benefit Firms Seeking Financing', *American Sociological Review*, 64: 481–504.

VAN DUYN, ALINE, and MUNTER, PÄIVI. 2004. 'How Citigroup Shook Europe's Bond Markets with Two Minutes of Trading', *Financial Times*, 10 September: 17.

VICTOR, DAVID G., and HOUSE, JOSHUA C. 2006. 'BP's Emissions Trading Scheme', *Energy Policy*, 34: 2100–12.

VINTCENT, CHARLES. 2002. *How to Win at Financial Spread Betting*. London: Pearson.

VOGEL, STEVEN K. 1996. *Freer Markets, More Rules: Regulatory Reform in Advanced Industrial Countries*. Ithaca, NY: Cornell University Press.

VOLCOVICI, VALERIE. 2007. 'The RGGI Experiment', *Trading Carbon*, 1/1 (December): 28–9.

WALTON, PETER, HALLER, AXEL, and RAFFOURNIER, BERNARD (eds.). 2003. *International Accounting*. London: Thomson.

WARA, MICHAEL. 2007. 'Is the Global Carbon Market Working?' *Nature*, 445 (8 February): 595–6.

WEBER, MAX. 1970. 'Class, Status, Party'. Pp. 180–95 in *From Max Weber: Essays in Sociology*, edited by H. H. Gerth and C. Wright Mills. London: Routledge and Kegan Paul.

—— 2000a. 'Stock and Commodity Exchanges [Die Börse (1894)]', *Theory and Society*, 29: 305–38.

—— 2000b. 'Commerce on the Stock and Commodity Exchanges [Die Börsenverkehr]', *Theory and Society*, 29: 339–71.

WEITZMAN, HAL. 2005. 'Ecuador Paves Way for $750m Bond Issue', *Financial Times*, 5 December: 8.

WETTESTAD, JØRGEN. 2005. 'The Making of the 2003 EU Emissions Directive: An Ultra-Quick Process due to Entrepreneurial Proficiency?' *Global Environmental Politics*, 5: 1–23.

WHITE, HARRISON C. 1981. 'Where Do Markets Come From?' *American Journal of Sociology*, 87: 517–47.

—— 2001. *Markets from Networks*. Princeton: Princeton University Press.

WIDICK, RICHARD. 2003. 'Flesh and the Free Market (On Taking Bourdieu to the Options Exchange)', *Theory and Society*, 32: 677–723.

WILLMAN, JOHN. 2007. 'The City v Wall Street: The Smart Money is on (and in) London', *Financial Times*, 27–8 January: 11.

WINNER, LANGDON. 1980. 'Do Artifacts Have Politics?' *Daedalus*, 109/1: 121–36.

Wise, J. Macgregor. 2005. 'Assemblage'. Pp. 77–87 in *Gilles Deleuze: Key Concepts*, edited by Charles J. Stivale. Chesham: Acumen.

Wittgenstein, Ludwig. 1967. *Philosophical Investigations*. Oxford: Blackwell.

Wyns, Tomas. 2007. 'NAP II Court Cases: A Double-Edged Sword', *Carbon Market Europe*, 6/21 (1 June): 1.

Yamin, Farhana (ed.). 2005. *Climate Change and Carbon Markets: A Handbook of Emissions Reduction Mechanisms*. London: Earthscan.

Yule, George Udny. 1927. 'On Reading a Scale', *Journal of the Royal Statistical Society*, 90: 570–87.

Zaloom, Caitlin. 2003. 'Ambiguous Numbers: Trading Technologies and Interpretation in Financial Markets', *American Ethnologist*, 30: 258–72.

——— 2004. 'The Productive Life of Risk', *Cultural Anthropology*, 19: 365–91.

——— 2006. *Out of the Pits: Trading and Technology from Chicago to London*. Chicago: Chicago University Press.

Zapfel, Peter, and Vainio, Matti. 2002. 'Pathways to European Greenhouse Gas Emissions Trading History and Misconceptions'. Available at <http://ssrn.com/abstract=342924>, accessed 19 September 2006.

Zeff, Stephen A. 1984. 'Some Junctures in the Evolution of the Process of Establishing Accounting Principles in the U.S.A.: 1917–1972', *Accounting Review*, 59: 447–68.

Zorn, Dirk M. 2004. 'Here a Chief, There a Chief: The Rise of the CFO in the American Firm', *American Sociological Review*, 69: 345–64.

Zuckerman, Ezra W. 1999. 'The Categorical Imperative: Securities Analysts and the Illegitimacy Discount', *American Journal of Sociology*, 104: 1398–438.

——— 2004. 'Structural Incoherence and Stock Market Activity', *American Sociological Review*, 69: 405–32.

INDEX